THE NEW HERETICS

The New Heretics

Skepticism, Secularism, and Progressive Christianity

Rebekka King

NEW YORK UNIVERSITY PRESS
New York

NEW YORK UNIVERSITY PRESS
New York
www.nyupress.org

© 2023 by New York University
All rights reserved

References to Internet websites (URLs) were accurate at the time of writing. Neither the author nor New York University Press is responsible for URLs that may have expired or changed since the manuscript was prepared.

Please contact the Library of Congress for Cataloging-in-Publication data.
ISBN: 9781479822065 (hardback)
ISBN: 9781479836147 (paperback)
ISBN: 9781479873630 (library ebook)
ISBN: 9781479899340 (consumer ebook)

New York University Press books are printed on acid-free paper, and their binding materials are chosen for strength and durability. We strive to use environmentally responsible suppliers and materials to the greatest extent possible in publishing our books.

Manufactured in the United States of America

10 9 8 7 6 5 4 3 2 1

Also available as an ebook

CONTENTS

Introduction: Believers in Exile   1

1. "Not Christian Like That": Exploring the Contours of Progressive Christian Congregations   37

2. To Mine the Text: Textual Interpretations and Reading Praxis   79

3. Deconversion: Progressive Christians and the Protestant Proximate Other   111

4. *Still, Already, Yet*: Imagining the End of Progressive Christianity   145

Conclusion: "We Are All Heretics Now"   175

Epilogue: There Will Be Cake and Dancing   199

Acknowledgments   205

Appendix: The Eight Points (American and Canadian Versions)   209

Notes   211

References   223

Index   243

About the Author   257

Introduction

Believers in Exile

I don't believe in God, I don't believe in Christianity. Really,
I like to tell people that I am an atheist who goes to church.
—Suzan, West Hill United Church

Suzan and I sat down for lunch in a crowded deli at a busy intersection not far from where I lived and a stone's throw from Suzan's workplace. The lunchtime crowd was a mix of medical professionals from the nearby hospital network where Suzan worked as a nurse. I was struck by how strange it was to see her in this setting. The bustle of downtown was markedly different from the suburban tree-lined streets where she lived and where I had gotten to know her during the previous year and a half through her work as the coordinator of adult education programming at West Hill United Church. Suzan had served as a critical interlocutor in my study of progressive Christianity, a variety of Christianity that promotes intellectual integrity, biblical criticism, liberal humanism, and scientific empiricism.

Several of Suzan's colleagues stopped by our table to say hello, and she introduced me as a friend, noting that our meeting involved an interview, so we needed privacy.

"I almost said you were a friend from church," she laughed as I pulled out my digital recorder. "That would have been uncomfortable," she said and shrugged her shoulders.

I asked how she understood herself as a Christian, and Suzan acknowledged that she was reticent to use terms like *church* or *Christian* when she talked about her weekend activities. "I don't want people to think I'm like Richard Dawkins, but I also don't want them to think I'm like Jerry Falwell.[1] I guess we're Christian because that's what we've always been. It's our heritage," She smiled and continued: "I don't personally use the term *Christian* anymore. I usually tell people I'm an atheist who goes to church."

But even this description was imprecise as it did not quite reflect the type of church that Suzan attended. West Hill had assumed a place in the public spotlight, capitalizing on the popular profile of its outspoken minister, Gretta Vosper, and had set itself apart as a church where atheists and skeptics might feel comfortable. Here they found common ground in tradition, heritage, and commitments to amorphous concepts like love, justice, and fidelity. West Hill offered a space to be Christian without the need to assent to specific beliefs (either literally or metaphorically) as a condition of membership. To a certain extent, it created a space for religious identification in which "belonging without believing" was not only made possible but actively generated and promoted through the rejection of specific beliefs and practices (Bullock 2018; Francis and Robbins 2004; Oakes 2015; cf. Day 2011; G. Davie 1994; Voas 2003; Zwissler 2007).

To illustrate her departure from traditional Christianity, Suzan related how, despite the fact that she took her children to church every Sunday, they lacked basic knowledge of Christianity. For example, many of her daughter's friends were Muslim, and Suzan proudly reported that her daughter knew far more about Muslim beliefs and practices than she did about her own religion. Suzan liked this example because it reflected her values of multiculturalism and religious pluralism—values that she saw as setting her religious affiliation apart from other Christian denominations. "Last Friday night, my daughter's school choir was singing a benefit concert at an old Baptist church," she told me. "My son couldn't sit still at all . . . he was playing with the hymnals, the order of service, and then at one point, he pulled out the Bible." Mimicking the slow cadence of her son's voice, she continued: "Ho-oly Bi-ble. What's this?"

Suzan's church did not read the Bible anymore. After years of deconstructing biblical texts, the members had determined that it was time for other voices—poetry, literature, philosophy, and self-help books—to occupy the place of privilege in their church's selection of readings. West Hill's members rejected the power attributed to the Bible and instead focused their energies on revealing how it has been used as a tool of oppression. This preference informed not only how the congregation read scripture or performed exegesis but also its approach to Christianity more generally. After all, it saw itself as the driving force of a larger movement within Christianity to challenge anything that impedes the development of a new socially progressive and empirically verifiable model of religion. With these revisions, the congregation eventually might abandon even concepts like *church* and *Christian*, should the members deem them obstacles.[2]

Indeed, West Hill was not alone. Something was happening in church basements, local pubs, and fellowship halls across North America. United under the moniker "progressive Christianity," groups of Christians like Suzan gathered to read the theological works of popular authors and scholars. Certainly, the act of Christians meeting to discuss theology and the Bible is not new (Bielo 2009c; Juzwik 2014; Malley 2004), but these particular Christians stood apart because they were questioning and rejecting both traditional beliefs and the historical accuracy of the Bible. In their place, these groups were attempting to assemble an understanding of Christianity in line with their own experiences, one that lends authority to science over faith, humanism over dogma, and freethinking over fiat. When asked, many reported that they "no longer believe in God" or, like Suzan, were "atheists who go to church." They were part of a growing movement of Christians who identify as progressive, post-Christian, or believers in exile. In choosing these locutions, progressive Christians consciously and proudly construct a social and religious identity that renders them heretics and skeptics within North American Christianity.

In short, this book is about Christians who don't believe in Jesus. To be more specific, it is about Christians who see rejecting belief in Jesus as a divine figure to be part of a larger moral imperative in which they regard the act of rejection as an ethical one. Central to this book's overall argument is the notion of *conviction*, in the form of skepticism, a term offered as a means of settling larger debates about the role of belief as a category of analysis within the scholarly study of religion. Too often, belief is understood as a noun or an object rather than an action or a practice (Elisha 2008). Even when framed an action, it is derived from Christian analytical categories and seen as affirmative: belief in *x* or about *y* (Asad 1993, 2003; Day 2010; Lindquist and Coleman 2008; Ruel 2002). Yet closer investigation reveals that disbelief, skepticism, and dissent are among the core characteristics of contemporary American Christianity, at least as far as Protestantism is concerned.[3] For example, in evangelical and conservative religious circles, "belief against" such hot topics as evolution, abortion, or other religions occupies public and popular debate (Alumkal 2017; Bielo 2018; Veldman 2019). These beliefs serve as a litmus test of denominational affiliation (Bebbington 1989; Reimer 2003). Among progressive Christians, similar conceptions of "believing against" emerge when they read the Bible in the context of their understanding of history, science, and humanism.

While not believing in Jesus might be framed within a larger narrative of secularization (Callum Brown 2012; Bruce 2011; Calhoun, Juergensmeyer, and VanAntwerpen 2011; Clarke and Macdonald 2017) or nonreligion (Baggett 2019; Baker and Smith 2015; Beaman and Tomlins 2015; Cotter 2020; Lee 2015; Thiessen and Wilkens-LaFlamme 2020), doing so misses the opportunity to examine doubt and disbelief as religious expressions. The scholarly focus on secularization depicts cultural processes of differentiation and accommodation as outside forces imposed upon religion. It emphasizes a weakening of beliefs and a decline of religious influences on society. Studies of nonreligion focus on disbelief as a departure from religious adherence. While progressive Christians reject much of their religious tradition, central to this book's argument is their ongoing retention of Christian affiliations and identities.[4]

In contrast to secularization and nonreligion, skepticism serves as a broader category for understanding how people make sense of their religious experiences. In the case of progressive Christians, skepticism about the existence of God or the divinity of Jesus can be best understood in relation to how belief is made palpable as an ethical stance or a conviction, as opposed to an experience of faith. Skepticism takes the form of a resolve to disbelieve based on a moral framework that regards belief as possible only when accompanied by evidence and proof.[5] When paired with skepticism, conviction offers a more dynamic way of thinking about religious processes *as* processes—that is, as positions generated within a religious tradition.

Situated within the subfield known as the anthropology of Christianity, this book stands as the first ethnographic and scholarly study of progressive Christianity. It is based on my two-and-a-half years of ethnographic fieldwork at five churches between the fall of 2008 and the spring of 2010. I conducted fieldwork in southern Ontario, Canada, in communities that can more or less be described as suburban or bedroom communities to the city of Toronto. This research featured five mainline liberal Protestant churches that identified as progressive and regularly engaged in studying popular books by progressive Christian authors that challenge traditional theology. My initial foray into these churches was as a participant in their book study groups because this was where I had been told progressive Christianity was happening. I also attended church services, potluck dinners, movie nights, conferences, speaker series, and coffee hours. I supplemented my participation in these communities with seventy in-depth interviews. The congregations' Sunday attendance averaged fifty to eighty people. The churches reflected the demographics of mainline Protestantism in North America and were predominately white and middle class (Jones 2016).

This book seeks to shed light on how one decides what constitutes one's religious self in contrast to one's secular self. In other words, what are the boundaries that demarcate what everyday adherents see as part of their religious and secular lives? While one might presume that religious identity takes prominence over a secular one, progressive Christians invert such assumptions and even relish those instances when endorsing secular frameworks result in heresy charges. For progressive Christians, being seen as heretics creates a powerful opportunity to reconfigure the Christian tradition—its beliefs, practices, and identity markers. When a progressive Christian rejects God but maintains a Christian identity, the act of first doubting and then rejecting is a religious one. Progressive Christians perceive this reconfiguration as the point, not a side effect. In fact, it becomes the primary means whereby progressive Christians understand themselves to still be Christians despite, or because of, their heretical beliefs.

Defining Progressive Christianity

Progressive Christianity emerged in the mid-1990s and developed as an alternative to both evangelical and liberal Christianity.[6] It was adopted primarily by well-educated middle-class baby boomers in search of a form of Christianity that, in their eyes, does not conflict with modernity. Using slogans like "church for thinking people" and "no need to check your brain at the door," progressive Christians seek to integrate their secular ways of thinking with religious ones. When this is not possible, they privilege the secular over the sacred. They have proposed a version of Christianity that dismisses or deemphasizes supernatural and nonempirical beliefs and practices. Instead, progressive Christians see themselves as a religious movement that embraces scientific empiricism, a moral ethic derived from humanism, and the findings of biblical historical criticism (cf. Dorrien 2006). In place of traditionally held beliefs, progressive Christians emphasize inclusivity, liturgical revision, intellectual integrity, incorporation of non-Christian rituals and readings into their services, and increased participation in social justice causes (Taussig 2006, 25–34; cf. D. Brown 2008; Cobb 2008; Slessarev-Jamir 2011).

Progressive Christianity has surfaced in conversation with a corpus of popular books by religious figures that seek to challenge Christian paradigms. While several authors have served as prominent figures in this movement, none was as conspicuous as the late Episcopal bishop John Shelby Spong, who provided many of the terms and ideas that progressive Christians use. Spong first proposed the term *believer in exile* in his best-selling work *Why Christianity Must Change or Die: A Bishop Speaks to Believers in Exile* (1998). In it Spong, who passed away in 2021, draws parallels between modern Christians' experience and the biblical Judean exile in Babylon, suggesting that progressive Christians have been forcibly dislocated from the broader Christian tradition. Exile is understood as having been imposed by those within the church unwilling to accept the idea that Christianity should change in order to align itself with modern science, liberal humanism, and historical evidence. Spong explains this experience as follows: "I live in a state of exile from the presuppositions of my own religious past. I am exiled from the literal understandings that shaped the creed at its creation. I am exiled from the worldview in which the creed was formed" (1998, 20). Though he uses the biblical term *exile*, Spong is clear that he does not desire to return to a previous position within the fold. Rather, those in the church who maintain what he sees as antiquated doctrines and traditions have required that he and other believers in exile choose to either leave the church or live a lie. With Spong's backing, progressive Christians have forged a third way.

Spong's earlier writings inspired a movement. As progressive Christianity gained momentum in the late 1990s and the early 2000s, it positioned itself as an alternative to leaving Christianity or remaining mum about doubts and disbelief.[7] The Center for Progressive Christianity (TCPC) was established in 1996 in the United States under the leadership of the Episcopal priest Jim Adams as a network for skeptics and agnostics within the church. Across the country, congregations affiliated themselves with the center, and its website listed them as "safe places" for skeptics. Congregations that became affiliated did so based on their recognition of, and alignment with, TCPC's Eight Points (see the appendix). In 2004, the Canadian Centre for Progressive Christianity formed, setting itself up as an even more radical variation of the movement. Initially, the Canadians adopted TCPC's Eight Points; however, the Canadian Centre for Progressive Christianity perceived the TCPC as too Christocentric and later rejected the TCPC's Eight Points. Instead, the Canadians created their own Eight Points, which espouse a similar social justice orientation but with no references to Jesus or God (see appendix). There are several other prominent progressive Christian organizations in North America, such as Progressive Christians Uniting, Sojourners, CrossLeft, and Wild Goose, with new ones forming regularly.

The term *progressive Christian* might be misleading to the casual observer of North American religions. This movement does not conflate *progressive* with its use by the evangelical Left, Third Wave Christianity, Red Letter Christians, and the Emergent Church, which, in certain instances, appear to share many of the political ideologies of the progressive Christians that I discuss in this book. These are distinct movements with different histories, approaches to biblical hermeneutics, and views of the church's role in the world (see Bielo 2011a; Bialecki 2009; Packard 2012; Marti and Ganiel 2014). The sociologist Laura Desfor Edles describes such progressive evangelicals as prophetic progressive Christians, noting that they retain traditional understandings of Jesus and God and "may even lament that progressive 'mainliners' (such as [Marcus] Borg) 'demythologize' the Bible" (2013, 6). She positions them on a continuum with a second ideal type, self-proclaimed progressive Christians. This second category, which denotes those who explicitly set themselves in opposition to the religious right, more closely resembles the progressive Christians featured in this book.[8]

Furthermore, the term *progressive* is not intended to indicate that progressive Christianity is a direct descendant of the late nineteenth- and early twentieth-century Christian progressivism characterized by the Social Gospel. While many progressive Christians certainly agree with the tenets of the Social Gospel and see its proponents as their denominational forerunners (see Airhart 2013), they are two distinct movements with no direct genealogical link. Nor should they be linked with the long-standing tradition of progressive Catholicism exemplified in such movements as Catholic Worker. Progressive Christianity emerges within different intellectual, political, and social dynamics. Most prominent is the fact that other progressive versions of Christianity possess comparatively traditional beliefs regarding notions of divine immanence and incarnation.

Instead, progressive Christians' chosen descriptor, progressive, is meant to contrast theologically with conservative, evangelical, and fundamentalist Christians, whom the progressives perceive as backward and unwilling to engage with critical scholarly sources (D. Brown 2008). Moreover, and perhaps more surprisingly, the term also aims to distinguish them from their near neighbor, liberal Christianity, which the progressives see as irrelevant, indecisive, and unnecessarily rooted in Enlightenment thought and universal notions of truth (Cobb 2008). Although progressive Christians are liberal in terms of their politics and theology, they see themselves as a distinct movement that diverges from liberal Christianity. While liberal Christians may reject Christianity's beliefs in unverifiable miracles, unlike progressive Christians they retain its language in their services, understanding it as metaphorical or symbolic.

It is challenging to pin down the exact numbers of progressive Christians. In the United States, the term *progressive* primarily refers to a political rather than theological stance. American progressive Christians see their religiosity as intertwined with voting practices, political advocacy, social agenda, and economic policies (see Jones 2008; Mockabee, Wald, and Leege 2012; L. Olson 2007, 2011). For example, in her analysis of the symbolic dynamics of progressive Christianity, Edles identifies the 2008 election of "one of their own," Barack Obama, as "perhaps their greatest achievement yet" (2013, 4). A 2013 study by the Public Religion Research Institute classified 19 percent of Americans as religious progressives. Inclusive of both Christian and other religious progressives, this percentage is a composite calculation that results from certain values assigned to theological, social, and economic orientations to create a profile of religious progressives (Jones et al. 2013). These numbers serve as a helpful starting point for understanding the populations involved in progressive religious discourses but do not provide an accurate account of progressive Christians—especially those who might see themselves as kin to the progressive Christians described in this book.

Religious affiliation in Canada, in contrast to that in the United States, is not as politically charged. Indeed, while some Canadians link their religious and political identities, these are not as tightly enmeshed for several political, cultural, and historical reasons (see Bean 2014; Noll 2006; Reimer 2003). Canadians see religion as properly located in a private and domestic realm.[9] For this reason, attempts to measure religion in Canada have centered on religious commitment measured through participation and attendance at services. The sociologist Reginald Bibby argues that by the second half of the twentieth century, a shift had occurred wherein religious participation was no longer seen as an obligation but rather a choice motivated by whether or not one found it worthwhile (2017, 25–29). Bibby identifies "religious lows"—those who neither embrace nor reject religion—as the biggest religious cohort, comprising 45 percent of the Canadian population (2017, 81; see also Thiessen 2015). In his assessment of the religious low, Bibby concludes that many were exposed to religion at a young age and notes that religion is "still in their system." About a quarter of this population comes from mainline denominations. Many indicate an openness to increased religious involvement if they perceived it worthwhile (Bibby 2017, 81). It is this group that progressive Christians see as potential members.

At the 2009 biannual national conference of the Canadian Centre for Progressive Christianity, which I attended, Gretta Vosper, the organization's president, discussed the distinctions between progressive, liberal, and conservative Christianity. She explained to the audience: "In the early days of the Canadian Centre for Progressive Christianity, when we reflected upon what church was like for us, people talked about experiences of isolation—either because they felt like they couldn't speak openly or because the only church they could find was a conservative one." While many looked to more liberal churches for a safe space to express doubts, they found themselves isolated by their esoteric liturgical language and elite intellectualism. Vosper criticized liberal Christianity's reliance on academic deconstructions, arguing that it does not go far enough. From her perspective, liberal Christians study Christianity's historical context and adopt a more nuanced theology without altering their language, practices, or beliefs. She sees this approach as a problem because only those who have undergone extensive study are able to grasp the metaphorical and symbolic meanings that liberal Christians endorse. Concerned about being accessible to everyone, she focused her address on the question of where those who are unfamiliar with these new readings will find a spiritual home: "People won't be fed by a message that uses language that they don't have the tools to deconstruct. No, obviously, people are going to end up in evangelical settings, which tell them that their needs will be met and that they will be better off with the church." In Vosper's view, beliefs and rituals need to be transparent; they need to communicate what is going on to someone who is an outsider or not well versed in Christianity.

Along the same lines, in *Rescuing the Bible from Fundamentalism* (1991), Spong predicts that the liberal church is doomed to fail, commenting that the liberal Protestant main line and liberal Catholic minority are "by definition fuzzy, imprecise, and relatively unappealing. They might claim to be honest, but for the most part they have no real message. They tinker with words, redefine concepts, and retreat slowly behind the rear guard protection of a few pseudoradical thinkers" (1991, 35–36). Turning his attention to the shortcomings of conservative Christianity, Spong observes that the conservatives expend "all of their meager energy on the hopeless task of doing a facelift on the corpse of the traditional Christian religion, employing images that have lost their meaning. They, too, will ultimately fail" (1991, 36). Amid such ominous predictions and expectations, Spong, Vosper, and the progressive Christians featured in this book attempt to forge a version of Christianity that is neither liberal nor conservative; it is not a middle path but rather one that charts a novel direction.

Echoing Spong's rallying cry that Christianity must "change or die," progressive Christians see themselves as proselytizers of a new Reformation that they believe will reinvigorate the church. Under its auspices they foresee a return of those former adherents who left because they could not speak openly about their doubts. Many new initiates report that they are grateful to have finally found a congregation where they can be themselves and express their skepticism without fear of persecution. This new Reformation insists that progressive Christians must question or reject components of Christianity when they do not align with so-called secular evidence and experience. This supposition allows progressive Christians to exclude beliefs and practices that might otherwise be thought of as central, including the miracles of Jesus, the authority of scripture, sacrificial atonement theology, and the notion of a God who intervenes in human history. Many reject the existence of a deity altogether because they regard the idea that God might intervene on behalf of some humans and not others as not only nonempirical but also immoral. Thus, in contrast to more traditional versions of Christianity, the progressive Christians featured in this book understand their Christianity as without God and consider that humans, not a divine force, wrote the Bible and prayers.

A commitment to intellectual investigation and a willingness to evaluate religion using secular knowledge is imperative to progressive Christians' faith. While secular knowledge might denote a variety of content and epistemologies, for progressive Christians it refers to knowledge derived from historical and scientific research and aligned broadly with ethical humanism. They believe that without such secular knowledge, one cannot determine what is true and what is false when reading the Bible. For example, without historical biblical criticism, one would not know that Matthew's use of the term *virgin* in reference to Jesus's mother, Mary, is the result of a mistranslation of Isaiah in the Septuagint. Likewise, without modern science, one might not know that individuals are not miraculously healed of infectious diseases or that a human cannot walk on water. Finally, without humanism, one might assent to biblical mandates to stone people identified as homosexuals or witches. In each of these examples, widely cited by progressive Christians, secular knowledge trumps religious tradition.

Secular knowledge is more than just intellectually reliable—for progressive Christians, it denotes personal integrity. It enables or, put more strongly, compels a progressive Christian to reject certain traditions and doctrines. Failure to reject those beliefs that one knows to be false or those practices that one knows to be wrong reveals not only a lack of understanding but also a lack of character. Secular knowledge thus inspires a moral directive. One cannot simply believe something because one has always believed it. Instead, one must weigh beliefs against evidence and experience.

In order to undertake such an evaluation based on evidence, progressive Christians read popular theological books by authors claiming expertise in the historical study of biblical texts. The most notable works attend to scholarly reconstructions of the historical Jesus to advocate for a dismissal of the view that he is divine. While Spong is exemplary, other prominent authors include the biblical scholars John Dominic Crossan (*God and Empire*) and Marcus Borg (*The Heart of Christianity*), the Anglican priest and journalist Tom Harpur (*The Pagan Christ*), and Gretta Vosper (*With or Without God*), minister of West Hill United Church. Many read these popular works in church book study groups that facilitated their initial foray into progressive Christianity. One early example in my fieldwork at West Hill United Church provides a sense of a typical progressive Christian gathering.

A Novel Variety

James, our facilitator for the evening book study group, counted us off into four groups of five or six members and directed us to the different parts of the church where we were to meet and have a discussion for approximately thirty minutes. I held three fingers together, as a child does, so I would not forget my assigned group. I smiled as I checked to see who else had been assigned to group 3. The other members cringed as James instructed us to meet at the front of the church's sanctuary, which was always dark and clammy at night. It did, however, afford a different view of the church in which I spent many Sunday mornings and every other Friday night for the better part of a year.

James hastily handed out two sheets of paper. "These sheets list the greatest commandments from different religious traditions," he explained, drawing air quotes around *greatest commandments*.

I glanced down at the papers, and sure enough, they listed slight variations of the Christian adage "Do unto others as you would have them do unto you." Also on the page were religious symbols: a picture of the

Buddha, the Star of David, and so forth, so that we would know to which religion the statements belonged. The second sheet listed versions of the Ten Commandments as they appear in the New Revised Standard Version of the Bible (Exod. 20:2–17 and Deut. 5:6–21).

"The problem with the Ten Commandments," James remarked, "is that they reflect the cultural context of the Bible, not our current world." Heads around the room nodded in agreement. "It doesn't make sense for us to follow all those rules. The rules about food, homosexuality, treatment of women, treatment of people with diseases—we *know* those teachings are wrong! What I want you to do today is break into your small groups and think about what commandments you think are important. We're going to rewrite the Ten Commandments for us to use today, here, at West Hill United Church." With that, James began to distribute large pieces of construction paper shaped to look like the stone tablets that Charlton Heston carried down the mountain as Moses in the 1956 film *The Ten Commandments*.

As we began to gather our belongings and move to our assigned locations, James called over his shoulder, almost as an afterthought, "You only need to do six. The first four of the original Ten Commandments are religious. So we can automatically exclude them. Just do six." No one objected or even really took note of what might, in other Christian contexts, be understood as a heretical statement. "We'll break for our snack time in thirty minutes."

As we pulled up chairs in the choir area near the altar at the front of the church, we quickly introduced ourselves: the group consisted of Steve, Kassy, Jane, Karen, and me. The other members of my group were typical of the demographics within a progressive Christian church. All four were in their mid- to late sixties and had attended mainline liberal churches on and off for most of their lives. Referencing their religious upbringing, they told stories about former Sunday school teachers and ministers who had made them memorize the Ten Commandments. For the most part, they felt that these experiences had been a waste of time. They talked about how they did not like the tone of the Ten Commandments. Kassy explained, "The Ten Commandments are too negative. They all start 'Thou shalt not ___.' They should be about what you should do, not what you shouldn't do."

From there we moved on to a discussion about the historical context and purpose of the Ten Commandments and the legal system recorded in the Pentateuch. Steve was sure this larger legal system was about power and attempts to control the masses, while Jane took a functionalist approach, pointing out that the food restrictions, especially, served as a rudimentary medical science. Soon enough, James came by and pointed out that we had only ten minutes left. It was time to get down to business. We talked about the values West Hill held. We identified justice, love, and caring for others and the environment as at the core of the church's worldview. Picking up Kassy's point, we decided that we would issue a series of positive commandments because we did not like the negative tone of the Ten Commandments. With my eye on the clock, I tentatively suggested "Share" as a straightforward and simple commandment rooted in the Christian tradition and inclusive enough to reflect a progressive Christian worldview. My group loved it, and before time was up, we had come up with a total of four commandments. We were running behind, and Steve quickly wrote them down on our construction paper stone tablet:

1. Share.
2. Have compassion.
3. Take responsibility for own actions.
4. Leave no footprint.

It was not quite the six James wanted, but we were confident that they epitomized the congregation's values.

During the break, church members stood over an elaborate spread of crackers, hummus, and dessert squares and buzzed about the group activity. James's Ten Commandment tablets were a hit. The book study group was more accustomed to breaking into small groups to discuss and debate a text. Most of its activities were cerebral. The opportunity to do something creative and produce something was novel. The atmosphere was lively, and every group was excited to share its new commandments with everyone else. After the snack and social time, we returned to the church's main hall to present our commandments. Steve stood up and volunteered to go first, and he proudly held up our construction paper tablet. In a loud voice, he began to read.

"Number one, Share."

"Share what? Share poison?" quipped Kevin, a vocal member of the book study group and a respected lay leader in the congregation.

Everyone laughed. Kevin was a known joker.

"No, I'm serious," Kevin insisted, furrowing his brow and leaning forward in his chair. "This is what got us into trouble in the first place. You can't just say, 'Share.' People might misinterpret it. There's a lot of things I'd rather you not share with me."

Steve shrugged his shoulders and glanced sideways at our group. Kassy sighed and shook her head. Since we offered no defense, Steve forged on with the presentation of our new commandments. Fortunately, our next three commandments required no explanation. After he finished, representatives from other groups stepped up to share their commandments. Common themes around respect, love, environmental stewardship, and self-awareness emerged from the remaining presentations. A brief discussion ensued, highlighting these themes and their presumed universality. As he summed up our evening, James bore the grin of someone who has shepherded a successful activity. Satisfied, he concluded, "I think all cultures would have similar values." The majority of heads around the room nodded. I glanced over at Kevin, whose eyes were fixed on a particular place on the carpet. I couldn't help but smile. Having watched Kevin both in the book study group and at church for several months, I was pretty sure that he was letting this particular comment slide because it was getting late.

It was well past 10:00 p.m. by the time I reached my car in the parking lot. It would take me almost an hour to get home. As I drove, I thought more about Kevin's dismissal of my group's suggestion of Share.

Kevin's assertion that the church should be wary of any statements that could be misinterpreted is consistent with the attention to detail that progressive Christians employ when it comes to interpretation. Kevin worried that "Share" could be taken out of context and purposely manipulated in order to poison someone. His critique resembled those that progressive Christians raise about Christianity and biblical hermeneutics: they feel that the Bible has been used for similar nefarious means in the past. For progressive Christians, nothing—not even the Bible—is inherently sacred. They see themselves as part of a movement that is decentralizing and deconstructing Christian dogma and creed. In so doing, they rely on the findings of contemporary biblical scholarship alongside general scientific empiricism and humanism.[10]

I recount the example of Kevin's objection, which occurred about six months into my fieldwork, because it points to one of my key observations: for progressive Christians, the Bible serves simultaneously as a raw resource that they might refine for greater access to real religion and as an obstacle that blocks access to authentic Christianity. The Ten Commandments might retain some usefulness but only after they are reconsidered and rewritten for a contemporary audience. While perhaps surprising to contemporary observers accustomed to thinking of the Bible as static, this practice of entextualization situates progressive Christians within an enduring tradition of rewritten scripture.[11] Indeed, they embody a strategic rereading of texts: from the parabiblical expansion literature of antiquity (Mroczek 2016; Reed 2008) and the apocryphal corpus of early Christianity (Burke 2017) to the austere revisions of the New Testament proffered by Thomas Jefferson and Leo Tolstoy that reject the miracle components of the Christian narrative to recast Jesus as an ethical, religious teacher (Manseau 2020; Levitsky 1979).

While Kevin was a vocal member of West Hill and a prominent advocate for pushing the limits of language and representation in religious contexts, others at the church were not as familiar with the types of critique he wanted to raise. Kevin's restraint at the end of the night reflected a second characteristic of progressive Christianity, which encourages an interlacing of ethics, discipline, and conviction. In his view, the church must be vigilant about its language yet sensitive to the fact that these changes will take time for some to digest. Kevin did not want others to feel isolated in the process. Like many progressive Christians, he saw the movement as on the cusp of a new Reformation that will change Christianity's fundamental features. He was uncertain, however, as to when and how this new Reformation would come about.

A few Sundays later, at church, I asked Kevin about the Ten Commandments.

"The good, the ethical, the moral, these things are constructions," he told me. "It was a fun exercise because we need to deconstruct our own stories and practices, but we can't say that these qualities reflect the truth, capital *T*." I offered what I hoped was a responsive nod. Kevin continued, "I never know with this group, when to push them and when to sit back and wait and see. Some of these people have been attending for a long time." He began to trail off, adding, "Progressive Christianity is a journey, not a destination."

Lived Secularity: Skepticism, Sincerity, and Accidental Speech

Kevin's insistence that the journey matters more than the destination speaks to the necessity of looking beyond official definitions and classifications when studying religious people. The example of rewriting the Ten Commandments is informative about the approach members of the West Hill book study group adopted in regard to religious dictates and ethics. The virtues they offered in place of traditional commandments require a different relationship to ethical action and suggest a diminished emphasis on religious authority. It is revealing that the process carries forward the framework of enumerated rules from the Christian tradition, albeit into a secular model. At the end of the day, the newly generated commandments were not as significant as the process itself or the experiences of the members of the study group.

The concept of lived religion provides insight into such experiences. Many scholars have advocated for the study of lived religion because it shifts our focus from institutional religion, theology, and doctrines to the everyday practices of ordinary religious people without resorting to classifying them as misguided, inauthentic, or folk practitioners (Hall 1997; McGuire 2008; Orsi 2003; see especially Bielo 2011a, 101–17). Lived religion emphasizes the religious significance of everyday items and people even when they lie outside traditional hierarchies such as sacred and profane or institutional and popular (Kaell 2014, 11). It takes seriously the multiple and incongruous layers of meaning making that religious adherents employ. Furthermore, it underscores the messiness of religious belonging. It provides more insight into people's capabilities to hold contradictory ideas about the significance of their religious beliefs and practices without reducing religion to specific domains, activities, or ways of thinking. Instead, lived religion relates beliefs and practices to their broader cultural context and the particular experiences of a religious individual or group.

While lived religion expands our capacity as scholars of religion to make sense of the experiences of religious adherents, it retains religion as its foundation for analysis. As a framework employed by scholars, lived religion can be problematic. The anthropologist Jennifer Selby notes that it is sometimes used "as a shorthand for real or authentic religion" (Selby 2019, 63; see also Ramey 2015, 62). In doing so, it presumes that religion occupies a privileged place in the minds of both adherents and the scholars who study them.[12] But what of those groups, such as progressive Christians, for whom religion is not the point of departure? As this book reveals, progressive Christians start with what they see as secular assumptions. In the same ways scholars have considered lived religion, it is possible to likewise think about lived secularism or, more accurately, lived secularity as further blurring the binaries between sacred and profane entities, institutional and folk practices, and religious and nonreligious experiences.

Both the human geographer Philippa Williams (2012) and the religious studies scholar Anna Bigelow (2019) have proposed the concept of lived secularism, although they do not set it in contrast to lived religion. Williams sees lived secularism as embodied within notions of citizenship as they relate to "the bundle of practices that constitute encounters between the citizen and the state" (2012, 982). In a similar vein, Bigelow locates it as "one of the key means by which people come to understand the scope and shape of political, state-structured secularism" (2019, 729). Williams and Bigelow apply the concept to better understand the ways that minority religious groups are able to reconfigure institutional structures and political imaginaries in order to negotiate their place within multireligious contexts.

Secularism has supplanted secularization as a theoretical model for thinking about religious responses to contemporary social contexts. It incorporates a broad range of philosophical, political, and cultural "behaviors, knowledges, and sensibilities" (Asad 2003, 25). As an analytical category, secularism often is tied to secularization theory, which posits a steady and irreversible decline of religion (Casanova 1994; Zuckerman, Galen, and Pasquale 2016). This conflation of the two is deceptive; secularization directs its attention to the withdrawal or decline of religion in public life, whereas secularism has a point of origin related to religion but is not necessarily dependent upon it. According to the anthropologist Talal Asad, it is necessary to distinguish between *secular, secularism,* and *secularization*. Like religion, secularism can be analyzed as a socially embedded system of representation and power (Asad 2003). Further distinctions can be drawn between secularity and secularism, whereby the former refers to a state of being and the latter implies an ideological and epistemological commitment that provides a guiding sense of how the world ought to be (Zuckerman, Galen, and Pasquale 2016, 21–22).

There are many different ways to be secular. The behaviors, knowledges, and sensibilities associated with the secular depend on social context (Asad 2003; Berlinerblau 2012; Casanova 1994; Keane 2007; Mahmood 2015). While often framed as a political or social force with an emphasis on macrolevel examinations, secularism can also be conceptualized as a lived experience that ordinary people negotiate and embody (Scheer, Johansen, and Fadil 2019). The anthropologist Ashley Lebner (2015) argues that continued focus on the secular as a political analytic is an obstacle for ethnographic inquiry. Lebner critiques the perspective of secularism as entangled—perhaps irreversibly—in institutionality and governance, which gives it a transcendent-like quality that makes secularism challenging to locate in everyday lived experiences. In its place, she proposes ethnographic investigations of *secularity* (a term borrowed from the philosopher Charles Taylor). While noting that Taylor's concept emerges from Eurocentric and Christocentric perspectives, Lebner argues that secularity shifts the focus from an inaccessible political imaginary to one with the "potential to elucidate how religious and secular lives are lived" (2015, 64).

Lebner's advancement of secularity illuminates the social frameworks that progressive Christians employ. Taylor argues that the primary framework of secularity is religious pluralism, wherein "exclusive humanism" as a new condition of belief emerges as a possibility.[13] Exclusive humanism constitutes a framework for navigating the world without presuming the necessity of the transcendent or other claims that "go beyond human flourishing" (Taylor 2007, 21). Under these conditions, one might retain religious frameworks, but it is not necessary. In other words, in secularity one might choose to be religious or not, or both; religious and secular identities can and do coexist in a larger social milieu. Lebner calls for ethnographic investigations of secularity, noting that the concept is potentially useful precisely because it is imperfect. Rather, its "potential openness as a concept" may help avoid larger disciplinary pitfalls (Lebner 2015, 70).

Similarly, in an edited volume that brings together scholars examining the intersections of religion and secularism within a broad European context, Monique Scheer, Birgitte Schepelern Johansen, and Nadia Fadil have called for a study of secularity centered on embodiment, affect, and everyday practices. While they contend that such approaches have become standard for scholars of religion, they note its lack when it comes to understanding the secular. As they frame it, "the study of the secular should not so much lie in an attempt to capture what it *is*, but rather to reveal what it *does* and how it *works*" (Scheer, Johansen, and Fadil 2019, 3). Likewise, this book takes up the question of how secularism, or secularity, works as a popular category.

While many people tend to think of popular secularism as a discursive realm set in strong opposition to religion and populated by the likes of the atheist thinkers Christopher Hitchens and Richard Dawkins, it can also be seen as an embodied experience, a set of practices, and an ethical system that directs individuals' lives. Progressive Christians understand the secular to denote knowledge garnered from empirical experience and common sense. This knowledge stands in contrast to the implausible and unverifiable claims of religion. Religion is thus entangled in and subsumed by secular knowledge, which progressive Christians frequently privilege over religion (cf. Bender 2012; Cimino and Smith 2015). Of course, the categories and assumptions progressive Christians bring to their understanding of what it means to be secular (and religious) depart from those outlined by scholars. Central to this discussion is Lebner's point that the value of focusing on secularity lies in its imprecision. While religion remains the primary descriptive category used by progressive Christians, they presume that it must be dominated by a larger adherence to practices, ideas, and moral frameworks generated from an overarching secularity.

It is noteworthy that this commitment to secularity involves an ethical stance that evokes a sense of what one ought to do and an expectation that one should privilege secular behaviors, knowledges, and sensibilities when evaluating moral choices (see Zuckerman, Galen, and Pasquale 2016). For progressive Christians, this assessment attaches moral significance to both *what* and *if* one believes. In this context, belief takes an empirical form; it can be examined and therefore endorsed or disqualified alongside other elements of Christian practice. For example, in the mid-1990s, Jim Adams, the founder of the Center for Progressive Christianity, proposed that some Christians may be able to believe in Christianity's claims of miracles; however, such faith was never intended for all Christians. In Adams's view, faith is merely one of several gifts identified by the apostle Paul alongside spiritual gifts like tongues or prophecy, which some Christians reported they had received, but others did not (Adams 1996, 32). In the eyes of progressive Christians, these gifts are undesirable. They were associated with certain conservative Christian denominations, were available only to some, and relied on miraculous occurrences and nonempirical presumptions. Thus, since faith is classified with these other undesirable gifts and is already contentious, it is not difficult for Adams to conclude that believing is not necessary—or even desirable—in order to be a progressive Christian. Others, as I will explain, make the jump that it may indeed be unethical to believe.

Within the anthropology of Christianity, the dominant paradigm has twinned belief with sincerity as the essential modality by which adherents classify and evaluate their religious commitments. The temptation for anthropologists has been to accept interlocutors' understanding of belief as something amassed through acts of Christian surrender (Elisha 2008) and various forms of piety (Bartel 2016; Bell 2002; Strhan 2015). While belief and believing are hallmarks of Christian epistemologies, the supremacy of belief lies not in assent or rejection but rather in its capacity to generate conviction. Conviction stands as the missing link between belief and experience. One need only consider the fervor with which evangelicals attest to their "personal relationship with Jesus" as the defining aspect of their faith as an indication that belief is primarily an experience (Elisha 2008; cf. Bebbington 1989). For many Christians, an expressed belief that is gauged to be sincere is thought to reveal an adherent's moral nature (see, for example, Keane 2002; Keller 2005; Robbins 2008). For progressive Christians, however, conviction in the form of skepticism does not strengthen but rather weakens faith. Skepticism acts not as a gift but as an ethical imperative. In this respect, doubt mirrors the function of belief. Because their secular convictions are consistent with empirical experience, progressive Christians understand them to be more sincere and authentic than their former religious ones.

In the context of progressive Christianity, lived secularity places skepticism and doubt at the forefront of generating and evaluating knowledge and discerning ethical or moral choices. This concept is more than just a reversal of lived religion (such as when one might ambiguously impose religious-like practices in a secular, differentiated realm). Rather, it accounts for instances in which secular categories (or those presumed by adherents to be secular) take preeminence and direct religious ones. Herein lies the value of lived secularity: the experience of no longer believing something or believing against something can be as profound as assenting to traditional doctrines and tenets. Lived secularity thus makes two contributions. First, the concept allows a more complete investigation of how religious doubt and skepticism parallel faith and belief, accomplishing similar tasks and engendering conviction. In the case of progressive Christianity, it is essential to examine as examples of religious activity occasions when beliefs and practices are challenged or jettisoned. Incorporating lived secularity allows scholars of religion to highlight moments of simultaneous doubt and conviction as they occur within faith communities and are experienced by proponents of the tradition (cf. C. Smith 2003). Second, it expands our scholarly understanding of how notions about what knowledge does and how evidence works discipline the presumed sincerity of the inner self. An example shows these two factors at work.

Progressive Christians have frequent conversations about the ways that their former religious beliefs and practices impinge upon their more recently developed progressive and/or secular ones. The problem of accidental prayer emerged as a common theme throughout my fieldwork. These were occasions, often insignificant ones, in which a progressive Christian inadvertently uttered a prayer and then immediately regretted the action because prayer is perceived to be outdated and unethical. Whether spontaneous or scripted, supported or spurred, prayer is a central practice in Christianity. Thus, its elimination provides insight into progressive Christianity specifically and North American Christianity in general. It directs attention to Christian notions of how language operates, to human capacities to communicate, and to the nature of private thoughts.

As a relatively new discipline, the anthropology of Christianity has devoted significant attention to the role of language in constructing

Christian subjectivities. Scholars interested in the study of Christian language practices have sought to extend or substantiate the anthropologist Webb Keane's (2002; 2007) suggestion that sincerity is the central animating concern for Christians regarding the purpose and consequences of language. In Keane's view, sincerity is pertinent "because of the links it forges among language, social interaction, personal character, freedom, regimes of truth, and some narratives of modernity" (2002, 65). Most important is the perceived intentionality and ethic attached to a linguistic act. North American Christians assume a high degree of intentionality regarding religious speech acts, such as prayer, sermons, rituals, or discussions about faith. This intentionality is evaluated to see if it aligns with words and actions (e.g., when a Christian proclaims they have been "born again," they are laying claim to an inner transformation determined to have in fact occurred when they model the behavior and beliefs of a born-again Christian). Sincerity is difficult enough to decipher with one agent; an individual might lie or be misunderstood. Christian notions of sincerity are even more challenging to discern when they involve multiple actors, particularly supernatural ones. That is, God's words and actions are difficult to observe and assess. Adherents must often contend with competing claims from rival spokespersons about God's motivations.

But, for the progressive Christians, there are not multiple actors—or at least not divine ones. They consider the existence of God implausible and deem belief in God immoral. By privileging secular knowledge and sensibilities, they frame disbelief as an ethical act. They have determined that it is unethical to believe what historical and scientific evidence says is false. Alongside the scientific and historical evidence, they critically assess the biblical narrative and find it reveals that God's character is deficient. Spong's interpretation is illustrative. In discussing the biblical depiction of God, Spong points out that the deity comes across as "clearly pro-Jewish" in his interventions: "God had freed the Jews from slavery in Egypt by visiting great violence on the Egyptians. God had led the marauding Israelites in their conquest of the land of Canaan. God had championed his people in their continuing conflict with the Philistines. One can only imagine that such a view of God was wildly popular among the Jews. It was not, however, a very pleasant view of God if you happen to be an Egyptian, a Canaanite, or a Philistine. A universal

God of love this deity was not" (Spong 1998, 30). Here God intervenes on behalf of one side (the Israelites) and not the other (the Egyptians, Canaanites, or Philistines). Reading the narrative through the universalizing lens of Christian monotheism, Spong finds it problematic that God would favor one group of people over another. He labels this intervening God immoral because of its unequal treatment of people and transgression of humanist teachings about universal equality. Additionally, for progressive Christians, anyone who claims to believe in a God that intervenes in this manner is likewise judged to be unethical. These assumptions necessitate that progressive Christians reject the notion of God's intervening in their lives in any way—a task that for some is easier said than done.

With this imperative in mind, progressive Christians generally look down on prayer directed toward God and regard seeking intervention as a sign of moral or ethical weakness. To avoid it, progressive Christians monitor and discipline their language in both religious and nonreligious settings. Many draw upon the example of not being able to locate a convenient parking place in the mall and the inadvertent, spontaneous thought, "Please let me find a spot," as a mistaken invocation of God. They perceive this request, directed toward an otherworldly force with the power to intervene and materialize a parking spot, as not only an empirical error but also an unethical act. Whether the progressive Christian actually believes in God and God's ability to generate a parking spot or not is irrelevant. According to progressive Christian thinking, such a request, even if it is only thought and not spoken aloud, is problematic. It aligns its thinker with the notion of an interventionist God who would just as soon slaughter the innocent children of Egyptians, Canaanites, or Philistines as make a free parking spot available miraculously. The inadvertent prayer presupposes a (potentially) wrathful God. A passive participation in this discourse generates guilt on the part of progressive Christians.[14]

While this example may appear to be superficial, it points to critical questions about the ethics of believing. Christian sincerity is often conceptualized as spontaneous and natural. In reality, it requires careful discipline to achieve and maintain. The weaving together of sincerity and skepticism points to the ways in which conviction operates in progressive Christianity. What one believes is less important than consistency with the secular behaviors, knowledge, and sensibilities related to historical evidence, liberal humanism, and scientific empiricism.

The preceding discussion involves everyday speech acts; however, progressive Christians apply a similar approach to ritual prayers. When a church adopts progressive Christianity, one of the congregation's first steps is to rewrite prayers and liturgies to more accurately reflect a progressive Christian worldview. For example, congregants at West Hill United Church no longer recited the Lord's Prayer; instead, the children led the congregation in reciting a version of the Prayer of St. Francis. Likewise, at Holy Cross Lutheran Church, another progressive Christian congregation, the wording of the communion service omitted Jesus's sacrifice and references to blood and death. Instead, the liturgy emphasized fellowship and sharing. Finally, at St. Matthias Anglican Church, the community received special permission from its diocesan bishop to use an overhead projector, rather than a book of services, to alter the words of the service as they saw fit.

Through a complex process of revision and reconfiguration, progressive Christians self-consciously redefine their religion as simultaneously Christian by choice and secular by necessity. Belief becomes meaningful when it is jettisoned; it is replaced by an ethical imperative that links skepticism and conviction. While they work to realign their practices and theologies to their secular knowledge and experiences, the very process of doing so buttresses their identity. Progressive Christians provide an ideal case study for introducing lived secularity as a framework because they resist attempts to categorize people according to belief (e.g., either atheist first or Christian first). Instead, their nonbelief is dependent on secular forms of knowledge, which enables them to maintain their religious identities. In this way, they parallel the messiness found within the model of lived religion.

Anthropology of Christianity, Research Methods, and Reflexivity

As a work focused on the development of progressive Christianity in the context of the broader study of Christianities, this ethnography evokes two prominent themes within the anthropology of Christianity. First, it examines the role of language and discourse in demarcating religious frameworks, experiences, and identities (Bialecki 2011). Second, it addresses the need for a self-consciously comparative anthropological study of Christianity that highlights divergences rather than similarities (Robbins 2003; cf. Engelke 2004; Harris 2006).

Concerning the first theme, this book contributes to anthropological explorations of the ways that the Christian subject is constructed and legitimized through language (Stromberg 1993; Harding 2000; Keane 2007) and initiated and maintained through collective reading (Bielo 2009c; Boyarin 1993; Cannell 2006; Wuthnow 1994a, 1994b). In investigating how progressive Christians read about and endorse a version of Christianity that is both secular and religious, this book adds to more extensive discussions of religious boundaries and notions of belonging. This book asks what can be made of Christian subjects who adopt the rhetoric of secularism to subvert traditional definitions of Christianity while continuing to describe themselves as real Christians. The goal is not to determine whether their version is authentic but rather to delineate the social processes through which they negotiate claims to authenticity (cf. Bielo 2011a).

Second, this book proposes that examining the discursive processes by which progressive Christians articulate their religious identities provides the anthropology of Christianity with an opportunity for comparison that has been missing. As Chris Hann (2007) maintains, "We still do not have much by way of ethnographic studies of mainstream Christianity in countries such as Britain and the United States," where the institutional homes of most anthropologists are located (2007, 384).[15] While Hann calls for an extension of ethnographic research to more familiar landscapes, most anthropologists focus on regions where Christianity is primarily a missionary or convert culture (Hann 2007; Howell 2005). Many anthropologists remain hesitant to study mainstream Christians because they are not sufficiently other; that is, they have inherited and contributed to the same hegemonic social systems as many anthropologists themselves (Cannell 2005; Robbins 2003). Although those working within North America have begun to respond to the call to study Christians perceived to be both geographically and culturally proximate (Bialecki 2017a; Bielo 2009c, 2011a; Elisha 2011; Kaell 2014), their works generally explore communities that retain an element of other in terms of social practices, political ideologies, or beliefs about the supernatural (Harding 1991). In contrast, as mainline Protestants in North America, progressive Christians are located in a familiar position; they share many of the ideological and ontological assumptions that anthropologists and scholars of religion make and have similar socioeconomic, political, and ethnic identities (cf. Bender 2010; Zwissler 2018). Thus, this book responds to Hann's call by extending the anthropology of Christianity and bringing it closer to home.

Like members of other movements within North American Christianity, progressive Christians fluctuate between the heretical and hegemonic (Klassen 2011; cf. Albanese 2007; Emberley 2002; Schmidt 2005). Methodologically, this point raises the question of whether the seemingly dual role of both familiar and other affects the analysis of progressive Christianity. Since scholars and Christians subvert their own terms to reinscribe Christianity, the study of progressive Christianity interrogates the means through which both groups define the tradition. One potential route for analysis is to adopt a dialogical approach, which underscores the perceptual ambiguity of who is and who is not a Christian, a classic problem that also preoccupies adherents (Garriott and O'Neill 2008). Progressive Christians debate such classifications both within their local congregations and under the auspices of the broader progressive Christian movement. While they often disagree about what counts as progressive or Christian, such debates reveal more about the nature of progressive Christianity than an examination of what they hold in common.

This book highlights those disagreements and differences in its description of progressive Christianity. I studied five churches—two United Church of Canada (George Street United Church and West Hill United Church), two Anglican (St. Matthias Anglican Church and St. Peter's Anglican Church), and one Lutheran (Holy Cross Lutheran Church). I spent at least six months with each community, although at some, like West Hill United Church, I attended events and services and participated in their book studies throughout my two-and-a-half years of fieldwork. I am using, with permission, the actual names of four of the five churches. The fifth congregation, an Anglican church I call St. Peter's, is not actually a progressive church but featured a reading group that engaged progressive texts. I met with this reading group for a full year, and this small group, averaging from four to ten members, was, surprisingly, the most diverse in its theological positions. While St.

Peter's is not a progressive Christian church, the presence of progressive thinkers in its community provides relevant comparative data. It helps expand an understanding of what is characteristic of Christians in general and what is unusual in the collective reading of progressive theological texts.

The diversity of theological opinions within the study group at St. Peter's became remarkably clear during the first meeting. To break the ice, the leader asked us to position ourselves in the study room according to our own theological beliefs. Most members stood in the middle of the room, one woman at the far north side (to indicate that she was conservative) and a few others at the far south side (declaring their liberal leanings). Another member left the room entirely by the south side exit to have a cigarette. A third opted to stand above us in the choir loft to indicate that he felt that he was above these sorts of exercises and that his theology transcended arrangement on a linear continuum.

In private conversations and formal interviews, members of this group explained that they did not feel that they could openly espouse a progressive theology. For this reason, to protect the identity of the members of this book study group, I have elected not to include the name and location of this church. They may be surprised to find themselves included in this study of progressive Christianity. They differ from the other congregations in this book and knew little about progressive Christianity before meeting me. I found my time at St. Peter's to be especially important because I suspect that for every congregation like West Hill United Church's, there are several congregations like the one at St. Peter's. Churches that feature a few members exploring progressive theology in small study groups and a few members who identify themselves as atheists or nontheists and often feel like those in the St. Peter's book study group: that they cannot be honest about their beliefs with their families and other congregants. I am grateful to this group for the candor with which they shared their thoughts and personal journeys and the openness with which they invited me into their conversations.

Many consider participant observation to be an art form. It is a way of life rather than a set of prescribed skills. Practitioners resist attempts to formulate a concrete methodology (Jorgensen 1989, 8) and advocate that students learn it organically in the field by using the body as an instrument of knowing (Coleman 2006, 32; Ortner 1995, 173). Anthropological fieldwork requires the researcher to develop relationships and is as contingent upon the researcher's personality as it is upon theories and methods. In the words of Amira Mittermaier, the anthropologist "offer[s] neither an objective account nor a final interpretation but a *re-telling* of [their] interlocutors' stories and one particular perspective of them" (2011, 28). It is inevitable that the anthropologist shows up in the very image they seek to capture. Of course, in focusing in, the anthropologist can sometimes lose track of the larger picture.

When I was in my first year of university, a woman in my dormitory purchased a photomosaic poster of Bob Marley. Photomosaics use thousands of different tiny images to create a larger picture. When viewed from far away, one saw a cohesive image of Bob Marley, but when one stood closer to the picture, it revealed multiple different images of the Rastafarian musician. One evening her roommate cut out a tiny picture of herself and pasted it over one of the images. From a distance nothing appeared to have changed, but closer examination revealed a smiling college student with her hair pulled back in a loose ponytail. This image was a striking contrast amid the sea of ganja-smoking, peace sign-flashing Marleys.

By focusing closely on her community of study, the ethnographer provides insight into the many tiny images that make up its more substantial picture. No matter how careful the ethnographer is, they also leave their own image behind. To account for this inevitable imprint, anthropology insists on a reflexive account from ethnographers (Clifford and Marcus 1986). "At its worst," the anthropologist James Bielo warns, "'being reflexive' amounts to little more than unnecessary autobiography (navel gazing as it were)." But "at its best, 'being reflexive' scrutinizes how research is conducted and the experience of doing fieldwork, all in the pursuit of helping readers better understand the claims being made" (2009c, 22).

Anthropologists are well prepared for reflexive questions; those who study religion in particular are prepared to account for their own religious beliefs, practices, and affiliation. The field asks us to address our own relationship to the religious claims of the subjects we study. The anthropologist Susan Harding provides a model, writing honestly and compassionately about how the language of the conservative Christians she studied influenced her thoughts. Her decision to study Christian fundamentalists was often under scrutiny by other anthropologists. While conducting her fieldwork, other scholars frequently asked Harding about her religious background and whether she considers herself to be (or as having been) a born-again Christian (1991, 375).

Likewise, our subjects of study often pose questions about our religious beliefs and practices. My experience within progressive Christianity was unlike that of my colleagues studying evangelicals as these anthropologists sometimes struggle with attempts to convert them and are often forced to define their theology or identify themselves as religious agents (see, for example, O'Neill 2010, xiii). Armed with accounts of reflexivity and the advice of other fieldworkers, I was prepared to discuss my religious background with progressive Christians. To my surprise, the topic rarely came up. I had entered fieldwork determined to espouse methodological atheism, which is the default position for most anthropologists (see Bialecki 2014; Bielo 2009c; Blanes 2006; Harding 1987; Howell 2007), but I was never once asked what I believe, and only twice did anyone address the question of my religious affiliation in a way that attached any significance to the answer. On one occasion, in my introductory meeting with the small study group at St. Peter's Anglican Church, a slightly more conservative member of the book study group asked if I was Anglican. The question followed my presentation of my research proposal to the group when I asked if they had any further questions or concerns about my potential participation in their study group. While I cannot be certain, I interpreted the question, based upon the tone with which it was asked, as suggesting that they may have raised concern had my answer been no. I cannot determine whether this was the case because I responded affirmatively, that I had been baptized in the Anglican tradition. They dropped the subject of my affiliation and raised no further questions (or objections).

On another occasion, after we spent an evening debating what it means to be a progressive Christian, my hosts, a couple in their late thirties, asked for my definition of progressive Christianity and whether I am a progressive Christian. In this instance, I drew upon Hal Taussig's definition (2006, 25–34) and acknowledged that, while I share many of the social commitments of progressive Christianity and feel that their theological project is meaningful, I do not consider myself to be a progressive Christian. From there, the conversation shifted to my religious background. While the couple belonged to St. Matthias Anglican Church and had baptized their son in this community, the husband had been raised Roman Catholic and the wife grew up in the United Church. They were interested to learn what it had been like to grow up in the Anglican Communion. On other occasions, denominational background came up as a less significant reference point. The Lutheran community in Newmarket, Ontario, included a former Anglican priest and his wife. Both formally joined the Lutheran Church during my fieldwork there, and we often joked together that Lutherans were like Anglicans but with beer instead of sherry.

While my religious affiliation was not contentious and my religious beliefs were not broached, I tried as much as possible to fit into the churches that I was studying. From the beginning of my research project, I was determined to participate fully in church services. This participation included reciting prayers, taking communion, singing hymns, bringing baked goods to social events, and contributing to the offering plate. I suspect that most congregants saw me as an insider because I knew the words and melodies and, in certain instances, the actions that accompanied their songs. I was also familiar with the biblical and theological contexts of discussions and the fancy—albeit outdated—church words that are important within the Anglican tradition in particular. I worked hard to be a member of the congregations I studied and believe that I was successful, as evidenced by comments from church members. For example, at George Street United Church, a woman whose pew I often shared turned to me after one service and remarked, "I always love to watch you sing the hymns. I can see in your eyes how much you love the songs." She was not wrong. Likewise, I knew that I had fully immersed myself in Holy Cross Lutheran Church when, at one point, I stood up after the service to make an announcement about my research, and Pastor Dawn remarked to the congregation, "I don't know how Rebekka is going to study us—she's one of us!"

While I chose to participate fully in church life and theological discussions, I made a conscious effort to participate in such a way that my contribution would not alter its trajectory. When asked direct questions, I offered responses that were true to my own stance but also reflected a middle-of-the-road progressive Christian one. Because I had studied this movement with an interest in how language operates within it, I did not find it challenging to adopt rhetorical tropes that would position me as an insider during such conversations. The ease with which I did so is a testament to the fact that progressive Christian language is inherently secular and not dissimilar from conversations I regularly had at my university with my peers or social gatherings with friends and family.

Like R. Marie Griffith (1997), I found that my age was the most significant point of distinction within the communities I studied (I estimate that at least 90 percent of congregants were older than fifty, and many were in their seventies, eighties, and nineties). In many instances, my participation in the congregation provided members with an opportunity to pick my brain about attracting youth to church. In group discussions, they often called upon me to report what young people wanted in terms of religious activities. On one occasion, Holy Cross Lutheran Church held what the congregation called an Agape meal.[16] Members gathered at different parishioners' homes to discuss their vision for the future of the church. After addressing various issues, my group of twenty or so discussed the absence of young people at their church. I initially sat back until the conversation turned to how and where the community could find young people. Potential locations included the mall, schools, sports clubs, and the internet. Participants held up evangelical and conservative churches as examples that had managed to attract and retain youth. I interrupted to say, "Maybe you don't need to worry about where the young people are. At those other churches, they don't sit around and brainstorm about where they can find old people." My remark garnered laughter. One woman picked up the point, declaring, "That's right! They're not coming into the Tim Horton's and saying, 'Let's find some old people to come to our churches. We've gotta get those old people into our pews!'"

I often felt like a peculiar insider, so I let my interlocutors form their own assumptions about me. While I was asked only once whether I am a progressive Christian, most members probably assumed that I am. Likewise, they seemed to assume that I shared their political perspectives. Unlike my colleagues who study conservative denominations, I was never once asked where I stood on topics like sexuality, women's ordination, reproductive rights, or immigration laws. For the most part, I share their liberal humanism and left-leaning politics, although I will be the first to acknowledge that many of the older members of these churches are far more radical than I am. For instance, when one congregation decided to hide a refugee seeking asylum in the church basement, they did not conceal this from me. A member did request that I not name their church when discussing this course of action. During the provincial elections in Ontario, the congregants at George Street United Church assumed that I supported local social democratic politicians. Again, this was not an off-the-mark conclusion, given my age, education level, and presence at a United Church of Canada.

In his discussion of reflexivity, Bielo points out that his role as an academic was a thorny issue among the evangelicals he studied. Evangelicals often see academia as a "breeding ground of 'liberalism,' 'humanism,' and 'secularism'" (2009c, 40). In contrast, progressive Christians saw me as an affirmation that their theology is of scholarly interest. On several occasions, I felt as though I was being "shown off" at conferences and community events. My training in religious studies and biblical exegesis was an asset, and members often called upon me to provide dates and the names of texts or theological movements when someone drew a blank on specific details.

I was the only anthropologist in the book study group, but many others had advanced degrees in religious studies, theology, history, and other fields. Courtney Bender's experience conducting ethnographic research among practitioners of metaphysical traditions was akin to my own. Her subjects were often as familiar with the ivory tower as she was, frequently dropping academic names and referencing their own scholarly pedigrees (2010, 15). Because she and her interlocutors shared a linguistic, educational, and geographical perspective, and in many cases held the same understanding of what professors and researchers do, Bender found herself caught by her presumptions that her subjects of study approached the world in the same way (2010, 15–16). Each of the congregations I studied included university professors and members who had completed master's degrees, doctorates, or other advanced professional degrees and were acquainted with the type of research I was conducting. For example, one member of West Hill United Church was completing a master's in my department, and another worked for the University of Toronto's research ethics board. Surprisingly—or perhaps not so surprisingly—these were the members of the communities around whom I often felt the most uncomfortable but to whom I am most indebted for reminding me of the importance of honesty, reflexivity, and rigorous transparency throughout ethnographic research.

Outline of Chapters

This book highlights the core themes of ethics, conviction, and skepticism, which are hallmarks of progressive Christian thinking. It argues that progressive Christianity provides an opportunity to consider what it means to be religious when religion itself is not the starting point. As members of a movement that spurned Christian orthodoxy in pursuit of a resolutely skeptical faith, progressive Christians privilege other forms of knowledge in place of traditionally religious ones. Through various acts of revision and reconsideration, they construct a form of Christianity that aligns with contemporary notions of science, historical knowledge, and liberal humanism. My project in this book was not to rehash antiquated binaries or competitive hierarchies between religious and secular but to chart a process in which they collapse; my hope is that doing so provides fodder for a new framework for understanding religious identity and affiliation.

The first chapter describes the congregations featured in this book. It explores notions of whiteness, being middle class, and suburban religiosity as a means of investigating not only the religious worlds inhabited by progressive Christians but also their socioeconomic, ethnic, and cultural identities. This chapter attends to the lived religion of progressive Christians by focusing on their everyday experiences in their ecclesiastical settings as they articulate their values and identities.

The subsequent chapters draw from ethnographic examples to analyze the perspectives and practices of progressive Christians. Chapter 2 looks at the interpretive practices that progressive Christians employ as they read and discuss biblical criticism. While their interpretations draw on traditionally Protestant interactions with text and ways of being textual, they lend agency and authority to historical analyses by scholars rather than the Bible itself. The shift to history in place of scripture results in a textual ideology that both overly privileges and simultaneously rejects the idea that there is meaning within the biblical text. Progressive Christians afford the Bible the position of a simulacrum, a faithful reproduction intentionally distorted to provide an authentic representation (Baudrillard 1994). In attempting to provide a historically accurate and authentic reading of the Bible, progressive Christians whittle their narratives of origins to such a point that key parts of the story, such as the figure of Jesus, become virtually nonexistent and inaccessible. Yet the congregants remain focused on the Bible as an object of study, and their focus on Christian origins takes precedence over other periods of Christian history. This approach to the Bible reflects what Bruno Latour (1993) describes as the "purification impulse" inherent in modernity. This impulse leaves progressive Christians haunted by an inaccessible point of origin that retains authority over them even as they seek to exclude it from their collective narrative.

Chapter 3 picks up the theme of collective narratives, examining how individuals' stories about their past and their journey toward progressive Christianity reflect shared experiences with other progressive Christians. They present this journey as a process of contemplation, conversation, and contestation, culminating in the rejection of a traditional Christian worldview. They deem traditional Christianity to be unempirical and unethical and replace it with progressive Christianity. They recount this process through a deconversion narrative. Like conversion testimonies, deconversion stories involve reconstructing one's past actions and beliefs in a way that sustains one's current position and status within a religious community.

For many progressive Christians, the ultimate end of their religion is atheism. They describe this future outcome in a way that bears a resemblance to the eschatological language found more broadly within contemporary Christianity. Chapter 4 pays attention to the emphasis that progressive Christians place on temporal adverbs (*still*, *already*, and *yet*), arguing that these words enable progressive Christians to situate themselves in the present discursively but with an eye to a future in which their current religious identities will cease to exist. It is, however, a future that appears to be continuously displaced, never realized.

The conclusion returns to the concept of lived secularity. It considers both its limitations in the context of studying progressive Christianity and ways in which it might be extended into the study of other religious phenomena such as Muslim apostates, Christian creation scientists, and the newly emerging demographic of the religious "nones." While not a perfect category, lived secularity is intended to help scholars of religion think more broadly about the binaries we employ to study religious and nonreligious subjects.

Throughout my fieldwork, I was often struck by the lengths to which progressive Christians would represent themselves as departing from an older, traditional, conservative variant of Christianity while simultaneously maintaining that theirs was a version of Christianity that was somehow, in comparison, purer or more authentic. Jonathan Z. Smith's admonition— "What a difference a difference makes" (J. Smith 2004)— ran through my mind on many occasions. Initially, I looked for ways to reconcile competing claims of simultaneous novelty and antiquity, expose their imbalances, and convince whomever might listen that the tensions within the progressive Christian psyche demanded sorting out. In many ways, I was not alone in this quest as other book study interlocutors sought similar resolutions—albeit as adherents rather than as anthropologists. Ultimately, I found the ease with which my subjects of study assumed and promoted contradictory worldviews to be the most interesting point. As this book's title, *The New Heretics*, suggests, the moniker of heretic is one that they assume with pride: difference *does* make a difference, and a label that is self-designated rather than imposed takes on new meanings in this context. I hope that this book reveals that it is in the negotiation of differences—how they are imagined, consumed, and represented—that scholars of religion can begin to locate progressive Christianity and its vision for the future of the tradition. While progressive Christians see themselves as believers in exile, they are not wandering aimlessly through the desert. Instead, they have begun the work of digging trenches and installing irrigation systems, which they hope will allow for a new religious flourishing and perhaps an offering of refreshment to what they see as a parched and dying church.

1

"Not Christian Like That"

Exploring the Contours of Progressive Christian Congregations

The early Sunday morning drive to Peterborough, Ontario, was just under two hours from downtown Toronto. My route took me up the Don Valley Parkway, across the 401 highway, and along the scenic Algonquin Trail. For four months, I watched the leaves change and the snowfall as I sped along the highway to the sleepy city. There were twelve United Church congregations in Peterborough and the surrounding area. Although there was some discussion of amalgamating several parishes into one, church leadership had taken few steps to bring the congregations together. George Street United Church, an enormous gothic construction, towered over the downtown core, much as it did in its Methodist heyday at the turn of the twentieth century, when the Reverend Edwin Arthur Pearson, the father of former Canadian prime minister Lester B. Pearson, served as its minister.[1]

It is safe to say that theological diversity was a core tenet at George Street. With so many United Church congregations in the region, the members spoke of making a clear choice to worship at this particular location. While many grew up in the denomination, others were attracted to George Street's inclusive teachings. The opening statement on the church's website proudly pronounced: "Literalist? Progressive? Traditionalist? Skeptic? Humanist? You are welcome at George Street United Church." It went on to explain the church's view of Jesus and conditions of membership, and it warned that George Street might not feel as familiar or comfortable as other churches:

> In a time when Christians are deeply divided, we are trying to have new conversations about Jesus Christ. Who was he? What did he really teach us? Why does he still matter today? He was a religious revolutionary who brought transformation—both personal and political—not doctrine. The

original name of the Jesus movement was The Way. At George Street, we are trying to discern the way, and follow it.

That means all are welcome to our grand old building with our brand new thinking. We are a diverse group. The liturgy, while familiar, includes the congregation as leaders. We do more than speak out against injustice; we act out. There is a lot of questioning going on; it is not always comfortable, but it is deeply caring. Through our leadership, our guests, our congregational ministry, we are trying on new ways of seeing; a new perspective that we think can overcome the differences between the literalists and the progressives. You are welcome.

The website also advertised the church's many activities, namely its speaker series featuring prominent progressive Christian theologians, meditation group, children's services, special events, local and international outreach organizations, and the Theological Studies Group with which I spent the majority of my time. Facilitated by the congregation's minister, Karen, the Theological Studies Group met on Sundays following the 10:00 a.m. service, immediately after coffee hour. Members brought brown-bag lunches and eagerly took up their stated task, reeducation.

My first visit to George Street United Church was on a crisp fall morning in early September. The attendance of approximately eighty to one hundred people was greater than I expected. Even with that number, the cavernous church appeared sparsely populated. Like many mainline Protestant churches, George Street followed an order of service that included hymns, prayers, a children's story, Bible readings, a sermon, communion on occasion, and announcements. Some young families were present, but most congregants were baby boomers and members of the greatest generation (demographics that I would soon learn were reflective of progressive congregations). Like many mainline Protestant churches and like the other churches featured in this book, the church's demographic broadly encapsulated the category of white Anglo-Saxon descent.

Toward the end of the service, Reverend Karen warmly invited everyone to move to the fellowship hall for coffee and conversation. An elderly couple sitting next to me turned slightly and smiled. Leaning across her husband, the woman said, "We have a student's group; I don't see any of the members here today, but Karen can tell you all about it."

The congregation sang the closing hymn and slowly filed out of the sanctuary. I followed the crowd into the gathering hall. Surveying the room, I stood to the side, balancing my lunch bag, my notebook, and a copy of John Spong's most recent publication, *Jesus for the Non-Religious*. A few children ran around the hall. I looked around and tried to determine to whom they belonged, but no one seemed to be watching them closely. Whoever their parents (or perhaps grandparents) were, they were otherwise occupied. I was at least thirty years younger than most everyone in the room and felt out of place. As I made my way to the line for tea and cookies, I thought about my friends and colleagues who were studying evangelical Christians and how eager their research subjects were to interact with them. Their stories of overwhelming and enthusiastic proselytizers seemed different from my current experience.

As I added sugar to the thick orange pekoe tea, which looked like it had been steeping for several hours, the woman who had sat next to me during the service approached me. "Are you new here, dear?" I responded affirmatively. She followed up with questions about whether I was a student and what I was studying. I rattled off details about my thesis. Like many graduate students, I was uncomfortable describing my research topic. I worried about revealing too many mundane details and leaving my listener wishing that she had not asked.

"Interesting!" my new friend exclaimed. With that, she took my arm and led me over to meet Elizabeth, a core member of the Theological Studies Group.

"Elizabeth, this is Rachel."

"Rebekka," I corrected.

"Right! Rebekka, sorry! I always get those two names confused." She smiled widely and carried on, explaining who I was and why I was there. "Rebekka is a student in Toronto. She's here to study the Theological Studies Group."

Elizabeth raised her eyebrows and asked where I was going to school. "Are you at the Toronto School of Theology?"

"No," I replied. "I am at the Centre for the Study of Religion." My response generated blank looks. "It's the nondenominational secular study of religion." I heard my voice go up at the end of the sentence as if I was asking a question rather than making a statement. I was immediately unsure why I had said nondenominational and wished I had not done so; I was wary of scaring them off with the term *secular* and judged that *nondenominational* might somehow soften the word. Later I would learn that *secular* would be a selling point for progressive Christians.

"Like comparative religion?" asked my new friend, whose name I never obtained.

I nodded thankfully and said, "Yes, sort of like comparative religion, but I study contemporary Christianity."

"I went to Trinity," Elizabeth interrupted, referring to the liberal Anglican divinity school located on the campus of the University of Toronto. She added that she once had been an Anglican priest. "I considered doing a PhD, but I was older." As she spoke, I saw that Elizabeth was looking me over. I assumed she was trying to gauge my age. "And I had kids at home."

In the subsequent weeks, Elizabeth became one of my key informants at George Street. I appreciated that the former Anglican priest was direct in her criticisms of the church's hierarchical structures. Furthermore, her habit of peppering intense theological debates with curse words was both amusing and refreshing. Many months later, when we sat down for a formal interview, Elizabeth told me about studying theology in the 1980s and how she had planned to pursue doctoral work. She had been preparing for language exams and putting together a research prospectus while working part time as a parish priest in the east end of Toronto. "Life has a habit of falling apart and exploding in various ways and directions," she explained. Following her ordination, Elizabeth fell in love with a woman and divorced her husband; the diocese asked her to resign voluntarily. Elizabeth became a teacher but remained involved in church life, working as an advocate for LGBTQ+ equality in the Anglican Church of Canada.

After she retired, Elizabeth and her partner moved to Peterborough. Initially, Elizabeth continued to commute to a small Anglican church in Toronto known for its inclusivity and radical theology. Eventually, the drive became untenable. Unable to find an Anglican church that suited her theological and liturgical needs in Peterborough, she started attending the speaker series at George Street and soon began attending services there. When I met Elizabeth, she was part of the leadership team responsible for coordinating the Theological Studies Group, the speaker series, and religious worship. Ultimately, at George Street, she returned to priestly duties as one of two former Anglican priests who presided over a small Eucharist service in the chapel on odd Sundays.

Elizabeth ushered me into the boardroom to find Karen and meet the rest of the Theological Studies Group. My previous correspondence with Karen had been over email, and this was our first time meeting face to face. She smiled and introduced me to the other group leaders. After a period of small talk, she made introductory remarks to the entire group of fifteen or so individuals and invited me to explain my project. I told them the working title of my book, "The New Heretics."

"We certainly are that!" chortled Jerry, a gregarious man in his seventies, as he looked around the room. Jerry, who had grown up during the Second World War, was in many ways the official spokesperson of the group and seemed pleased with the characterization.

Bringing the group back to logistics, Karen asked about the research process. I explained that I would take notes and participate at times in their conversation. I asked them to treat me like any other member of the Theological Studies Group.

"How did you come to study this project?" asked Mary-Beth, a slender woman with bony wrists. I explained to them that I had happened to be near Peterborough visiting family four years previously and attended a lecture by Spong at George Street. I described how witnessing the large crowds and the packed sanctuary had piqued my interest.

"I guess you could say my project was born in this church," I told them.

"That's great!" exclaimed Jerry. "Just great!"

I was appreciative of the enthusiastic response of the Theological Studies Group at George Street United Church. Their genuine interest in explaining progressive Christianity as a movement arising from reading and discussing popular theological books shaped my interactions with the churches that I subsequently studied. The world of book studies, lectures, and biblical criticism was not far removed from my life as a graduate student studying religion in Toronto. Like the anthropologist Karen McCarthy Brown (2002), my experience was one of dual learning, far from the classic image of the anthropologist as a "heroic traveler," crossing boundaries and learning local languages (131–32). Clearly, I would not report on the exotic practices of young retirees in suburban Canada. Instead, I was exploring a world similar to both the rural farming community in which I had grown up and the urban environment of Toronto where I lived. It was, after all, a social space shaped by modern middle-class habits and derived from particular political and ideological perspectives formed within mainline Christianity in Canada. From the George Street group, I gained insights into the formative and circuitous roles that texts and authors play in progressive Christianity.

As readers, the members of the Theological Studies Group privileged specific authors over others. They formed a cohesive theological stance by drawing from a variety of preferred thinkers. Most prominent at George Street was John Shelby Spong. In our discussion that day, we looked at the first section of *Jesus for the Non-Religious*. The opening chapters recapitulate Spong's earlier works and argue in favor of historical biblical criticism and a scientific understanding of the world at the expense of traditional Christian doctrines. Spong's perspective, which might be controversial in other Christian circles, represents a normative approach for progressive Christians. He rejects traditions such as Jesus's birth in Bethlehem, his station in life as the son of a carpenter, his selection of twelve specific individuals to serve as disciples, and his performance of miracles as he traveled the countryside. For Spong, these and other fictitious details of the Jesus story "are part of a developing mythology that must be separated from Jesus if we are ever going to see him as he really was" (2007, 20).

As we discussed Spong's assessment of the Gospels, it became apparent that the group was both familiar and highly comfortable with the historical analysis of the Bible. They drew from various popular texts by biblical scholars to highlight the historical context of first-century Palestine. Several members complained that they had grown bored when reading the opening chapters of *Jesus for the Non-Religious*, noting that it largely comprised an overview of Spong's previous works. The consensus that week and in subsequent weeks was that the book represented a review for most members of the Theological Studies Group. Indeed, as this book reveals, many had already concluded that Spong's desire to see Jesus "as he really was" was outdated and misguided. Instead, they contended that biblical scholarship ultimately provides little insight into the historical Jesus. That said, they also agreed that their study afforded an opportunity to review Spong's writings in anticipation of his next visit to George Street, then less than two months away. The group hoped that

Spong's return to Peterborough, as with his visit four years earlier, would fill the church building to capacity.

Sure enough, in early November, the members of the Theological Studies Group were not disappointed. Spong returned and lectured to a packed audience. As he reviewed the key points from his book, members of the Theological Studies Group bobbed their heads energetically in agreement. Among the most energetic was Jerry, whose face clearly displayed his admiration for Spong and excitement about the bishop's message. Jerry's esteem stemmed from the fact that Spong had provided the language for Jerry to describe himself as a nontheist.

"You have to understand what theism is," Jerry explained when I asked him about his religious background. "If you reject theism, then your knee-jerk reaction is to call one an atheist, which is not the case." Talking rapidly, he continued, "Although an atheist is one who rejects theism. But a nontheist does not necessarily reject God, and this is the difference that I find people have a hard time understanding."

Jerry saw Christianity as divided into three groups of people with corresponding fault lines. First, the nontheists like himself who may or may not believe in a divine "God-like" force, but they certainly do not believe in the traditional Christian God. Second, the theists, who adopt traditional Christian beliefs and practices and hinder attempts to incorporate progressive ideas. As Jerry explained it, theists are concentrated in certain denominations, such as "the Baptists, the evangelicals, the Roman Catholics, and many of the Presbyterians." Jerry paused as if he were about to tell me a secret, then added, "and many of the United Church folks are still theists." The final group includes members of what Jerry, following Spong, calls the CAA (the church alumni association). The CAA is a lighthearted term used to describe those individuals who attended church as children but do so now only for weddings, funerals, and the occasional holiday.

> They're the ones who grew up in the traditional church, as I did, or almost in an evangelical church, as [Spong] did. They have grown and developed and finally decided this doesn't work. If you can't get your mind around it, how can you get your heart around it? And so there's this group that have not gone out slamming the door. They've just quietly drifted away. They do other things. They work for the United Way, and they work for

the Kiwanis, and they work for the food banks, and so forth. They do lots of wonderful works and they still have a wonderful life, but it's not the formal "Christian-in-church-every-Sunday" Christian life. This is the target audience that [Spong] has and I always try to have around here. Try and do something that's going to attract the CAA; get them to come back and see that church has changed, approach has changed, understanding has changed, and that it's a place to be comfortable in.

While Jerry did not say so explicitly, he shared with many other progressive Christians the assumption that the CAA are also nontheists. In his eyes, the CAA had stopped attending because they found theism off-putting.

In our conversation, Jerry vented his frustration with the holiday services at George Street. He described a battle between the progressive nontheists and the traditional theists in the congregation that culminated in a staging of the nativity play. Jerry reported that Christmas was one of the rare occasions when the CAA came to church to celebrate the holiday with family. He saw the holiday season as an opportunity to demonstrate that the CAA would be welcome at George Street regardless of their religious beliefs and practices. But this year, according to Jerry, the theists in the church had won out. The congregation's children performed a traditional nativity play and sang traditional carols as part of their Christmas programming.

While one might suggest that Christmas is about tradition and need not be subject to such a critique, for Jerry this way of thinking missed the point. "Was the bishop even here?" he asked in an exasperated tone. "The CAA come back and they say, 'Here we go. We've got the animals talking to each other and we've got all sorts of strange stars and strange magical things.' And nobody really explains it. It's all the same, same-old, same-old. 'Well, we'll come back next year and see what happens.'" Jerry worried about losing any positive marketing derived from Spong's weekend and the opportunity to appeal to a demographic of could-be parishioners. The nativity conflict revealed Jerry's conviction that Christianity is appealing only when it is historically and scientifically verifiable. The decision to have a nativity play, replete with talking animals, heavenly choirs, magical stars, and the divine birth of Jesus, transgresses an ethic of believing common within progressive Christianity. This ethic contends that ritualized acts must correspond with the interior beliefs of their audience. They must maintain what progressive Christians call intellectual integrity. To do otherwise is perceived as insincere.

Jerry's apprehension regarding the nativity play stands at the forefront of several key themes necessary to an understanding of progressive Christianity. These themes bring to light what several scholars have noted is a Protestant preoccupation with sincerity and authenticity (Keane 2007; cf. Bielo 2008; Robbins 2008). The larger animating question for many progressive Christians is whether it is ethical to retain those elements of the Christian tradition that have been revealed to be scientifically, historically, or morally flawed. Such concerns emerge from liberal Protestants' attempts to make sense of the competing claims of faith and the supposedly secular realms of science, history, and morality (C. Smith 2003; see also Hatch 1989; Modern 2011; Turner 1985).

Derived from religious worldviews, these assumptions are also the by-product of social location. Christianity can be conceptualized as a performative ontology encompassing religious, political, and economic practices. As a movement that values intellectual engagement, reading, and progressive politics, that progressive Christianity grew out of mainline liberal Protestant churches is not surprising. It likewise is not surprising that the members of these congregations are predominately white middle-class baby boomers. This chapter highlights these social dimensions by addressing what it means to be middle class and mainline and this group's ensuing social concerns. Rather than presenting a repetitive description of each of the five congregations featured in this book, this chapter focuses on key themes I found in each congregation's social dynamics. In providing ethnographic snapshots, this chapter explores concepts of membership, like-mindedness, congregational dynamics, and (for some) the fear of rejection if their families and friends were to learn their true identity as a progressive Christian.

The Field Sites

For thirty months, I participated in book studies, discussion groups, pub nights, speaker series, and adult education programs at five different congregations. I chose these churches because they had book study and adult education groups that featured progressive theology and expressed interest in popular literature by progressive theologians. Four out of the five churches identified themselves as progressive on their websites. One book study group was hosted at a more conservative congregation and provided invaluable insight into how progressive congregants and clergy position themselves in more traditional settings.

Participant observation fieldwork can often be disembodying. It runs the risk of overlooking certain components of one's identity in favor of a central focus. Throughout this book and especially in this chapter, I have attempted to show rather than merely tell how participants experienced and performed different identity components within each church. I based the selection of ethnographic sites on the similarities of the congregations. For the most part, they held similar beliefs and had similar demographics and geographies. However, as many ethnographers quickly realize, the differences between congregations, even within denominational families, are striking (McCloud 2007, 135–66; Bielo 2009c; Elisha 2011; Wilcox 2003).

While these variances might be attributable to the churches' individual histories, their clergy's pastoral styles, and their institutional affiliations, such explanations do not tell the whole story. Time and time again, I found that these variations were of interest not only to me as an ethnographer seeking a lucid picture of progressive Christianity but also to the members of the different congregations. As I struggled to make sense of how each church's denominational structures and social histories contributed to such variations, my awareness of these differences strengthened my assessment. Thus, members of one congregation or another might find that the definitions and descriptions of progressive Christianity in this book do not necessarily match their definitions and descriptions. I hope, however, they will hear echoes of the many conversations we shared about their congregation in relation to the larger progressive Christian movement. Furthermore, I hope that they will consider the paths that they did not pursue and the possibilities that they did not entertain and learn more about their own perspectives through reading this book.

This chapter paints a picture of my time in the field and attends to each congregation's particularities. It highlights both the significant and mundane: the worship services and the moments between, casual conversations and formal interviews, times when I saw myself as being in the field and those instances when I unexpectedly bumped into my interlocutors while living my life (shopping at the grocery store, presenting at academic conferences, and vacationing with my family). As I noted earlier, most congregants at the churches were baby boomers or members of the generation that came of age during the Great Depression. While a few notable exceptions exist, for the most part, their narratives point to events such as the Depression, World War II, the Kennedy assassination, the civil rights movement, the moon landing, Vietnam, and the Cold War as formative. I offer the ethnographic snapshots in this chapter and throughout this book to provide insight into these particular communities and the ethnographic lens through which I observed them.

Of course, mere representation will never suffice. Along with the necessary reflexive analysis, this book seeks to analyze the lives of these congregations beyond their church-related beliefs and practices. In doing so, the book provides a sense of what might be called, following Bourdieu, a progressive Christian habitus that develops and inscribes itself on progressive Christians as they read, worship, and converse together. The analysis owes a debt to scholarly works on the demographics and characteristics of white, middle-class, and suburban communities. I have already set the stage by describing the social setting and dynamics within the Theological Studies Group at George Street United Church. My next example shows how assumptions that certain activities and spaces are comfortable serve as an indicator of class.

Leadership, Location, and Like-mindedness (Holy Cross Lutheran Church)

When Pastor Dawn arrived at Holy Cross Lutheran Church in 1999, the church had been around for only twelve years.[2] The building, purchased in 1998, is a small white structure that resembles a house and was formerly a Montessori school. The sanctuary has no permanent installments, which allows the congregation to use the space flexibly for various purposes. Located twenty-five kilometers north of Toronto, Newmarket is a rapidly growing city. According to the 2006 census, the population had more than doubled in twenty-five years to almost seventy-five thousand. The city maintained its historic downtown center but, not surprisingly, had a suburban feel to it since many residents commuted to Toronto for work. The Lutheran synod had designated Holy Cross as a mission church. Pastor Dawn was selected to help the church grow and increase its membership. Although the church leadership had instructed her to recruit new members, she saw building personal relationships as her primary role. Reflecting on this aim, she explained: "It was sort of my theory that if they were enjoying themselves and growing that it [the congregation] would naturally grow in numbers by itself."

As she recalled, her first task was to tackle the liturgy and raise the issue of inclusive language. In sermons and study sessions, Dawn led the congregation through conversations about the content of their music, prayers, and creeds. It was important for Dawn that these discussions occur slowly and deliberately; her intention was for them to be a learning opportunity for both her and the congregation. She began by exploring different versions of the Jesus Prayer, which is what progressive Christians call the Lord's Prayer to avoid calling Jesus "Lord" and to emphasize the human, as opposed to divine, authorship of the prayer:

> We started with Greek and Hebrew and looking at the different sources in the Greek that we have of the Jesus prayers, looking at the Vulgate and tracing through all these different translations, [and] the German—we have German speakers who would look at the early German and not be able to fathom what they said. I had some other older English versions, so that sort of freed people up to realize that "Oh, it didn't come down in the King James Version." Because up until that point, their argument was, "Do we use the contemporary or the traditional interpretation?" And then slowly [we started] adding different interpretations of the prayer. So that happened over a period of three years. It didn't happen overnight.

According to Dawn, this dialogue method allowed each member of the church to participate in rewording the liturgy.

In 2006, a group of evangelists staged a revival in town. Dawn said that "they did a big show, they had all kinds of advertising, hundreds of people showed up." Members of Holy Cross were intrigued. They wanted to know why they were unable to promote themselves similarly and galvanize people about progressive Christianity. The congregation had just sold its parsonage and found itself with a large sum of money. "The wise thing to do would have been to use that money to invest in building," Dawn recalled, "but that wasn't what they wanted to do. They wanted to invest in programs." So the church began by hosting several wine-and-cheese events for its congregants.

Before the wine-and-cheese events, Dawn asked the congregants to have conversations with their adult children about why they did not attend church. She smirked slightly as she recounted the wine-and-cheese sessions. "It was fascinating because people came with all kinds of stories about having spoken to their adult children for the first time about God and stuff. They found out where the members of their family were at in terms of religion." A common theme emerged. Many reported that reading was a crucial part of their religious practice. Both the members of Holy Cross and their nonattending adult children shared an appreciation for popular religious and theological authors. Inspired by this information, Dawn and another member of the congregation went to a local bookstore just before Easter to find out what people in Newmarket were reading. "We discovered [books by] people like Tom Harpur, Spong, [and] Barbara Rossing's books were there, [also] Marcus Borg and John Dominic Crossan. All of the people that we sort of suspected people were reading, but the fact that they were on the center aisle at Chapters [the largest bookstore chain in Canada], with a big prominent display for Holy Week, we figured that they must be selling!" With that, the Rethinking Christianity lecture series was born.

The series began with a guest lecture by the former Anglican priest Tom Harpur, whose 2004 work, *The Pagan Christ*, suggests that Jesus never existed. Instead, early church leaders combined popular pagan myths with prophetic expectations garnered from the Hebrew Bible to create a composite figure. Church circles and popular media had been sites of hot debates about Harpur's work, and Holy Cross hoped that he would draw a crowd. To make the event more accessible to those who might be uncomfortable in a church setting, the congregation rented a meeting room at the local country club. During the event, the church promoted itself in a manner that Dawn called a soft sell: brochures about the church were available, but there was little focus on Holy Cross. Church members invited those in attendance to discuss the lecture at a local pub the following week. "Drinking beer and discussing theology is a true Lutheran experience," members of the congregation were quick to point out, a joke that references Martin Luther's wife, Katharina, who was a brewer. The pub night was a success and became a monthly event. During the first year of the Rethinking Christianity lecture series, Dawn forbade congregants to directly invite anyone at the pub to church. "This is about giving a gift to the community," she told them. "It isn't about filling up our church on Sunday morning."

The events hosted by Holy Cross were as revealing about the social spaces occupied by its congregants as they were about their theology. Their choices demonstrate middle-class notions of desirability and like-mindedness. Pub nights and wine-and-cheese socials suggest a particular socioeconomic status. The initial decision to go to the local bookstore to find out what people in Newmarket were reading assumed certain disposable income levels and education. Furthermore, the idea that people will be more comfortable at the country club than the church reveals something about the social spaces they found familiar. From the beginning, their perceived audience was, at least in part, limited to people who could afford to buy the books (often hardcover editions since authors tour to promote their most recent works) and were at ease in what arguably are middle-class social settings.

Defining the middle class is difficult because of the divergences in worldviews, values, and practices across regions, ethnicities, religious and cultural communities, and subsections of the middle class (Newman 1999, x). The very notion of being in the middle means not being defined as one extreme or the other. Unlike most other identity markers, class is fluid and is often conceived to be less visible than rank, gender, or ethnicity (although these categories have become increasingly fluid). One might expect to move upward or downward within class structures (Bledstein 2001, 7). Often one's income bracket, occupation, educational status, and sociocultural practices denote class status, but these categories in and of themselves are not sufficient to form a comprehensive definition (Bledstein 2001, 2, 18–19). Instead, these elements are elastic at best and are often deployed as a means to buttress middle-class identity (see, for example, Ehrenreich 1990).

The study of the middle class is ultimately a study of cultural performances that delineate but never explicitly define the middle class. The anthropologist Kathryn Dudley points out that identifying as middle class "requires the unremitting performance of a distinctive *moral character*—one which, in every community, is as much culturally-defined as it is economically-based" (1999, 4). For understanding the cultural transformations of the middle class, material items are as crucial as shifting family structures, political affiliations, and value systems. For example, in his study of middle-class notions of domesticity and respectability, the sociologist Richard Wilk argues that the La-Z-Boy recliner serves as the pinnacle signifier of class status as it points to both disposable income and leisure activities (1999, 106–7). The La-Z-Boy is perhaps an outdated example for the early twenty-first century. A better technocentric example might be the iPhone, which exemplifies the individualism that drives middle-class North American culture (see Martin 2014; E. Smith 2015). Material items used as a means of allocating values and worldviews differ depending on the context but nonetheless make it possible to understand the larger factors at play in the construction and continuous reconstruction of the middle class. Being middle class is as much about the coffee one drinks as it is about one's occupation, education, or even neighborhood (Roseberry 1996). Or, put more succinctly, it is about the ethics and aesthetics implied in purchasing one brand of coffee instead of another. The selection of one's coffee brand (or smartphone or neighborhood) for ethical or aesthetic reasons, as in the purchase of fair trade coffee, rests on personal choices alongside ideological directives rooted in class norms (see Wolfe 1998).[3]

Those scholars of religion who have addressed questions of class offer an understanding articulated through discursive practices. The scholar of religion Sean McCloud (2007) calls attention to how class enables religious adherents to indicate group status and to set boundaries between themselves and outsiders. The anthropologist Omri Elisha (2011) points to the ideological conflicts and misunderstandings that emerge when members of different socioeconomic groups converge. Most pertinent to this study is the argument of the scholar of religion Craig Martin (2014): the consumption patterns of the middle class render particularly appealing religious ideologies that endorse productivity, individualism, and quietism. Martin sees this process at work in popular spirituality and self-help books. In these genres, he finds a legitimating discourse for the American dream of economic and social success achieved by self-directed, autonomous individuals (Martin 2014; cf. E. Smith 2015, 157–98; Newman 1999, 8). Similarly, the books that progressive Christians read favor a comparable individualism that takes the form of an intellectual and ethical endeavor. There is an understanding among progressive Christians that anyone who sets aside preconceived beliefs and rationally engages the evidence can discern which components of Christianity are accurate and authentic. Certain interpretive practices that favor autonomous, intellectually capable individuals promote these values.

Barry, a wealthy physician who attended Holy Cross, explained how finding a church whose members were intelligent, like-minded individuals was an important part of his religious journey. When he was in his forties, even though he was the son of an evangelical Presbyterian minister, Barry gave up on church. "I'd gotten into a bad habit, I guess, when attending church, to be very critical and to think that they just didn't get it," he explained as we sat down for coffee one sunny winter afternoon in the basement of Holy Cross. "I am biased towards the intellectual. I am biased towards questions. I am biased towards understanding something. I am biased towards history." While he labeled these traits *biases*, for Barry, they were necessary preconditions for church participation.

Eventually, Barry found the online forum of Grace Cathedral, a liberal Episcopal church located in San Francisco. The simultaneously solitary and participatory nature of Barry's worship strategies are noteworthy. He distinguished himself as a critical intellectual capable of finding community and spiritual nourishment only among like-minded devotees with whom he could engage in conversation and ask questions. "I would worship Sundays on the internet with Alan Jones at Grace Cathedral. That's where I got my weekly spiritual nourishment and [it's] important that I mention that because that's where I had fellowship," he told me. "They had a discussion group that would meet first, and it was a discussion group where you could participate online with questions. And they had very, very good people—it's an amazing webpage. That was very important: you could participate in those discussions via the internet."

For Barry, religious activities had to include personal introspection and cognitive exploration. His approach represents a form of online religiosity that the cultural theorist Robert Glenn Howard (2010) identifies as "radically vernacular." Rather than emerging from a centralizing institution, the community forms as "a result of the individual choices that everyday believers make about how they deploy network media" (Howard 2010, 731; cf. Campbell and Tsuria 2021; Elisha 2011, 165).

When Barry and I sat down for a formal interview, he had been attending Holy Cross for only a couple of months. He had first heard about the church through Spong's newsletter. Based on the bishop's assessment, Barry decided that it was time to return to a physical church after a hiatus of several decades. At Holy Cross, he found a community that was open to change. Drawing an analogy from his career as a physician, Barry explained that it would be unacceptable if medical practitioners refused to engage new ideas and practices. Echoing Spong and other progressive thinkers, Barry pointed out that many of the ideas he encountered at Holy Cross had been taught in seminaries for quite some time.

> This has been around in seminaries for a long time, and it just hasn't gone out in[to] the church. I understand that there's a lot of different reasons. I was talking to a minister, and he was commenting on the fact that I spend a lot of time going to medical conferences and whatnot. I pointed out to him that was necessary in terms of my licensure and that we accumulated a certain number of hours for continuing medical training. And not only that, I enjoy doing it because it makes me a better doctor. I am not just collecting frequent flyer points. It makes me a better doctor. And his comment was, "Well, it's a good thing that we don't have to do that in theology: God's the same—yesterday, today, and tomorrow." When I heard that, I said, "There's the problem."

For Barry, the church must be open to change and innovation. "People would ask me, 'Why aren't you going to church any longer?' And the answer was, 'Because I take my Christianity seriously.'" Continuing his analogy, Barry observed that the church had forced congregants to do all of the work of theological reflection themselves. Shaking his head, he explained, "It's like going to a doctor and not getting proper answers and having to go on the internet and having to figure it out for yourself." Pointing to the absurdity of self-diagnosis, Barry continued, "Imagine going back to your doctor's office and saying, 'Well, I think this is what

I have.' And having the doctor respond, 'Oh, yeah, good idea, good thought.'"

Barry's analogy demonstrates larger assumptions that congregation members made about how they had invested financially and religiously in the church. These were investments for which they anticipated a return in the form of active and intellectually informed congregants. At Holy Cross, Barry said that he had found a congregation that also took Christianity seriously. Dawn picked up this point when she talked about the impact of the Rethinking Christianity lecture series upon the church. As more and more people came to the lecture series and the pub nights, some also began to attend Holy Cross. Many wanted to learn more about the historical context of the Bible and started attending the adult education class held before church on Sunday mornings. As Dawn related, they began to stay for the morning service and then they began to ask questions. "Most of the folks who have started coming as a result of the speaker series and the outreach program have been away from church for a long time," she said. Because of this absence, Dawn observed that they had a different set of questions about Jesus and God that forced the long-term members to rethink some of their own preconceptions.

Like many progressive Christian congregations, Dawn and the members of Holy Cross presented their theology as fluid. For Dawn, this process was part and parcel of Holy Cross's location in Newmarket: "People tend to move here for four or five years and then move on. So we always have kind of a movability," she said. "Usually, new people are coming in all the time and then people moving out." That said, she noted that the changing demographics of the congregation could be challenging "with people coming from other denominations or no denomination and trying to figure out how to be a community with all these kinds of questions."

Just as I was finishing up my fieldwork at Holy Cross, the members engaged in a debate about the Communion liturgy. Holy Cross, like most Lutheran churches in North America, celebrated Communion every Sunday. While Dawn reworked the traditional prayers to make them more inclusive and removed references to theologies of atonement, some of the members of Holy Cross found the ritual troubling. They reported that the images associated with blood and sacrifice felt barbaric. The experience of hearing the familiar liturgical words recited was painful. But for other congregants, the ritual and phrasing of the Communion service were so meaningful that they could not imagine removing it from their weekly routines.

Dawn struggled to find a balance for those in her community for whom the traditional liturgy evoked fond memories and those for whom it was painful. In our conversation, she confided that one member of the parish was traumatized by what Dawn called "the old words" of the liturgy:

> I'm thinking of one member of the parish who grew up believing that she was going to hell because she wasn't good enough and she never would be good enough. Then [for her] to suddenly realize that she is beautifully and wonderfully made and is capable of wonderful things. To be asked to go back to that fearful place, where those words take her really quickly because she's heard them so many more times than she's heard that she is beautifully and wonderfully made. She has a real visceral reaction to those old words. So much so that if I am going to use the Old Order, I warn this person. She shows up after it's over. Because it's just too hard and too painful. There are other places where that pain can show up in different ways and more subtle ways. But . . . I get that, where it feels like an assault. Someone is really, really smacking. The church has done that for centuries to so many people.

This focus upon old language as having the capacity to take an individual back in time to an emotionally or psychologically painful space is a recurrent theme within progressive Christianity. The decision to include or exclude the Old Order becomes an ethical one.

At some progressive Christian churches, the decision would be simple: they would exclude performed language that departs from a referential language ideology. But Dawn ascribed a certain power to religious language when used in a performative or ritualized context. On more than one occasion, she explained to the congregation that certain words or phrases are "in our bones." Language contributes to the way people see themselves and their community. Ultimately, it shapes ways of being Christian. Dawn recognized the power of words to hurt and cause pain but also their creative potential. She allowed limited access to ritualized language, a decision that she justified by warning in advance the member of her community for whom the language of the Old Order was too painful.

Progressive Christians understand their theology as continuously developing. It emerges out of an intellectual endeavor and is forged through conflicting perspectives and contested ideas. They mitigate potential or real disagreements through discussion, debate, and continued examination. Their confidence in their ability to overcome disputes points to shared values and assumed like-mindedness, which is derived from common social locations and convictions and engenders a tangible sense of community.[4] At Holy Cross, the congregants saw each other, potential members, and, most important, Dawn as invested in shared goals by virtue of their shared worldviews. The interlacing of membership and shared values, ethics, and beliefs is a common theme within progressive Christianity. At West Hill United Church, one of the other churches I studied, membership realigned as the church took an increasingly prominent and public role within progressive Christianity.

Who's in and Who's Out?—Membership and Community (West Hill United Church)

At West Hill, members raised questions of what it means to be a progressive Christian alongside an understanding that, as the home of the Canadian Centre for Progressive Christianity, the church should serve as a model of progressive Christianity for the general public. This assumption, however, was subject to criticisms and tensions regarding the relationship of the church and the center. About halfway through my fieldwork, several congregants left the church and began attending a different United Church congregation. This departure signified a growing discomfort with the church's atheist stance.

West Hill United Church sat on the edge of Scarborough, the easternmost edge of Toronto. The building was an unassuming red brick construction that was built in the 1950s. At West Hill, the nontheist and atheist perspectives were dominant. While a core cohort of congregants had been members for many years, most members first heard about the church through newspaper articles outlining the controversial teachings of West Hill's minister, Gretta Vosper, about the existence of God and the purpose of religion.

According to the church's records, it had 145 members during my fieldwork. West Hill drew congregants from Scarborough and from neighboring municipalities, as well as from the downtown core of Toronto. Many parishioners drove quite a distance to attend West Hill because it allowed them to be completely open about their controversial beliefs. Those who lived too far away to attend church every week came once a month for a special "visitors and travelers" service and luncheon. Others attended virtually by downloading videos and podcasts of the service and participating in West Hill's online forums and Facebook page. Such participation allowed the congregants to expand their conception of membership. For example, in the fall of 2010, West Hill sought to create a space for those members who lived too far away to attend services by inviting them to become symbolic members in an online, real-time service.[5]

Those who were present that day were noticeably excited at the prospect of initiating new members from far away. With little ceremonial gesture, someone placed a computer atop the altar at the front of the church. One of the church leaders tinkered with the Wi-Fi, sound, and resolution. A microphone was set in front of the speakers, and the congregants in the pews waved at the screen and passed along their greetings to Karl from West Virginia, who would soon be the newest member of West Hill United Church. Karl joined ten members who were in the sanctuary and individuals from England, Australia, and the United States; the names of those online were read aloud during a special service called Journey of Transformation. To mark his membership, a piece of colored fabric was tied in Karl's name to the sculpture of a tree that symbolized community, new life, and the future and stood at the rear of the sanctuary.

This service, celebrated on World Communion Sunday, was an opportunity for individuals worldwide to participate in the service at West Hill in real time. While only Karl was present in a visual sense (through Skype), others were encouraged to participate by taking Communion at their home kitchen table and reading a special prayer that Vosper had written. Those of us in the church stood around Vosper's kitchen table, which had been brought into the sanctuary for the occasion. Together we read a special litany that began by evoking the theme of community:

> We are born into family.
> As we grow, our families grow into communities.
> Friends and acquaintances become connected to us
> through our play, our work, our commitments.
> The web of connections we live and share
> is thickened each time we care for one another,
> celebrate each other's joys,
> shoulder burdens together,
> and stand in a shelter created by love.

The reading expressed the idea that a simple kitchen table represents sharing, hospitality, and love—values that progressive Christians see as essential. The reading attempted to eliminate the gap between the church and its online adherents. It closed by suggesting that anyone might actively participate in the community, if through nothing else than the merit of shared values.

> Today, my table is enormous because,
> through the work of West Hill United,
> I share it with many people,
> across Canada and in other countries in the world.
> And I share in the work of the United Church of Canada
> through that connection.
> Through the UCC,
> I share love in communities I may never visit,
> in countries I may never see,
> in dreams I may never share,
> and in lives I may never know.
> This morning, those lives and dreams are here at my table.
> And here, I remember, that I am a dreamer, too,
> and in the world of my dreams
> I see a world of peace, justice, beauty, and truth.

After we completed the reading, Vosper instructed us to "take a moment to consider some of [your] dreams," "break the bread, fill your cup, eat, drink," and "know that you are never alone." At the church Vosper followed these instructions with a simple Communion ritual. She encouraged those at home to participate with their own bread and wine or grape juice. Several days later, two online members from Saskatchewan posted on West Hill's Facebook site a photograph of their kitchen table adorned with a loaf of bread and the glasses of grape juice they consumed during their Journey of Transformation ritual.

This process of constructing, performing, and providing evidence of church membership through an online mediatory extends the traditional Christian separation of materiality and self. It enabled West Hill United Church members to demarcate and create an imagined community simultaneously present and distant (Anderson 1983). It spoke to assumptions about shared values that transcend geographical locations and notions that religion is primarily a cognitive rather than a corporeal experience.

This understanding of religion as made up of social relationships situates West Hill alongside other progressive Christian churches within what the historian Peter J. Thuesen calls the logic of mainline liberal Protestantism. This logic includes "a reasonable tolerance of ethical differences, a thoroughgoing commitment to ecumenical cooperation, and an all-embracing conception of the church's public role" (2002, 27). To these intellectual positions, the historian Elesha Coffman adds an embodied understanding of place manifested not only in the physical structure of church buildings but, more important, in shared assumptions made about human nature, social hierarchy, and the purpose of life. As Coffman terms it, the mainline "was, and is, embodied by individuals whose social location predisposed them to see some things and miss others" (2013, 6).

The Journey of Transformation service provided a new organic way of understanding and practicing membership, forging a connection among those who shared West Hill's progressive theology. Its occurrence in the aftermath of the departure of several members of the congregation is noteworthy. This was not the first time that the church had experienced a decline in members. After the first round of articles featuring Vosper and West Hill appeared in the early 2000s, several congregants were surprised to learn that many other parishioners did not believe in God. At that point, several longtime members departed. The remaining congregants levied substantial criticism against these former members, pointing out that they had unknowingly and happily worshipped in an environment that did not explicitly reference God and other traditional tenets in prayers, songs, or liturgy, leaving only after they became aware of these practices.

The more recent departure, however, was different. Several members left to join a nearby United Church congregation with more traditional services. One longtime member who had been sick with cancer started attending a nearby United Church congregation three weeks before she died. Members of West Hill were shocked and disappointed when the woman's husband and family decided to hold her funeral service at the new church. Many of the remaining members at West Hill were hesitant to discuss these events. Pauline, who was in her midsixties and described herself as "less progressive" than most members at West Hill, explained to me that for many, their reasons for leaving were personal. Pauline told me that another woman left the church after a service in which Vosper had explained that she did not believe in God. The woman's young son had asked his mother what that meant. She decided that she wanted her son to have exposure to biblical content and traditional Christianity and decide for himself rather than be indoctrinated in an atheist form of Christianity.

Pauline recounted that she loved having a minister in the public spotlight. "She was voted in the top forty women in Canada," Pauline told me proudly, referring to the spring 2009 issue of *More Magazine* that featured Gretta Vosper as a prominent mover and shaker. "When I see people come to the church because they saw her on television, that just pleases me so much. She's definitely leading edge," Pauline continued. But she was quick to note that not everyone shared her enthusiasm: "I guess people either love her or they don't. It's disappointing that the church isn't crowded. I don't know why the church isn't overflowing." Pauline paused and considered her own question. "Perhaps it is too early," she mused. I asked her about West Hill's position within the United Church of Canada, and Pauline's response highlighted some growing tensions between Vosper and the denomination. "I think the United Church tolerates Gretta," Pauline told me. "I think they probably grudgingly admire her, and they allow her to function. I know my old friends from Westminster say, 'Well you're going to that church where they don't talk about God.'" Pauline laughed. "That's the description: the church where they don't talk about God." Still laughing, Pauline clarified this point. "We just don't call it God; we have many different names. I go through the 101 different words for God that Gretta has listed in her book. So that's my response." Here Pauline was concerned with the quick judgments levied by her friends from her previous church. I started to move to my next question, but Pauline returned to the problem of language. "I often wonder if the word *church* is a stumbling block," she explained. "Maybe we should just be the Centre for Progressive Christianity." For Pauline, the question of membership was more important than ecclesiastical affiliation. She pondered whether it would be better to sever ties with their denomination and position themselves as an independent movement.

During a formal interview, I asked Bill, a former Presbyterian who had been attending West Hill for a few years, about the departure. He explained that many missed the traditional liturgy. While they affirmed progressive Christian beliefs, they wanted to continue with the traditional practices, including some recognition of the importance of Jesus. "There was still this sort of, 'I'd like to keep one hand on this fence and reach across to the other fence,'" Bill explained. "It's a matter of gradation at this point. We're in a very stressful situation; we've lost a lot of membership." For Bill, this loss was frustrating because he felt that there was only a minimal difference between Vosper and the minister of the other church. I asked for clarification, and he recounted a conversation he had with the minister of the other church: "I was talking to him at a funeral that he was officiating at about a year ago. He saw me there, and after the ceremony was over, we had quite a chat. I said, 'Are you fairly close to Gretta's thinking?' He said, 'I'm not that far behind.'"

Bill's assessment was that the other church's attraction rested in its leadership and the familiarity of its services. As he explained it, Vosper's public profile made it challenging for some congregants who disliked West Hill's notoriety and yearned for tradition. In contrast, Pauline found the notoriety to be a selling point for attending West Hill and was willing to give up the label of church should it prove to be an obstacle. Both Pauline and Bill indicated that the church's position stemmed from their minister and the transparency of her teachings. Those who did not affirm Vosper's teachings were therefore required to find a different church. This discrepancy between minister and members came up in a different form at St. Matthias Anglican Church, where the theological position of the minister departed from that of his congregants.

Contested Spaces—A Congregational Meeting (St. Matthias Anglican Church)

Brian, the interim deacon-in-charge of St. Matthias Anglican Church, and I played phone tag for several weeks before we finally connected in mid-December. As I described my research to him, he enthusiastically declared, "This is the congregation for you!" A few weeks later, I sat on a surprisingly comfortable padded pew in the sunny sanctuary of St. Matthias, which congregants affectionately called St. Matt's. Built in the 1980s, the church reflected the congregation's initial desire to have a functional space where they could host concerts and meetings along with their regular services. The church walls were decorated with banners featuring words like *passion* and *creativity*, which represented the core values of the congregation. To the left of the raised platform that held the altar was an area with a keyboard and music stands. Above that was a projection screen upon which scrolled the morning announcements.[6]

The church was located on the corner of a busy suburban intersection in Guelph, Ontario. As Brian told the congregation during a Sunday morning sermon, its location was the envy of many within its diocese, the Diocese of Niagara. There were two Sunday morning services at St. Matthias. The first, known as Come into the Quiet, was a small gathering of six to ten individuals without music. This first service, held at 8:30 a.m., used the Anglican Church of Canada's *Book of Alternative Services*. The second more lively service usually included twenty to sixty people and followed a liturgy that had been compiled from a variety of sources and was used with special permission from the diocesan office.

Before the service, many of the congregants approached me and welcomed me to their church with wide smiles. Located not far from the University of Guelph, St. Matt's was familiar with the occasional church-shopping student. While none had recently chosen to attend regularly, the congregation remained eager to present itself as a welcoming place for young adults. During the Peace, Brian made a special effort to approach me and shake my hand. I reminded him that we had planned for this to be my first Sunday. Brian nodded. "There are several people you should meet," he told me. "I'll introduce you after the service." I smiled appreciatively and sat back in the pew, preparing to take in my first service at St. Matthias.

The singing at St. Matthias was lively and drew from various Christian traditions, including hymns, mass settings, spirituals, praise music, and children's songs. The music team had altered the lyrics, which were projected on a screen, to more fully reflect the language that progressive Christians prefer. This practice of changing or substituting words is typical of many progressive Christian congregations, originating with a desire to make the language more gender inclusive. In 2005, after the community ran several Living the Questions study groups, the members began to think about other ways that they could alter the language.[7] They sought to remove references to divine entities, miraculous occurrences, and ahistorical stories. When asked about the use of language in music, one of the longtime church members responded by saying: "Words mean everything. In a service, all you have are the words. You have to think hard and deep to get around them. You have to manipulate them." The notion that "all you have are the words" contradicts other Christian traditions that regard the words used in rituals, such as biblical readings, prophecy, or tongues, as having been inspired by God and the Holy Spirit, who remain the main focus of the service (see, for example, Bielo 2011b). For progressive Christians, however, ritualized and performed words are neither the product of nor directed toward a divine being. Instead, the congregation alone produces and interprets the words.

For example, a popular hymn at St. Matthias was "He Came Down," a traditional song from Cameroon. The song's lyrics paint Jesus as a transcendent and superior heavenly being bestowed upon Earth from above:

> He came down that we may have love;
> he came down that we may have love;
> he came down that we may have love.
> Hallelujah forevermore. (Why did he come?)

From a progressive Christian perspective, the vision of Jesus as transcendent is both scientifically and historically inaccurate. Humans do not come down from heaven. Furthermore, progressive Christians frame as unethical the notion that a superior being bestows love. They object to the idea that love is external to the human condition. In response, they have altered the words of the song. Instead of using the word *down*, members of the congregation sing *so* (e.g., "he came SO that we may have love"). This subtle revision places Jesus on an equal level with the rest of humanity, who could just as easily bestow love on other humans. It represents him as a great teacher or prophet rather than as a divine figure.

The emphasis that St. Matthias placed upon words became a central theme throughout my fieldwork. During my visit that first Sunday, I was surprised by the traditional theology and language in Brian's sermon. The Gospel reading was from the first chapter of Mark and recounted the story of the baptism of Jesus. That Sunday, a little girl was baptized. In his sermon, Brian reflected on the importance of baptism to the Christian tradition. Brian spoke as if the baptism of Jesus by John the Baptist was a historical event. My heart sank. I wondered if I had somehow misrepresented the subject of my book. This did not sound like progressive Christianity to me. I shifted uncomfortably in my seat. What I had failed to notice at that moment, but soon became apparent, was that I was not the only one in the congregation shifting uncomfortably. I was not the only one who was confused about the place of this more traditional teaching at St. Matthias.

In the coming weeks, I met with congregation members and learned that St. Matthias was in the middle of a crisis. A much-beloved minister who had served the church for many years had recently moved to a new parish. It turned out that the diocese had assigned Brian to the community as an interim clergy because the congregation could no longer afford a full-time minister. Independently wealthy from a previous career in medical research, Brian had recently been called to ministry. Because deacons cannot celebrate the Eucharist, they rarely are put in charge of an Anglican congregation. The diocese had made an exception for St. Matthias because a retired elderly priest in the congregation could perform sacramental duties and supervise Brian as he finished his seminary studies.

The congregation struggled with Brian's presence at St. Matthias. Because he donated his salary to the church, the bishop's decision to assign Brian as their interim deacon made sense. But it was challenging for him to pastor a community whose theology departed from his own. As one member asserted, Brian had allowed the "old words to creep back into the services. He doesn't realize that for some of us, these words are painful." Some congregants felt that Brian's assignment to their church was a punishment for their progressive theology. However, when I asked Philip, one of the church wardens, he quickly pointed out that this was not the case. "Brian is here so that he can learn from us," Philip said. "The bishop wants him to broaden his perspective." Others felt that the bishop was not sufficiently aware of St. Matthias's needs. Over and over again, community members told me that they had an uneasy relationship with their diocese and that they represented a kind of experiment.

A month into my fieldwork, I attended the annual church vestry meeting. It began as many church meetings do, with congregants milling around, drinking coffee, and eating sandwiches. "Are you able to stay?" Philip asked me as I volunteered to help move a table to the front of the sanctuary. "Of course," I said, smiling and resolving to grab an extra cookie. I had by now in my fieldwork sat through enough vestry and congregational meetings to know that they were typically dull and uninteresting. Few things are worse than sitting through a thirty-minute discussion of the water bill while also listening to the sound of one's stomach growling. Philip looked concerned. "I've been to my fair share of vestry meetings," I reassured him. "I know what to expect." We set the table down, and I quickly topped off my coffee and took a cookie offered by one of the church youth tasked with cleaning up the lunch.

"Can you please wear your name tags?" asked Janet, a younger woman who was on several of the church's various committees. "It will make it easier if we know everyone's names."

A chorus of "I've lost mine!" erupted.

"I don't have a name tag!" a woman exclaimed excitedly. "I've asked for one before, but no one made me one." She looked at Janet somewhat accusingly.

"I am so sorry," Janet responded calmly. "Is there anyone else who needs a name tag?" Two or three hands shot up throughout the gathered group. I timidly raised my hand. Janet passed me a piece of paper on which to write my name and any additional information I thought that the church should know about me. As I wrote my name and passed the sheet along to another of the attendees without a name tag, Janet expounded on the benefits of having one. "We have a filing cabinet at the entrance to the church," she noted. "You can put your name tag in there and take it out for church. You have to remember to put it back at the end of church, but it's okay if you lose it. Just let me know. You can leave a message in my file." The church also used the filing cabinet to leave messages and relevant documents for the members of the congregation.

A few members reluctantly went to the filing cabinet to pick up their name tags. Philip and the other board members gathered at the head table took this as their cue to begin the meeting. During the name tag discussion, I had failed to notice the board members at the front of the church. One woman volunteered to take notes and pulled out a laptop to record the meeting's minutes. The other members were rustling papers and staring down at the agenda in front of them. The meeting was called to order and opened with an uncomfortable prayer by Brian. The board swiftly approved the minutes from last year's vestry, and the meeting commenced with the warden's report.

Philip revealed that there had been a miscommunication between the diocese and the church board about the length of time that Brian would serve their community. As Philip explained the communication between the diocese and the church, his demeanor was calm and matter-of-fact. Despite his stoicism, a tension in the room was palpable. As another member of the board began to thank the various congregants who had helped maintain stability during the transition, a woman who regularly attended the more traditional morning service interrupted. Shaking slightly, she accused the board and Brian of "speaking around the issues" and being unclear. Members of the congregation shifted uncomfortably. This woman was part of a small minority disappointed with the progressive direction in which the congregation was moving. She looked at Brian, expecting support from him. He turned to her and said, "My understanding is that my theology is different from that of St. Matthias. I am sending out my résumé to other parishes." The woman shook her head. Another member of the board softly responded, "We want someone who fits our theology."

"But who decides our theology?" the woman asked, pressing the issue. A voice in the back answered, "We do. We choose people to represent us." Another man chimed in on the side of the opposition, asking, "How do you get our feedback?" Brian assured the man that his feedback had been received. Brian explained that the best way to provide feedback was to attend vestry meetings and speak with the wardens and the minister about any concerns.

Sensing frustration, Brian continued, "Don't worry about me. There are lots of churches that share my theology. It is this church that is a challenge. It will be a challenge for you to find someone who can minister to you the way you want."

The board carried on with the meeting, which featured various reports from the heads of different committees and fundraising groups. A few congregants were surprised by the news of the church's debt of $89,000. They were upset that the diocese was charging interest on a loan. A brief discussion ensued about the feasibility of paying it off. A few newer parishioners were unfamiliar with the Anglican Church of Canada's diocesan financial structure and were shocked that, even though the diocese owned the building and the property, St. Matthias was in charge of paying off the mortgage. As that news sank in, various members began to talk among themselves. "What good does it do us to be part of the diocese?" a woman asked. "We could try to go to a bank and get a better loan," suggested another member. "We don't own the church building; we don't have any collateral," another woman chimed in, responding to the earlier question about why the church did not pursue a bank loan.

Above the din of people talking, Janet said, "Exactly—we can't go to a bank. We don't own anything." Pausing, she reached down and held up her name tag, "except your name tags. You own your name tags. You can take those home with you." Janet's dry humor garnered some nervous laughter.

Finally, the retired priest interrupted and warned the congregation not to begin to think in an "us-them" fashion. "We have the debt and it is our reality. We are down to a half-time clergy person, and we are working towards paying off our debt." He added that the previous year had been the first year that the church had been capable of making all of its payments in full and on time. The congregation had paid a total of $21,000 in one year. In fact, the congregation had taken out a line of credit and hoped to pay off the debt to the diocese in two years. Then, as quickly as the discussion and dispute had erupted, the conversation ended. The board members led the congregation through a detailed breakdown of its projected expenses and earnings for the upcoming fiscal year.

Many of the changes predicted during the vestry meeting came to pass in the weeks and months that followed. By the beginning of March, Brian had found a new position in a nearby parish. Just in time for Easter, Elizabeth arrived as the new rector. She had grown up in nearby Hamilton, so her appointment to St. Matthias was a homecoming of sorts. Her father had served as an Anglican priest in the diocese for sixty-three years, and she had completed her undergraduate degree in sociology at a nearby university. Elizabeth completed her theological training at the Vancouver School of Theology and was ordained in 1995, then became a priest in Saskatchewan. Five years later, Elizabeth moved to the Diocese of Umzimvubu, South Africa, where she served as its sole female priest. During her time there, she advocated for HIV/AIDS education and served South Africa's only multiracial Anglican congregation. In conversations over coffee, Elizabeth spoke to me of her time in South Africa as life changing. After returning to Canada, she suffered from culture shock and was uncertain she wanted to pursue parish ministry. After many conversations with the bishop, she agreed to become a minister in her father's former diocese.

The move to St. Matthias was fortuitous for both Elizabeth and the congregation. The members of St. Matthias were thrilled to have a minister who supported and addressed their concerns about language and progressive theology. "She's familiar with the Living the Questions program," Philip explained to me when her hiring was first announced to the congregation. Additionally, Elizabeth challenged the church to be more inclusive of intercultural differences. Her preaching frequently drew upon her own experiences in South Africa. For Elizabeth, St. Matthias proved to be a welcoming and inclusive space for her partner, Joan, as they settled into their first year of marriage. That summer, members of the congregation joined together to celebrate the Blessing of Marriage between Elizabeth and Joan at St. Matthias. As she giddily danced down the aisle past a sea of smiling faces during the recessional song, "One Love" by Bob Marley, I could barely remember the community that had seemed so divided only a few months earlier.

As with the other churches I studied, St. Matthias, except for its interim clergy, had more or less committed to progressive Christianity's intellectual frameworks and practices. In contrast, at St. Peter's Anglican Church, only a few members, including the clergy, were interested in progressive Christianity.[8]

Directional Change: Progressive Christianity in the Closet (St. Peter's Anglican Church)

Built in the 1870s, St. Peter's boasted a breathtaking sanctuary. It was a mix of modern pews and older stained glass windows installed to commemorate the church's founding families. The church hall and administrative wing, built in the 1960s, stand next to the original chapel. They provide ample meeting and gathering spaces. On the same night that the book study group gathered, the church hosted an Alcoholics Anonymous meeting and an art therapy group in different areas of the church complex.

Organized and facilitated by the church's ministers, Stan and Mary-Ellen, the book study group met on a biweekly basis for eight months to discuss Marcus Borg's *The Heart of Christianity* (a book that progressive Christians regard as introductory). Like most of the participants in this study, the four to eight young retirees were white, middle class, and had grown up in the Christian tradition. While the members of this study group appeared to be similar demographically, I soon recognized their theological diversity in both beliefs and practices.

Each week, our intimate group gathered in chairs in a circle outside the church's cathedral-style sanctuary. Without exception, we began by lighting a candle and finished by reciting a progressive Christian version of the Lord's Prayer. Stan and Mary-Ellen led us through different activities and discussions in which we were expected to share personal stories and speak candidly about our deeply held beliefs, our dreams for the future, and our fears. Stan and Mary-Ellen made a point of insisting that everyone, including me, receive ample time to share. Often Stan would pause and say, "Is there anyone who hasn't had a chance to speak?"

Linda, a heavyset woman, was often reluctant to take part in conversations. Asked once to read her favorite passage from scripture (Psalm 23), she wept softly. Later Linda explained that while she found Borg's book interesting, she had to read a few chapters before she fully grasped its content. Linda confided in me that she worried that she lacked the vocabulary to discuss the book since she had not pursued postsecondary education. She compared herself with some outspoken male members of the book study who were more familiar with Borg and other popular progressive Christian authors and explained: "I feel like I am in kindergarten compared to some of the knowledge [possessed by others]. In that group, a lot of the men had read different books by different authors and by the same author, and they were very well versed in their opinions about those authors. I am just barely getting started. I am in kindergarten." Before participating in this book study group, Linda had been part of a group for women only. That group read Tina Beattie's *The Last Supper according to Mary and Martha*, which explores the life of Jesus from the perspective of his female followers. Linda reported that she felt much more comfortable speaking about the historical biblical context in relation to the women in that period.

Yet when I asked her about the effect that Borg's book had on her, Linda's face lit up. "This book study was really far out for me!" she explained. "I hadn't given any conscious thought to some of the different attitudes. I was brought up really traditionally. This book opened my eyes." Despite her difficulty with the book and her traditional upbringing, Linda thought that Borg reinforced ideas that she had previously formed but had been unable to articulate. "This book gives you permission to question, delve, and grow. I found that part of it very promising, very exciting."

Linda's comparison of herself and the men in the book study group at St. Peter's, combined with her analogy of feeling like she was in kindergarten, is revealing of the ways cultural practices and assumptions pattern religious communities. Linda participated in a gendered discourse that the anthropologist Catherine A. Lutz identifies as a "rhetoric of control" that deems the emotional experiences of women irrational, subjective, and dangerous, whereas it presents the men as rational, objective, and in control (1990, 69–70). While Linda was unable to contain her emotions, weeping softly when her favorite psalm was read, she depicted the men in the group as rational, possessing increased knowledge and familiarity with the topic and the setting of discussion and debate.

On the first day that we gathered for book study, Stan and Mary-Ellen asked us to position ourselves on an imaginary line depicting where we stood on certain church teachings. They explained that those of us who held liberal positions should stand at the north end of the room while those who were more conservative should stand toward the south side. They presented different issues to consider, such as the role of the Eucharist, the ordination of women, the Trinity, and so on. When I asked Linda about that exercise, she explained that her position had changed since she had completed the book study. Whereas she had once stood primarily at the south end of the room to mark her more conservative theological outlook, she now saw herself as standing in the middle. Borg's book had changed Linda's perspectives mainly on sexuality and interfaith dialogue. Although Borg's book covers neither topic directly, having the opportunity to ask questions and explore contemporary debates provided Linda with a venue to engage the larger social issues with which her church was then engrossed.

The practice of placing oneself theologically along a spectrum is common within progressive Christianity. For example, during a question-and-answer period at his workshop at Holy Cross, Spong used the analogy of the Israelites' crossing the Red Sea to describe his leadership role within progressive Christianity. "We are all more or less moving in the same direction. As a pastoral figure, I need to make sure that no one diverts too far off the path," he said. "Some are moving too quickly, and I need to remind them to slow down and wait for the group. Others are too slow and might get caught by the waters when they advance; I need to hurry them forward." This image of physically or chronologically moving forward is striking. It assumes that one's current position is temporally bound. While Linda saw herself as in kindergarten, she assumed that eventually she would move on to the next level. From the perspective of progressive Christianity, this advancement means moving toward more secular perspectives.

The members of St. Peter's book study group were more interested in reexamining the life and teachings of Jesus than were such groups at other progressive Christian churches, which see such studies as a necessary but introductory step toward progressive Christianity. Indeed, as this book shows, notions of belonging to progressive Christianity and of becoming a progressive Christian are tied to a rigorous investigation of the past. This past includes both a historical analysis of the biblical context and revisiting one's personal story through shared introspection. They undertake both of these activities in group settings. There is something about the progressive Christian habitus that encourages communal gatherings and exchanging knowledge with others.[9]

Paul attends a different Anglican church in town, which he described as "small *c* conservative." Paul enjoys the traditional worship style of his home church. He participated in the book study group at St. Peter's in order to engage intellectually with progressive Christianity but did not desire to switch congregations. When I asked him to describe his religiosity, Paul recounted that he saw himself as a closeted progressive Christian. He hid his progressive Christianity because he knew that his wife would be upset if she found out what he really believed. "I have no wish to upset her," he explained when we spoke over the telephone about the church he attended with his wife. "I'm not sure if I'm saying the right thing, but within our own parish, it is pretty traditional." He paused and pondered whether others at his church shared his view, saying, "Maybe there's a bunch of other people there like me? I don't know. My own personal faith? I'm definitely a progressive Christian."

Paul was raised in the Anglican Church, but he drifted away from the church as a young man. After he and his wife had their first child, they began to attend church out of a sense of duty rather than a desire to be religious. In the late 1970s, after they had been married for ten years, Paul and his wife attended an evangelical Anglican couples' retreat. Describing that event, Paul explained, "I was a reluctant participant, but I came out of that with an absolutely transformed view about my marriage and a completely reinvigorated view about faith." From that point on, Paul and his wife were active members of the Anglican church. Paul began leading Bible studies and became increasingly interested in biblical hermeneutics. Initially, Paul viewed the Bible as the literal word of God, but because of his background as an engineer, he struggled with the scientific inaccuracies and claims about miracles. For many years, Paul attempted to reconcile his faith and empiricism through private study, reading books by Borg, Spong, Crossan, and others.

As a closeted progressive Christian, Paul was representative of a larger subgroup of progressive Christians. These are individuals who find progressive Christianity intriguing but cannot find or are not interested in attending progressive Christian churches for a variety of reasons. Instead, they subtly integrate progressive theology into their current churches. As a Bible study leader at his home church, Paul tried to introduce progressive Christian thinking. These ideas are not always warmly received. In our conversation, Paul recounted an argument with another member of his Bible study group about the meaning of "Son of man" in the New Testament. As he remembered the debate, Paul's voice grew soft. "There was an individual there who was very, very sincere," he recalled. "[He was] very serious about his faith and so passionate that he tends to be overpowering. He'll make categorical statements in such a forceful way that it tends to shut down conversation."

Paul described the man's insistence that Son of man passages were the same as "Son of God" and interpreted as referring to the divinity of Jesus. "He was going on and on about Son of man in kind of a literal understanding," Paul related. "I shouldn't have allowed it to happen, but it was irking me. So I finally introduced the idea that the Son of man phrase goes back to Daniel and the Judaic period." Paul paused to ensure that I was following him, and I nodded to indicate that I was familiar with the scholarship that classifies this idiom as highlighting human, rather than divine, nature. "It can have a number of understandings. Certainly, in Judaism, it was not seen specifically as a literal Son of God. This was the connection that he was making: Son of God." Paul's objection to this man's interpretation was rooted in the man's refusal to consider other interpretations. In particular, Paul was annoyed at the man's privileging of a theological hermeneutic rather than a historical one. "And so I offered this as a 'by the way are you aware'—meaning the group at large—that there were other understandings of this particular phrase that were around a long time before Matthew wrote them in his Gospel."

The next day, another member of the Bible study group called Paul to follow up on the conversation. "We got into an awful discussion. He asked me some questions, and I told him the truth and that was quite upsetting to him," Paul said. The man decided that he would no longer participate in Paul's Bible study group. "He said to me, 'Well, I respect you for who you are and your beliefs, but I must tell you that I won't be participating in anything else that you lead at the church.'" I expressed to Paul my surprise that the man was not willing to participate in future studies. Paul sighed and related, "This is anecdotal, but I have found it's such a sensitive issue with some people. I haven't figured out ways to say things that might be meaningful to me in ways that won't be upsetting for them. So I must say, I tend to sit back and pick my times pretty carefully."

Sitting back and picking one's battles is common among progressive Christians. In this example, as Paul saw it, he knew the truth, but he had to exercise caution in introducing it. Many progressive Christians whom I met at conferences, workshops, and speakers' events recounted similar stories. For example, during Spong's visit to Holy Cross, a man from a local Baptist church explained that he was the only progressive Christian in his congregation. He asked the bishop what he could do to introduce progressive Christianity to his congregation.

"You're probably not the only one," Spong replied.

"It feels like I am," the man answered. Afraid that he might be asked to leave, he explained that he feared telling his pastor and the other congregants about his beliefs.

Spong paused and a look of genuine concern came over his face. "Be an uncomfortable voice for change," he said, looking the man directly in the eye. "There are so many people across North America who are the only progressive voices in their churches. It's difficult for them." Turning to the audience, he explained, "It is a lot easier to join a progressive church and be fed. But those who choose to stay in the traditional churches, those who act as an uncomfortable voice in conservative congregations, they're the ones who get to really make change happen."

There are similarities between Paul's experience and the fears of the man who had asked Spong for advice a few months earlier. Halfway through our interview, Paul turned the conversation around and started asking me questions.

> PAUL: You might be able to help me. I'm trying to help people prepare devotions. I said, "Well, Google *devotion* on the internet and you get a million pages." So someone did this, and I've done it, and then, in due course, she wrote me and said, "You know, these are all too evangelical for me." That's the Christian Right, this personal relationship with God and you're going to be saved. I couldn't find anything else. So my question to you is, Are you aware of some websites [where] one could get either Bible study material or devotional material of a more progressive or liberal, as opposed to an evangelical, way? I'm wading through fourteen million hits, [and] I can't.

Rebekka: Well, if you're looking for Bible study material, there is the Living the Questions program. Have you looked at it?

Paul: I haven't looked at it but I'm familiar with it. I just haven't forked out the money for it yet.

Rebekka: Yes, it's expensive.

Paul: That's through the progressive Christianity website?

Rebekka: Yes, it's fairly—it would make what we did with Borg seem fairly conservative, I think. It's sort of supposed to be based on the Alpha program. But it's an extensive engagement with biblical criticism and features people like Karen Armstrong and Spong and Borg and John Dominic Crossan, Elaine Pagels, and all those thinkers.

Paul: You said that it makes our conversation look conservative. [Do you mean] the conversation that we had in the study group or [that] the Living the Questions material is conservative?

Rebekka: I would say that Borg's work is much more—he's very obviously trying to walk a thin line and be as inclusive as possible to everyone, and I would say that's not as prevalent in the Living the Questions programs. They sometimes call it Alpha for liberals.

Paul: Okay. Well, you know Spong is right out there on the edge. I do understand: Borg tries to bridge the gap, whereas Spong says, "This is where I am and I'm not too worried about the rest of you."

Rebekka: Exactly.

Paul: What about devotions? I'm trying to get people, when we have small groups that meet on the advisory board, to spend ten or fifteen minutes at the beginning of the meeting on some sort of scriptural or devotional thing—getting people to up the curve so that they can lead it. Whether it's reading something or preparing something and having a question. At this juncture, I'm not particularly concerned, but I'm looking for material like that. That's why I sent this person to Google [the word] *devotion*. When she wrote back and [described] the problem she had, I knew it because that's the problem I had. I'd done it several times before myself and then I [would] get frustrated. I can't find anything that is less right wing. It sounds like Living the Questions is way on the other side of the perspective. I'm going to pursue that myself and look into, you know, some of that. But I'm not—that's not the material I'm thinking of to help people who say, "Where do I go to find devotional material that isn't quite stamped with this evangelical-style approach?"

REBEKKA: I don't have an answer for you, but I will send an email to a couple of people who I know who might have answers for you and email you and let you know what they suggest. I know a lot of liberal Christian ministers who would maybe have information about that. Devotions aren't really something that I've spent a lot of time researching. But I know people who will have those answers, so I will find out and get back to you on that if that's helpful.

PAUL: That would be great. The way I get around it is [that] I just take one of my study Bibles—almost all of them, again, tend to be more evangelical. Some of them have some pretty good summaries . . . on a topical basis: righteousness, justice, compassion, things like that. And sometimes [they have] some interesting questions alongside texts. So I'll pick a text or a topic in the text and just make up my own questions, often using that material as a bit of a guide, and I'll just frame the questions in a way that appeals to me. That works. It's fine for me, a study Bible. The more familiarity you have with the Bible, the easier something like that is. I find, you know, suggesting that to people tends to fall on deaf ears simply because they don't have a study Bible, or, if they have one, they wouldn't know really how to go about it. I will continue to explore and try to understand more about progressive Christianity. I think one day I'll go down and see Gretta Vosper, [and attend] one of her services or several of her services.

REBEKKA: Have you had a chance to read her book?

PAUL: I haven't. I have it, but I have not read it yet. But it's on my list to do shortly. So, yeah, I guess I would prefer to be with like-minded people. I don't find my friends at [my church] like-minded in the way that we've been talking about. But it's not that I want to leave, because of my wife and, you know, my longtime association with the parish. I would much prefer to help individuals broaden their own experience of God and wherever that takes them. I could do that here and I'm very happy doing that here.

These lengthy passages from my recorded discussion with Paul offer insight into the ways progressive Christians access resources. Congregations often find each other and new authors through their social networks and word of mouth. In this instance, in as much as Paul was one of my key informants, I aided his pursuit of progressive Christian reading materials.

Paul had more experience with conservative Christianity than most progressive Christians. He did not necessarily desire to see others become progressive Christians. Instead, he strategized about how to introduce progressive Christian thinking in ways that were, as Paul said, meant to "help them broaden" their perspectives rather than dramatically change their theology. For Paul and other progressive Christians who do not attend progressive Christian churches, this negotiation of practices, theology, and community is a fragile balancing act. While they might worry about what others say or think, their fears and frustrations are not enough to compel them to seek out new congregations. In Paul's case, he played an important leadership role, enjoyed the liturgy, and valued the company of his wife and friends. These were compelling reasons not to abandon his congregation because of theological differences.

Discernable Differences

The question of how many progressive Christians are closeted is outside the scope of this book. At the churches featured here, I met several married couples in which one partner was more committed to progressive Christianity than the other. Later I will discuss the case of Jodi, who was quite active in promoting progressive Christianity at St. Matthias. While Jodi's husband also was committed to progressive Christianity, he acknowledged that he was "not as far along" as his wife. In fact, Jodi adopted the identity of atheist as a tactic to push her church community to expand its theology. Her practice mirrored Paul's attempt to push his community to engage progressive ideas. Once again, the theme of progressive Christianity as progressing is observable in the example of Jodi.

As I have shown, progressive Christians adopt a certain habitus, certain ideologies, and certain performative tactics that are innate among primarily white, middle-class, and mainline Protestant churches. These social markers dictate the daily ebb and flow and lived experiences within each congregation. As with any social group, progressive Christians understand themselves in a variety of ways. They perform their values through their theological perspectives and social dispositions. This chapter has offered examples of both. The assumption on the part of the congregants at Holy Cross that everyone would be comfortable at the local country club is one side of the coin; on the other side, Linda worried that she did not have enough information to converse with the men in her book study group. A tension emerges between intellectual activity and loving relationships. It reveals itself in the struggle with Brian at St. Matthias, the hurt feelings at West Hill after members left because of theological disagreements, and is most fully realized in Paul's decision to remain a closeted progressive Christian out of respect for his wife. These tensions play out in the ways progressive Christians understand themselves in relationship to one another and to the Christian tradition. In the next chapter, I will turn to progressive Christian understandings of the role of the Bible and historical biblical criticism.

2

To Mine the Text

Textual Interpretations and Reading Praxis

Amid a wash of neon highlighters, dog-eared pages, and passages double- and sometimes triple-underlined or starred, the Bible stands at the center of most Protestant study groups. It is read by believers who figuratively inscribe their own narrative and perspective on its pages. Biblical references often serve as a central focus, and scripture maintains an authoritative status structuring the vocabularies and analogies available for use (Bielo 2009c; D. Olson 1994). While the Bible is understood as unchanging, it possesses a certain degree of fluidity, contingent upon circumstances. Christians often speak of the Bible as the *living Word*, a term derived from scripture that assigns to the text itself a form of agency or capacity to speak (Engelke 2009, 155; cf. Boyarin 1993b).

The possibility that the Bible might speak directly to an adherent resonates among those Christians for whom the Bible occupies a central space in both their personal and social lives (Hatch and Noll 1982; Malley 2004; Muse 2005). In most cases, however, the interpreter determines the Bible's capacity by naturally projecting their values and experiences onto the text and its key figures. A popular adage among scholars of religion notes that those who attempt to uncover the character of the historical Jesus, for example, will inevitably find a version of Jesus with whom they have much in common (Tyrrell 1913, 44; Martin 2009; see also Arnal 2005; Crossley 2015; Droge 2008). This maxim is apparent in the case of progressive Christians, whose understanding of Jesus derives from biblical scholarship by popular theologians whose version of Jesus reveals their progressive viewpoint has more weight than historical context. Here multiple interpretive layers so mute the Bible's capacity to speak that it is buried or lost.

The Bible is noticeably absent in progressive Christianity. The example in the introduction of Suzan's son, who did not even recognize the

Bible when he happened upon a copy at his sister's choir concert, epitomizes its absence. Unlike their evangelical kin, progressive Christians in reading groups focus on popular biblical exegesis and theology. Their church studies generally involve gathering around *a* text, as opposed to *the* text. They regard the Bible as an artifact from which readers are attempting to extract a kernel of truth. For progressive Christians, there is a sense that the truth may be buried deep within the biblical narrative, lurking somewhere behind or beyond the text itself (cf. Crapanzano 2000). Of course, such assumptions are not limited to progressive Christianity and have a long genealogy in the hermeneutical practices of both scholars and religious adherents. Distinctive to progressive Christians is the notion that locating this truth is an arduous, even impossible, undertaking—one that may ultimately require abandonment.

Progressive Christians hold a textual ideology in which absence authenticates the Bible. The Bible is both hyperpresent and hauntingly distant in progressive congregations. Only once during my research did it make a physical appearance. This occurred during a book study session at St. Peter's when we were asked to share our favorite biblical passages. Since most progressive Christians grew up understanding that church and Bible go hand in hand, its physical absence is intentional and noteworthy. The authority previously held by the Bible as God's word does not dissipate but rather is transferred to popular texts and authors that become authoritative by virtue of their proximity to the Bible's subject matter.

The idea that the Bible might be present through its absence is analogous to dynamics that emerged in the anthropologist Matthew Engelke's (2007) study of the Friday Masowe Apostolics of Zimbabwe. Known as Christians who don't read the Bible, the Masowe Apostolics reject the Bible in favor of a "live and direct" connection to God. In their eyes, the Bible is entrenched in its materiality and, as a physical object, it cannot be a source of spiritual inspiration (2007, 7). Engelke outlines how their rejection of the Bible serves several purposes, including a political critique of colonialism and European missionaries. The Masowe Apostolics have reoriented their focus, away from what they consider the Bible's original stale context and toward contemporary Africa and the struggles the Masowe Apostolics face. Rejection of the Bible enables a "symbolic obviation" generated through "the relationship of textual presence and absence" (Engelke 2004, 77). In its place, the Masowe Apostolics substitute a relationship with the divine mediated through religious leaders and prophetic figures. These religious leaders often are possessed by biblical figures or the Holy Spirit and revered for their adherence to Levitical law and their ability to speak a language that they claim is ancient Hebrew. The leaders serve as representatives and interpreters on behalf of God. While anyone is capable of achieving what the Masowe Apostolics call a "live and direct" experience of God, certain individuals seem to have particular authority because they have specialized knowledge correlated to the discursive content of the Bible.

While progressive Christians have not removed the Bible in the same manner or with a similar intention of gaining access to God, its absence synthesizes their religious and secular commitments. Like the Masowe Apostolics, they revere those who possess specialized knowledge related to the Bible. Progressive Christians, however, do not reject the materiality of the Bible but instead displace it. While adherents may not themselves read or study it regularly, the possibility to do so is always available. This point speaks to what the sociologist Max Weber (1959) saw as an inherent element of modern disenchantment. According to Weber, a recategorization of knowledge marks modernity and renders it mundane. Weber illustrated this argument with the example of the streetcar. For most riders, the streetcar's mechanical composition remains a mystery. In their use of it as a form of transportation, however, they are confident that should they pursue it, they could quickly come to comprehend its mechanics.

Weber's disenchantment highlights a democratizing approach to truth and knowledge that assumes a secular nature: "The knowledge or belief that if one but wished one *could* learn it at any time. Hence, it means that principally there are no mysterious incalculable forces that come into play, but rather that one can, in principle, master all things by calculation" (1959, 139). This logic is not unlike that of progressive Christians who derive their religious beliefs from biblical criticism. The hermeneutical exposé serves as an authoritative measure of truth. While progressive Christians may not understand the historical scholarship or philological translations, they share certain assumptions with Weber's streetcar rider. They are confident that were they to gather all of the necessary information (languages, history, social context, etc.), they would draw the same conclusion as the scholarly experts. Thus, they can validate their position based on the authority of the popular theological authors and claim to have rigorously examined the scholarly evidence, presenting it in an accessible and factual format for the general public.

Popular exegesis allows progressive Christians to jettison certain parts of scripture and, for some, the Bible in its entirety. The reasons for rejecting specific stories or passages are rooted in knowledge revealed by history, science, and a common sense of how the world ought to be. These justifications further support the claim that their stripped-down versions of the Bible are more historically accurate and theologically viable for a contemporary audience. Indeed, the specifics of the revised version are in certain ways rendered superfluous. Like the Masowe Apostolics, progressive Christians support a vast and at times vague oral tradition that does not rely on a physical Bible. Instead, their focus turns to debates about which parts of the Bible should be eliminated, why such a procedure is necessary, and the social consequences of abandoning certain texts. This process is further rooted in affiliating oneself with particular progressive Christian theologians who almost stand as a shorthand for its deployment.

Christian Sincerity: Fingers Crossed

Looking out over the packed sanctuary at George Street United Church, one can almost imagine what it must have been like during its heyday as an epicenter of Methodism at the turn of the twentieth century. On this day, a group of nearly eight hundred people, middle aged and older, sat in the gothic structure and hung on every word of Spong's series of lectures. Spong was there to outline the premise of his latest book, *Jesus for the Non-Religious*, in which he argues that the Christian narrative as it traditionally has been portrayed is wrong. No star shined over Bethlehem, the parents of Jesus are fictional composites, and all those miracles, which for many believers attest to the divine status of Jesus, never occurred.

As I noted earlier, the members of the Theological Studies Group at George Street had already concluded that this most recent book was a recap of material covered in other books. Regardless, in the preceding weeks, they had expressed excitement about Spong's visit, seeing it as an opportunity to reach out to those in the community who had never encountered his ideas. They regarded their invitation to the bishop to speak at the church as a form of progressive evangelism, and the massive number of attendees at the weekend event confirmed that their investment was a worthy one.

Those who heard Spong speak for the first time frequently remarked on how strikingly different he was in person, compared with the tone of his writing. His books, with such bombastic titles as *Rescuing the Bible from Fundamentalism* (1991), *Why Christianity Must Change or Die* (1998), *The Sins of Scripture* (2005), and *Biblical Literalism: A Gentile Heresy* (2016), created the expectation that the bishop would be outspoken and overbearing in his attack on fundamentalist and conservative Christianity. His humility often surprised those who were familiar with his work. The charismatic man, in his early seventies when he appeared at George Street, spoke passionately about biblical hermeneutics in a way that drew in his audience, as if he, too, was receiving the information for the first time. On this occasion, Spong's first lecture laid out an exegesis of the Jewish symbolism in Matthew's Gospel. Spong explained that Matthew had developed the plotline to reflect the Hebrew Bible stories rather than actual events. Spong's argument drew upon historical scholarship and was well received. A question period followed. People made their way to the front of the church, lining up behind two microphones. As was his custom, Spong contended that the church in general, and bishops in particular, have long suppressed women's voices and, in an effort to reverse this trend, said that he would begin with a question from a woman and then alternate speakers by gender.

Judith waited patiently in line to ask her question. Ahead of her, a woman and then a man asked for points of clarification about exegetical practices. The musty church heated up, the microphones squeaked, and people craned their necks to hear the questions and responses. Because more men than women had questions, Judith was moved ahead in line when the time came for another woman to speak.

"Bishop Spong," she began, pulling back the microphone so that her voice would not boom quite as loudly, "how come we've never heard any of this before?" Mumbled agreement echoed throughout the room.

The bishop smiled kindly at Judith. "Nothing I've told you today, nothing in my weekly column, nothing on my website, nothing in my books is new information. It's been taught in every mainline seminary in North America for the past fifty years. Don't ask me why you haven't heard any of this before! Ask your ministers, your priests, and your pastors. Ask those who have been trained in biblical interpretation, who have read the scholarly texts, and who have chosen to ignore them!" The room erupted in spontaneous applause. A few more questions followed, and then lunch was announced.

Over lunch, I approached Judith and her husband, Doug, and introduced myself. In their midforties, they were younger than most of the people at the lecture. The couple attended a Presbyterian church about an hour and a half away. Like everyone else, they were enthusiastic about Spong's visit. While this was the first time they had heard Spong speak, they had read his work avidly for several years. In fact, finding Spong's books had encouraged Judith to go back to school, and she was studying part time for a divinity degree. She balanced this task with raising her young son from a previous marriage and her work as a reporter for a local newspaper.

"We're excited to meet you!" she told me. "We saw your name in the bulletin and knew that we had to talk to you." That day's church bulletin had provided information about my research and told those willing to be interviewed how to contact me. We chatted briefly about my project and compared notes about life as a graduate student. The conversation turned to the day's lecture and the question-and-answer period.

"Bishop Spong is just so genuine!" Judith gushed. "You can really tell that he cares about all this stuff. It's made it easier for us to be Christians, you know, to actually *be* Christians."

"The church has got to change," Doug chimed in. "It's just got to. We've got all this new learning: science, technology, the universe. It's got to change."

Judith nodded, saying, "That's exactly what the bishop says. People like us, we went to church because we always did. Our friends were there, our families expected it, we wanted to raise our kids right. But, you know, after reading Spong, everything is different—"

Doug interrupted: "We don't have to cross our fingers during the creeds anymore! All that stuff about a virgin birth and the resurrection, who needs that? The church is going to change. Spong is a breath of fresh air."

While I doubt that Doug and Judith actually crossed their fingers during the creed, I heard people say this on more than one occasion throughout my fieldwork in regard to the presumed disconnect between personal beliefs and collective belief statements recited in the forms of creeds and hymns during church services. Folk wisdom has it that secretly crossing one's fingers when telling a lie absolves the individual of any responsibility for that lie (Leonard 1989). Often recounted as a joke, the idea that someone might cross their fingers during specific parts of a church service is intriguing. The joke presumes a specific form of engagement with words (written and spoken) that relies upon a referential language ideology thought to be clearly understood by all (Stromberg 1993, 6–9; Keane 2007).[1]

In this context, words and their speakers become available for evaluation. Their meaning can be discerned to be true or false. Furthermore, one can assess the animator's ethical character by attending to whether the words reflect a speaker's sincerely held beliefs. Creeds, such as the Apostles' Creed or the Nicene Creed, which are recited regularly in many mainline Protestant denominations, are examples. While they reflect traditional Christian beliefs, progressive Christians do not accept the creeds' claims about miracles. That is, progressive Christians *know* that God did not create the heavens and the earth, that Jesus was not conceived by a virgin, and that he did not rise again or ascend into heaven, nor do they anticipate a second coming, a future resurrection, or a life in the world to come. To say otherwise is deceptive. While crossing one's fingers or clarifying to others that one does not "really believe" in the creeds is an option, many struggle with the presumed inconsistencies that accompany their continued recitation. Others find the recitation of the creeds so disingenuous that they stop participating in religious services altogether.

Judith's case is representative: she stopped attending church after her divorce in her early thirties because her sense of hypocrisy became too much to handle amid a tumultuous personal life. Upon finding progressive Christianity, she was able to return to church and now regularly attended with Doug. When I asked her what compelled her to return, she explained that her initial foray into progressive Christianity was listening to a radio interview featuring Spong. She subsequently picked up a copy of *Why Christianity Must Change or Die*. "I read that, and it sent me out in a whole different direction of reading and sent me exploring all kinds of different ideas. So when I came back to the church, it was with a different sense of the possibilities of what church could be." In Judith's assessment, Spong provided both permission and justification to reject those components of Christianity that did not reflect her own experiences and expectations.

Likewise, Elizabeth, the former Anglican priest who now attended George Street United Church, reflected on the continued presence of implausible stories and false doctrines. For Elizabeth, they were a hindrance because they made it difficult to attract young people to Christianity. She criticized the church for not adequately communicating "the good stuff" and instead focusing on parts of the Christian story that are historically inaccurate. As she explained to me:

> I am sure that if we could get to a whole bunch of your peers who didn't have that "church image" from wherever it's from, we could talk about a passion for justice, and relationship, and the world, and blah, you know, the progressive stuff. People would go, "Oh! Is that what the church is? You know, maybe I should give it a look?" But then they would come in and see the stupid stuff going on in the church and go, "What? How do they do that shit?" You know? And as long as the church's worship is "O Little Town of Bethlehem" and it *really* has a star over it, there's no wonder they're not there. I don't blame them at all! Blame us! We didn't figure out how to tell people the good stuff!

In Elizabeth's view, there were positive elements to Christianity related to what she saw as universally attractive concepts like justice, humanitarianism, and social concern. But they were inaccessible because of the church's focus on outdated theological tenets extolled in songs, scripture, and teachings, as reflected in her example of the nativity story, which proposes that a celestial being led the shepherds and wise men to the stable where Jesus was born. For Elizabeth, the historical and scientific improbability of the traditional nativity story stands in the way of young people coming to church—people she believed would undoubtedly support the progressive and humanitarian commitments and programs at George Street. In order to attract young people, Elizabeth desired to see the church alter its stance. She advocated a revision of its theology, its doctrine, and its praxis to align with a modern, secular worldview.

Both Elizabeth and Judith spoke of a process of shifting their beliefs in light of new evidence, accumulated and evaluated as a collaborative process of reading, contemplating, and discussing popular texts that engage biblical exegesis. Progressive Christians understand book studies as one of their most important religious activities and forums for articulating a theology based on resistance to conservative Christianity.

It is helpful to discuss progressive Christian reading practices and to outline what I mean by a textual ideology. The most fruitful genre of scholarship on this topic emerged from a self-conscious methodological framework, the ethnography of reading. This field of study explores those cultural logics that direct not just reading practices but also the assumptions and strategies that one brings to reading anything. These include questions of who is permitted to read or interpret a text, where and when a text can or should be read, and how one should classify or engage with a text's subject (Boyarin 1993a; Bielo 2009c; Newton 2020).

Ethnography of Reading: A Study of Those Who Study

Progressive Christians read and study together. It is noteworthy that this enterprise occurs in an ecclesiastical setting. While their format may be similar to that of most Christian study groups', their subject and approach allow progressive Christians to differentiate themselves. To clarify, this is not a case of closeted theologians reading the Bible but rather a collective exploration of academic ideas in a popularized format. In this process, they use historical criticism to determine what they believe (or, as I have shown, what they *did not* believe or *no longer* believed) and subsequently to fashion their religious practices to these beliefs. Although collective reading is only one of many religious practices, progressive Christians feel that it makes them unique, and they frame their book studies as the first step toward becoming a progressive Christian.

Collective reading has a long history in religious traditions (Bielo 2009c; Boyarin 1993b; Lambek 1990; E. Smith 2015; Wimbush 2008). For text-based religions like Christianity, reading encapsulates both social and ritual practices, as in public and liturgical readings of scripture and prayers. Reading is more than a cognitive process. It is a socially embedded and linguistic practice used to construct and maintain relationships and to communicate intentions and meanings. In a collaborative setting, meaning is not only transmitted between the author and the reader but also between readers (Bloome and Green 2002, 395; Boyarin 1993a; Segovia and Tolbert 1995).[2] Collaborative reading situates the reader within a community of readers wherein a distinctive bond is forged alongside an inimitably personal experience of a text (Lofton 2011; Farr 2005; cf. Radway 1997, 219).

Several scholars have closely studied the contemporary upsurge of Christians meeting to discuss religious texts in small groups (Bielo 2008, 2009c; Boyarin 1993b; Cannell 2006; J. Davie 1995; Kort 1996; Nord 2004; D. Olson 1994; E. Smith 2015; Thuesen 1999). A reading or study group offers an opportunity to actively participate in a collaborative, unscripted discussion "to discover what biblical teachings *mean*" (Wuthnow 1994b, 352; cf. Wuthnow 1994a; see also Bielo 2009c: 6–7; Engelke 2009). Such groups operate as a location for articulating religious beliefs and affiliation, not only for active members of the reading group but also for the community that hosts it (J. Davie 1995; see also Wuthnow 1994a, 1994b). Reading groups often develop a "subtext of shared values," which has little to do with textual interpretation but rather allows for the development of new associations and ideas through conversation (Long 1993, 194). In this context, participants create "provisional collaborative identities using books" both in relationship with each other and in opposition to larger cultural authorities (Devlin-Glass 2001, 571).

James Bielo's work on evangelical Bible studies (2009c) offers acute insights about progressive Christian reading groups. He notes that, unlike other congregational activities, small group Bible study serves as a location for "knowledge production and disposition formation" (2009c, 11; cf. J. Davie 1995). According to Bielo's assessment, the collective setting of a Bible study is compelling because it creates a space where "individuals are able to critically and reflectively articulate the categories of meaning and action that are central to their spiritual and social life" (2009c, 12). A negotiation process is under way between not just the individual and their faith or the community and its comprehension of Christianity but also between specific group members who bring their personalities, worldviews, and experiences into the frame of reference of a particular text. Stated more definitively, Bielo argues that the act of reading is a strong cultural "forum for (and form of) social interaction, moral discourse, and epistemological formation" (2009c, 13).

Bielo's work with evangelical book study groups outlines two points relevant to this discussion of progressive Christianity. First, Bielo explores how books generate "a shared sense of belonging," or, following Benedict Anderson (1983), an imagined community (Bielo 2009c, 111). While readers of the same authors, books, or genres may have never met each other or may have little else in common, shared reverence for what particular books *do* or *signify* engenders solidarity (Bielo 2009c, 111; see also Candy Brown 2004; Klassen 2006, 818). Second, Bielo identifies the emergence of a "textual economy" that endows books, authors, genres, and even the broader category of text with social capital and meaning (2009c, 110–11). In the context of progressive Christianity, my interest is not just in the author's intentions or the effects of a book's message but also in the role the book plays as a book. A textual economy arises when a book is granted certain authority by virtue of its association with a particular genre or group of readers.

Progressive Christians build an imagined community around select books that explicitly dismiss what they perceive to be incorrect teachings held by a more powerful faction of Christianity. The process of engaging with biblical exegesis creates a criterion by which progressive Christians are able to demarcate themselves as having a distinct way of being Christian that is recognizable to other progressive Christians. Many connect through online forums and websites dedicated to progressive Christian authors, publications, and organizations outside their reading groups. In such settings, progressive Christians swap reading recommendations, share study guides, and engage in theological discussions with members of their tradition whom they may never meet face to face.

They generate social solidarity with other progressive Christians through a sense of shared ideologies and experiences as well as their canon of popular theology. Most of the members of the reading groups with which I worked frequently noted that, along with intellectual stimulation, their motivation for participating was therapeutic. Members speak of the reading group as providing a "sense of peace and assuredness," as a means of "making connections with the community," or as an outlet for conversing with others who are "thinking in Spong-type directions, in Borg-type directions, in Tom Harpur–type directions." For some, the group offers a forum in which to express doubt: "It was very refreshing to hear him [the author of a particular book] voicing a lot of the concerns that I was having in my heart." Others participate in order to contend with new ideas: "Something special is going on here, some honesty that a lot of other Christian churches in this town won't allow their congregants even to think about."[3]

What one might deduce from these statements is that at least some progressive Christians feel isolated and see these reading groups as providing a lifeline to intellectual conversation (cf. Long 1993, 198). For progressive Christians, an active and participatory negotiation of meaning in the smaller group setting not only promotes but in a sense embodies and ritualizes debate, dialogue, and doubt in lieu of accepting prefabricated doctrines and beliefs. Furthermore, the study group adds a social dimension because individuals are expected to participate in discussions and share and defend their opinions.[4]

Many progressive Christians feel that the reading group is the only venue in which to freely express their beliefs. The knowledge that they are participating in something larger than their own congregation emboldens a sense of belonging. For example, at George Street United Church, several individuals referred to themselves as "disciples of Spong." In explaining this term's effectiveness, one member, Jerry, whom I discussed in chapter 1, recounted a dinner party conversation that turned into a heated debate about theological relativism:

> You never talked about sex or God in my day at a dinner table. You still don't talk about sex at a dinner table, at least not at anything I've been to. But it's amazing that somebody brings up the word "God," or they say, "What church do you go to?" or you mention Spong. All of a sudden, everybody stops, and the discussion starts.
>
> At this one dinner party we were going to, I found it very interesting, we were talking back and forth, and the lady beside me was a Roman Catholic, a delightful lady, and the one over here (*points across from himself*) was an Anglican and . . . anyways there were two or three different faiths. There were certainly United Church folks there. . . . So anyways, we go back and forth. It was not too heated, but it was interesting. And then

somebody said, "Well, we all worship the same God anyways, so what does it really matter?" And I said, "Whoa, whoa, whoa, whoa, whoa!" And everybody said, "What?" I said, "I don't think we do!"

And there was just this intake of air. It was the first time anybody ever challenged that. It was just sort of the easy way to get out of these conversations. But I said, "I'm sorry, but the God that you Roman Catholics relate to is not my God. And the one of the Baptists' is certainly not my God. And the God of the Pentecostals' is certainly not my God! The Anglican God is sort of . . . depends which: Spong Anglicans or the other Anglicans." But I said, "This is the whole point."

For Jerry and other progressive Christians, differences *do* matter because it is through their differences that they articulate a shared identity. By aligning himself with Spong, Jerry not only distinguished himself from Roman Catholics, Baptists, Pentecostals, and nonprogressive Anglicans but he further affiliated with other progressive Christians who were also disciples or, at the very least, fans and consumers of Spong's books.

Jerry's evocation of Spong to delineate his own place speaks to Bielo's second point, the notion of a textual economy, which underscores the ways books gain meaning divorced from their textual content. Jerry and others shared stories about giving progressive theological texts to friends and family in the hope of providing them with "a place to ask questions" or "a different point of view." This practice serves as rudimentary proselytizing akin to evangelical witnessing tactics: the book's existence and the act of its being gifted and deemed giftable holds power. In her study of Oprah Winfrey's book club, Kathryn Lofton observes the social capital lavished on books by virtue of their being chosen by Oprah. Noting that the book club mirrors the religious practice of gathering around a text, Lofton explains that "the idea of a book is scriptural" (Lofton 2011, 155; see also Darnton 2002, 22). Already revered as significant religious objects, even books about religion have the potential to become religious.

The scholar of religion Richard Newton observes a similar phenomenon in his exploration of the scripturalizing role that Alex Haley's *Roots* has played in "the canonical narrative of America" (Newton 2020, 7). Newton offers an anthropology of scriptures that extends beyond the content of texts in order to interrogate how and why certain texts are used as part of what the political scientist Jean-François Bayart calls "operational acts of identification" (2005, 92). In the case of *Roots*, Newton points to the appearance of both the book itself and the 1977 television adaptation as a social actor in multiple settings. Its ubiquity emerges in both public and private forums: from its direct evocation by Republican senator Lamar Alexander at Barack Obama's presidential inauguration to more subtle allusions in American popular films, television shows, and music as well as its ever-present placement on personal bookshelves and family traditions of coming together to view the miniseries. Ultimately, it seems *Roots* assumes its status primarily because "it is not simply a story people read, but a story that *seems* to read readers back" (Newton 2020, 12).

The notion that books serve a purpose beyond their content became increasingly apparent as I spent more time in the homes of progressive Christians. As I have shown, the books themselves reflect economic status and life stage. Inevitably a visit to a progressive Christian's home included a perusal of their bookshelves. Often over a glass of wine, we would examine their collection as my hosts explained the significance of particular books or recounted the details of an author's recent visit to a nearby church. As my hosts gushed about figures like Spong, Borg, or Crossan, they rarely focused on a book's content, argument, or theoretical framework. Instead, the focus was on the role of a text or an author within a specific congregation or within progressive Christianity at large.

The question of how and why particular authors become authoritative and others do not is a multitiered process. It appears that the content of a particular text is less important than its author's ongoing relationship to progressive Christianity. Indeed, once progressive Christians gain knowledge of the questions specific figures are raising, it is easy to align themselves with that author's broader perspective. Throughout my fieldwork, I would often arrive at a book study session to find that I was the only one who had actually read the assigned chapters. Thus, while I have situated my work within the ethnography of reading, a more suitable subdiscipline would probably be the ethnography of interpretation. It is not so much the act of reading that defines progressive Christianity; rather, the community's impressions of a book and its author stand as the most critical consideration. With this stipulation in mind, a discussion of the authors themselves and the role their genre of books plays in collaborative reading environments is warranted.

Interpreting the Interpreters

As I have noted, one of the most popular forums for progressive Christians is a video program known as Living the Questions. Its curriculum features progressive theologians and biblical scholars along with clergy and laity discussing the contemporary relevance of Christianity. Rev. Jeff Procter-Murphy and Rev. David Felten created the series; both are United Methodist clergy from Arizona. According to its website, nearly five thousand churches worldwide have used the curriculum. The program offers a tried-and-true format: a twenty-minute video segment and a guide for subsequent discussions. For twelve weeks in the fall of 2009, Holy Cross Lutheran Church followed the Living the Questions curriculum for "Saving Jesus," a video series that promised to offer a new perspective on Jesus that is appropriate to the third millennium. Included in the promotional material distributed at the church was a flyer that asked the would-be participant: "Ever feel that Jesus has been kidnapped by the Christian Right?" From the program's perspective, greater familiarity with the biblical context and paying attention to discrepancies and inaccuracies within the New Testament are what save Jesus.

The observation that the Gospels are inconsistent with each other is not news to progressive Christians. For many of the congregants at Holy Cross, the Living the Questions series provided them with details that supported their already established position that Jesus was human, not divine. For example, one week during the season of Advent, we watched a video that featured contributions from the biblical scholars Marcus Borg, Walter Brueggemann, John Dominic Crossan, and Amy-Jill Levine, as well as the theologians John Cobb and John Shelby Spong. The discussion focused on the historical context of the nativity accounts featured in the Gospels of Matthew and Luke. One by one the theologians and scholars worked their way through the incarnation, noting that the New Testament offers five different explanations of how Jesus becomes God. Spong's summary is particularly telling. "I think we've got to start all over," he observes. "Jesus would not have been human if he had the Holy Spirit as a father." Noting that this view is derived from scholarly consensus, he repeats a recurring theme: "There is not a biblical scholar of any rank, Catholic or Protestant, who treats the birth narratives as history."

As the video ended, Pastor Dawn reiterated Spong's point. "There are five different, irreconcilable stories," she said, raising her eyebrows to emphasize the significance of this statement. "This gives us a clue that this was a problem to the early church." Pausing, she reflected on her own experience during her theological training. "When I studied religious studies and theology in seminary, the first thing they taught was all the heresies." She laughed. "Basically, they are teaching you what not to think."

Progressive Christians regard the heresies as important because they offer potential alternatives to an exclusionary model. From the perspective of progressive Christians, the fact that both the biblical canon and early church held such disparate views is hopeful and offers a potential avenue for moving forward. According to many progressive Christians, the church ran into problems when it tried to unite under the purview of church councils and creedal statements in the third and fourth centuries. Commenting on the corrupting effect of the creeds, Dawn explained, "I would have no problem with the Nicene Creed if it started with: 'Maybe it was something like this . . .' or if it said, 'Jesus was so incredible that we are explaining it like this.' But no, we get all of these 'I believes,' which came about when the church became powerful and needed to consolidate." Dawn went on to illustrate the necessity of multiple perspectives. "Think of yourself and who you are. Now think of three people in your life and how they might explain you." She paused and gave the congregation a chance to think. "They would each have a different view. That's what you would expect. The same can be said of Jesus and whether or not he is the son of God. But rather than celebrate that diversity, the church has eliminated it."

An older man, Richard, interjected an adoptionist Christology: "I really believe that Jesus had to be human and free to associate with the divine or to run from it. I think that a joining happened when Jesus said, 'It is finished' on the cross and gave himself up to death." Dawn nodded appreciatively, noting that this perspective departs from official church doctrine. She responded firmly, "That works for your cosmology, but for me, there is no joining." Richard looked disappointed and insisted, "But you need the joining!" Rather than furthering the debate, Dawn evoked a hagiographical legend and retorted, "Do you see why St. Nicholas punched Arius?" Everyone, including Richard, laughed. "We need to have this playfulness," she concluded.

In this example, both Dawn and Richard departed from orthodox theology, and their justification for doing so resided in their understanding of early church history and the biblical context. In redescribing early Christianity as a place where multiple perspectives and even heretical opinions coincided in harmony, progressive Christians salvage "a useable past" (E. Smith 2015, 277).[5] For the members of Holy Cross, it was not necessary or even desirable that they adopt the same perspective. Rather, their divergent views worked to further wrestle Jesus and the Christian faith away from those who insist on an all-encompassing, authoritative perspective.

Disputes about the legitimacy of different interpretations often hinge on disagreements surrounding the accuracy of biblical translation and historical context. Initially promoted for its ecumenical potential, the search for more accurate or scholarly translations of the Bible led to an ever-widening gap between liberals and conservatives. Throughout the twentieth century, debates ensued in seminaries and churches about the inclusion of new versions of the Bible that attended to the developing scholarly consensus. While biblical scholars posited the possibility of a scientific, historically accurate, and impartial translation, conservative Christians saw these revisions as a threat to theological or doctrinal tenets. Many mainline liberal congregations declared the King James Version of the Bible outdated and replaced it with the Revised Standard Version, assembled by a group of renowned historians and philologists (Thuesen 1999). Liberal Christians advocated for not only the inclusion of the new version in worship but also for educational programming that would outline for the laity the findings of historical biblical criticism in a popular and accessible format.

The desire for a popular and accessible version of the Bible speaks to more significant trends in contemporary Western culture. Many studies have been undertaken to explore the contributions of popular writers to the development of cultural opinions and ideological tropes in the twentieth century (Bhabha 1990; Sapiro 2004; E. Smith 2015). The social theorist Pierre Bourdieu shows that *popular* is often defined in relation to that which is excluded from legitimate language. It is an elastic concept fluidly applied to different circumstances and identities as the need arises (1991, 90–91). According to Bourdieu, the capacity to speak on behalf of the popular is a site of contestation about who might legitimately serve as an authorized spokesperson and what kinds of power this authority produces (1990, 150). With this point in mind, the following question arises: What happens when scholarly ideas move from the realm of specialized discourses into popular and public ones? Bourdieu suggests that specialized discourses derive their efficacy from a "hidden correspondence between the structure of the social space within which they are produced"—in this instance, the academy—and the "structure of the field of social classes within which the recipients are situated and in relation to which they interpret the message"—here, reading groups in progressive Christian churches (1991, 41).

In progressive Christianity, popular authors establish themselves as a medium through which scholarly ideas are made available to a lay audience. They present themselves as experts, or the next best thing, with training in critical exegesis. In doing so, they lay claim to both the symbolic capital and the social competence of leaders and authorized spokespersons. Bourdieu defines social competence as the ability to interact with a group whose statements might otherwise be semantically empty. That is, they mean nothing outside the community in which they are spoken. Instead, the group imposes authoritative power on a delegated representative based not on the actual content of a discourse or, if it is even understood, on the merit of the symbolic capital of collective identity (Bourdieu 1991). According to Bourdieu, "The efficacy of a discourse, its power to convince, depends on the authority of the person who utters it" (1977, 653). Spong, for example, spoke as an ordained bishop, but what was more important was that his authority came from being brave enough to share with laypeople what he regarded as the truth, a truth that is otherwise inaccessible to them.

Popular spokespersons will often locate their authority in the text, rather than its interpretation, in order to shield the audience from the fact that its meaning is derived from an interpretation rather than the text itself (Martin 2009, 6.4). Spong's authority came from historical exegesis, not the Bible. Regardless, the authoritative structure maintains a text-based focus: the reader receives a message from a book that derives its authority from Spong's interpretation of the Bible accessed through his own reading academic scholarship. The source of Spong's interpretive authority was likewise textual, coming from books produced by a collective of scholars known as the Jesus Seminar.

Founded by Robert W. Funk in 1985, the Jesus Seminar is a well-known but divisive example of attempts to bring scholarly historical studies of Jesus to everyday Christians.[6] Funk assembled thirty scholars "to identify an agreed inventory of sayings and actions by Jesus that could serve as a database for Jesus studies" (Jenks 2000, 2). As part of their methodology, the Jesus Seminar members set out to discuss, debate, and decide by majority vote the historical accuracy of more than five hundred New Testament passages. Voting made use of colored beads—red, pink, gray, and black—to register the participants' views regarding the historical likelihood that specific biblical passages denote the actual words or actions of Jesus. One by one, members dropped their beads into boxes to register their votes. Red signified an unequivocal yes vote: Jesus did this, Jesus said this. Pink indicated certain reservations. Black constituted a rejection of the passage: a determination that it was a later development by someone with a theological agenda. Finally, gray expressed a dismissal of the passage's reliability but suggested that it could still be useful in understanding the historical context of Jesus.

According to Funk, the initial regulations and requisite methodology were key to the seminar's scholarly work. In contrast to other institutions, the Jesus Seminar determined that with each passage, members "would *come to a decision*, no matter how provisional or tentative" (Funk 2000, 11). The decisiveness with which the seminar approached its data separates its work from that of other academics. Upon completing each debate, the Jesus Seminar announced its consensus and formed a conclusion—either Jesus did this and said this or he did not. Ultimately, seminar members presented their findings in two works: *The Five Gospels: The Search for the Authentic Words of Jesus* (1993) and *The Acts of Jesus: The Search for the Authentic Deeds of Jesus* (1998).

Funk claims that the Jesus Seminar's practice of publishing its work in "non-technical language" is an essential contribution to its popularity because it allows nonspecialists to access and understand the seminar's debates. When I interviewed Spong, he explained that his writing was necessary because it made the scholarly works of the Jesus Seminar more accessible to a general reading audience.[7] He told me,

> I make no bones about the fact that I'm not a primary scholar, I just read what the primary scholars write and try to communicate it, and that's a vital role. I don't denigrate that role, somebody's got to do that. I was the only member of the Jesus Seminar in America that didn't have an earned PhD. All of them speak Greek and Hebrew. I do a little bit of Greek and a little bit of Hebrew, but I sure don't come close, so I can't argue with them when they get to their technical analysis of these things. But what I can do is take their insights and communicate them to the average person on the street. That's what my books are for—I don't write for the academy, I write for the person in the pew.

There is presumed neutrality in Spong's appropriation of the Jesus Seminar's work and his own role as an intercessor. He posited that progressive Christians may garner the truth about what really happened through these multiple layers of interpretation. In this view, ideas move seamlessly and untarnished through the domains of research and translation by scholars, debate and election by the Jesus Seminar, and interpretation and presentation by Spong.

Like all scholarship, the work of the Jesus Seminar is firmly rooted in its historical context. As the biblical scholar James Crossley notes in his analysis of the Jesus Seminar through the figure of Burton Mack, one of its primary academic contributors, its presentation of Jesus develops in part as a response to "North American politics and culture wars emerging in the Reagan era" (Crossley 2021, 176; see also Arnal 2005; Crossley 2012). Crossley's interests rest not only in identifying the Jesus Seminar as a response to conservative Christian representations of Jesus but, more important, in understanding how its reading of Jesus tempers a more politically radical interpretation. In a similar vein, the biblical scholar Robert Myles (2016) explores how popular works by the biblical scholars John Dominic Crossan and N. T. Wright present subversive versions of Jesus that ultimately serve to reify the status quo of neoliberal Anglo-American culture. In the case of Crossan, who is much beloved by progressive Christians, Myles finds that Crossan's Jesus "sounds eerily familiar to a hipster-like Jesus" who, like progressive Christians, comes from a privileged socioeconomic background and draws attention to issues of poverty and injustice without requiring significant reform or political upheaval (Myles 2016, 63). According to both Crossley and Myles, the revisions proffered by the Jesus Seminar and in the popular works of other biblical scholars are as much a product of their ability to sell books as they are of historical analysis and critique (Crossley 2012, 85–98; Myles 2016, 67).

As I noted previously, many of Spong's works have provocative titles. He published more than twenty-five books, several of which have sold more than a million copies, and he maintained an e-newsletter to which many progressive Christians subscribed. His 2005 book, *The Sins of Scripture: Exposing the Bible's Texts of Hate to Reveal the God of Love*, provides insight into how Spong and many progressive Christians read the Bible. The phrase "sins of scripture" refers to "those terrible texts that have been quoted throughout Christian history to justify behavior that is today universally recognized as evil" (2005, 18). *The Sins of Scripture* outlines many of Spong's central criticisms of the Bible. The book addresses contemporary and historical examples of misused biblical passages and seeks to purge the Bible of its miracles and its ahistorical and antihumanitarian components.[8]

Spong's overriding assumption is that the content of the text is ethically neutral and the sins are committed by those who interpret them literally and adapt their worldview to this interpretation. In response, Spong aims to place biblical stories within their ancient milieu in order to dismiss their relevance today. In reality, he does more than merely contextualize. Spong criticizes contemporary Christians who subscribe to a literal reading of scripture, positioning them as naive at best and nefarious at worst. He shows how church officials and political authorities have used the Bible to justify beliefs and practices that depart from its original meaning. He argues that the Bible itself inspires violence and bigotry, which have no place in the contemporary world. Each chapter of the book examines scriptural passages that Spong thinks Christians should discard because they have been misused to justify such sins as environmental degradation, oppression of women and minorities, restrictions on same-sex relationships and equal marriage, racism, child abuse, antisemitism, and resistance to scientific advancements, historical study, and humanitarian compassion.

The Sins of Scripture is a product of its cultural location and supports the claim that everyone writes and reads books through their personal experiences and historical circumstances, reflecting the "social life of scriptures" (Bielo 2009b). In his preface, Spong recounts that initially he had been reluctant to write about the negative social impact of biblical passages because he felt that he "had moved beyond that debate and considered it to be essentially over" (2005, xii–xiii). He changed his mind after viewing the pervasive antisemitism in Mel Gibson's film *The Passion of the Christ* (2004). In discussing his qualifications to undertake this project, Spong claims two primary credentials: his long-standing "love affair" with the Bible and his status as a church insider who "yearns to see the church become what it was meant to be" (2005, 5). In offering these two validations, Spong claims ownership of the church and the Bible, situating himself and his readers as worthy interlocutors in the debate about the recognition, rejection, and revision of scripture.

While Spong casts off a literalist reading of scripture, he adopts a hermeneutical approach to the Bible similar to fundamentalist Christians. He assumes that certain theological or ideological truths exist apart from, but are revealed in, the biblical story. Thus, there exists a correct method of reading that enables the reader to extract these truths, which are otherwise ensnared by the "sins of scripture." In this approach, historical and scientific evidence, alongside ethical and moral assumptions, frame his evaluation of the Bible. He excises those biblical passages that are considered historically inaccurate, scientifically impossible, or morally repugnant. He promotes a form of neoliteralism, an approach to scripture that reads the Bible in a literal manner, but he ultimately rejects its authority because of his inability to reconcile the text with his contemporary worldview. This hermeneutic should be distinguished from literalism, whereby fundamentalist and conservative Christians allow a literal reading of the Bible to direct their worldview, beliefs, and lifestyle. Spong's literalism stems from a focus on history and science instead of tradition and faith (Crapanzano 2000; Johnson 1993, 458).

Naturally, Spong believes that contemporary scientific, historical, and ethical perspectives guide his reading of the Bible and his elimination or inclusion process. The Bible maintains what the anthropologist Vincent Crapanzano calls a "secure reference point." He sees it as containing an "original intention," which can be determined through common sense or a close reading of the text (Crapanzano 2000, 3). Undertaking biblical interpretation reifies the Bible's authority. Spong's purpose is not only to expose the "terrible texts of the Bible" but, more important, to recover the "ultimate depth of the texts," which continue to be worthwhile to Christians (2005, xiv). It is necessary for Spong's project that the Bible retains its "secure reference point," even as he seeks to diminish its authoritative power. He accomplishes this objective through a hermeneutic that renders the Bible personally relevant to both Spong and his readers by linking the ethical and the historical dimensions of the biblical text (cf. Malley 2004).

By historicizing the Bible, Spong is able to reject it or offer an alternative reading that privileges his and his readers' ethical stance. For example, Spong addresses the Bible's depiction of God as a reason to dismiss divine authority: "I do not understand how anyone can saddle God with the assumptions that are made by the biblical authors, warped as they are both by their lack of knowledge and by the tribal and sexist prejudices of that ancient time. Do we honor God when we assume that the primitive consciousness found on the pages of scripture, even when it is attributed to God, is somehow righteous? Do we really want to worship a God who plays favorites, who chooses one people to be God's people to the neglect of all the others?" (2005, 18). Here Spong subjects the biblical narrative to a contemporary moral lens and finds the biblical rendition to be lacking. He accomplishes this task by shifting the Bible's secure reference point to the contemporary moment, wherein it might be evaluated according to the reader's common sense and contemporary experiences and expectations.

In his second chapter, Spong challenges the scientific, ethical, and historical claims within the Bible. He offers a scientific critique, arguing that "the Bible makes assumptions that most of us who live in a post-Newtonian world of 'natural law' could never make" (2005, 21). The unscientific claims of the Bible that he finds scornful include the pillars of cloud and fire that led the Israelites through the wilderness for forty years (Exod. 13, 16:35); the powers granted to Elijah and Elisha to miraculously replenish food supplies (1 Kings 12:8–16, 17: 8–16); the unnatural levitation of the iron axe-head (2 Kings 6:5); and the raisings of the dead (1 Kings 17:17–24 and 2 Kings 4:8–37) (Spong 2005, 20–21). Likewise, Spong offers several specific examples of how the Bible's representation of God fails to correspond with contemporary morality. In the Bible, God sends a flood to kill everyone except Noah and his family (Gen. 6–9); stops the sun to enable Joshua to slaughter the Amorites (Josh. 10:12–15); commands King Saul to strike Amalek and destroy everything the population has without sparing any men, women, children, infants, or beasts (1 Sam. 15:3); allows his followers to sell their daughters into slavery (Exod. 21:7) and to possess slaves from other countries (Lev. 25:44); and mandates death to anyone who violates the Sabbath (Exod. 35:2), curses (Lev. 24:13–14), or blasphemes (Lev. 24:16) (Spong 2005, 18–19). Finally, alongside his ethical and scientific objections, Spong outlines the historical improbability and inconsistencies within the Bible. He draws on historical biblical criticism to dismiss traditional assumptions about authorship, pointing out, for example, that Moses was not the author of the Torah and David did not write the psalms. Spong further notes that in the synoptic Gospels Jesus incorrectly asserts Mosaic authorship of the Torah (Mark 1:44; Matt. 8:4, 19:7, 22:24; and Luke 5:14, 20:28, 24:27) and Davidic authorship of the psalms (Mark 12:36–37, Matt. 22:43–45, and Luke 20:42–44) (Spong 2005, 19–20). In this way Spong contests the accuracy of Jesus's teachings, and Spong locates his evidence in the very text that he seeks to undermine.

Directing his attention to Jesus, Spong explains that a literal reading of the Jesus story "will reveal either unbelievable miracles or a land of make-believe." Instead, the "only alternative is to be forced to face the fact that we have in the gospels only mythical accounts of Jesus' life" (2005, 21). To claim otherwise and to see the story of Jesus as part of God's masterplan for creation not only "violates everything we know about how the universe operates" but also "defines God as a super manipulator" (2005, 24). While Spong deconstructs the unbelievable elements of the biblical narrative, he contends that his reading of scripture is intended "to offer believers a new doorway into the biblical story" that moves beyond "the sins of scripture" (2005, 24–25). In doing so, Spong invites his followers to a figurative mountaintop where they can observe the destruction of the "idols of creed, scripture and church" (2005, 25). His hope is that his readers may ultimately take up the task of Jesus, to "build a world in which every person can live more fully" and "oppose everything that diminishes the life of a single human being, whether it is race, ethnicity, tribe, gender, sexual orientation or religion itself" (2005,

25–26). This transformation is what he claims was the ultimate goal of Jesus, to which Spong aligns his own purpose. Thus, in an intriguing reversal, he grounds his biblical revision in the tradition of Jesus and the authority of scripture.

Spong's animated syntax, multiple examples from scripture, and invocation of post-Newtonian reason are rhetorically persuasive and evidently appeal to his audience. Every year he spoke to sold-out crowds and standing-room-only auditoriums and church halls at more than two hundred speaking engagements. When I asked him in an interview to describe his audience, he indicated that he did not write for those who take the Bible at face value: "I clearly identify my audience. I don't write for the convinced. I don't write for the people who are in their churches. I'm not at war with them. If they want to stay there, that's fine with me." Instead, he returned to the image of the "believer in exile" and explained that his audience was those for whom Christianity retains an uneasy relevance: "I address the people who are either dropping out of organized religion because it doesn't make any sense to them or [who] are closing their minds and hanging on for dear life inside the institution. But they know it's a losing battle. And so I call them the 'church alumni association'; I call them 'believers in exile.' They're still close enough to their life of faith that they miss it when they leave it, and it's that missing that gives me the power to communicate another possibility." Spong's books offer his audience a clear sense of who they are. As is evident in the earlier example of Jerry's differentiation between "Spong Anglicans" and "other Anglicans," this identity is one they embrace. Not only did Spong provide a way to maintain a Christian identity, he also supplied accompanying linguistic tropes, interpretive practices, and consumer products. From his writings, progressive Christians gain a new version of the Bible that attends to their own empirical experiences, ethical expectations, and common sense.

Spong and others may claim their authority from scholarly sources, but their attention to scholarly method and historical detail is limited and read through the lens of their preconceived commitments. Instead, the authority of their knowledge rests on their repudiation of tradition. Herein lies the key to the reception of progressive interpretations that build upon scholarly exegesis instead of popular devotion. What these authorized spokespersons exclude from their writing may be as illuminating as what they include. Given what some might argue is biased use of scholarship, what is it about their rhetorical styles and strategies of argumentation that make the work of these authors resonate with their well-educated audiences?

Considering the centrality of the figure of Jesus, it is not surprising that revisionary accounts of Jesus are prominent. In trying to determine what the Bible actually *means*, progressive Christians begin with the traditional depiction of Jesus and demythologize it according to the version that the Jesus Seminar and other popular authors proffer. They revise, rewrite, and present the narrative anew to accommodate a more progressive worldview. Once again, that the quest for the historical Jesus generates a Jesus with whom its searcher has much affinity is a relevant observation.

Many of these revisions appeal to contemporary feminism and include further details about Jesus's relationships with women. For example, following the success of *The Da Vinci Code* and increased interest in the Gospel of Mary, an extracanonical text discovered at the turn of the nineteenth century, the feminist activist, Anglican priest, and former Roman Catholic nun Joanna Manning rewrote the story so that Jesus and Mary Magdalene are coteachers. In Manning's version, Mary is the favorite disciple, not an adulterous woman or a prostitute (Manning 2006, 28–30). In a similar vein, Spong suggests that Jesus and Mary Magdalene were married. He speculates that the wedding at Cana might have been Jesus's wedding to Mary Magdalene, which clarifies his concern about the diminishing wine supply. Of course, Spong rejects the idea that Jesus miraculously turns water into wine; instead, in Spong's version, Jesus rushes out to procure more wine in order to thwart the tears of his mother, the embarrassed hostess of the evening (1992, 187–99).

In his book *Born of a Woman: A Bishop Rethinks the Virgin Birth and the Treatment of Women by a Male-Dominated Church* (1992), Spong addresses the scientific implausibility of the virgin birth. Spong needs to attend to the biblical claim and knows that a virgin cannot give birth, so he rewrites the story to depict Mary as the victim of rape by a Roman soldier. Spong even goes so far as to claim that, now that he has brought to light what he declares to be the true story, he has liberated Mary and countless generations of Christian women from the impossible ideal of virgin motherhood (Spong 1992).[9] But are Mary and other Christian women actually liberated through rape? The power of this new "virgin birth narrative" lies not in its scholarly sources or in its presumed feminist emancipation but rather in its challenge to traditional discourses about the uniqueness of Jesus and the sexual activity of his mother. It seems that the currency of an interpretation is found in the arena of competition between two opposing groups. Progressive Christians find themselves struggling for social dominance against a traditional and conservative faction that they feel has marginalized and concealed the truth throughout history.

What is of particular interest is the means by which progressive Christians uncover the truth. They dismiss those parts of the biblical narrative that do not conform to their empirical experiences or ethical perspectives. In *Jesus for the Non-Religious* (2007), Spong writes that "destroying Jesus is not my goal; destroying the layers of ever-hardening concrete that have encased him is" (2007, 14). Spong explains his rejection of the nativity story, saying, "There were no stars, no angels, no wise men, no shepherds and no manger. This is our first conclusion. We move on from there" (2007, 24). In their desire to move on, many progressive Christians suggest that while certainly there are passages and biblical books that should be eliminated, some parts of scripture or ethical teachings might be retained. Others, however, feel that it is time to move on from the very process of determining what to include in or exclude from the Bible. It is time, they maintain, to move on from the Bible altogether.

Excavations and Extractions

Deborah was among the first members of the Theological Studies Group at George Street United Church to champion my research. At the age of seventy-five, she spoke from experience about shifts and changes within both the church and society at large. She spoke to me as a mother speaks to her daughter; her tone was often gentle and reassuring, punctuating her theological observations with wisdom and sage advice about the various transitions I could expect during my lifetime. Deborah jokingly called herself a "roaming Catholic," a nod to her Roman Catholic upbringing. She had roamed her way to George Street because of the

Theological Studies Group, and while she retained great admiration for the mystery of the liturgy in the Catholic faith, she felt more intellectually at home at George Street.

As we sat down together for tea one chilly afternoon in early December, our conversation gravitated toward the relevance of the Bible. She told me that she no longer read the Old Testament because she found it too gory and out of touch. While she recognized its historical relevance for scholars, she clarified that its worldview did not correspond with her own. "I don't think it helps to teach our kids in Sunday school those old stories and try to mine them enough to get out [of them] what you want," she said. Instead, Deborah thought that some of these stories could be reconfigured for children, but most were outdated. She continued, "If you take the David and Goliath kind of story, you know, that's not going to work itself out. Maybe we as adults can look at it and get something out of it, but I don't think teaching that in Sunday school is helpful. So I think we need stories about bullying in different ways. Something that they can see and say, 'Yeah, that makes sense. That makes sense for me today at school or at home.'" Although she was not interested in completely eliminating the Bible from church services, Deborah wondered if there is not a "better way" of providing moral teachings, especially to children. She suggested that "other books of wisdom" might prove to be more useful in the twenty-first century.

As we drank our tea, I pursued the question, asking: "Do you think there is anything special in Christian stories or the Bible?" Deborah sighed and said, "Certainly, the influence they have had has been very wide. I think because within it [the Bible] there are very good stories, very good messages that ring true with this intrinsic feeling that we have." Her tone was cautious. She continued by telling me that even those stories that did resonate with her created problems. Just as Kevin feared that the newly rewritten Ten Commandments would be taken out of context (see the introduction), Deborah worried about misunderstandings and misinterpretations. As she outlined her objections, her thinking became more resolved. Finally, concerning those stories that one might feel tempted to retain, she asserted, "I don't think there's that many of them. I think you have to twist and turn. As I say, it's like mining them. You're there for that little bit of truth, but you've got this mess around you that causes a lot of problems by saying, 'It's all true.'

So you have to mine for a bit of truth. And, you know, you could do it much easier. Find a better mine for better production and put that into service." Deborah's approach to the Bible is illustrative of progressive Christian reading strategies. She believed that there is something good at the core of the Bible, that "little bit of truth," as she called it, but she concluded that the process of accessing it is difficult and perhaps not worth the effort. Her image of mining the text is indicative of the relationship that progressive Christians have with the Bible and the authority they assign to it.

The French philosopher Bruno Latour's description of purification and hybridization as the pinnacle of modernity (1993) illuminates the metaphors of mining, extraction, and excavation that Deborah and other progressive Christians have employed. Latour argues that modernity is driven by a desire for purity, an impulse that originates with scientific empiricism and social differentiation. The scientific method posits the possibility of an objective analysis of nature removed from human error and corruption; a similar pattern appears in the modern demarcation of social domains, which advances a separation of such areas as politics, religion, technology, and economics. This worldview champions categorical divisions and sees fundamental differences between nature and society without recognizing their mutual dependence (1993, 6, 10–11).

Whereas the premodern era conflated the aforementioned categories, in Latour's assessment moderns endorse a perspective that views the present as entirely foreign to and separate from the past. His larger project shows how, although carving out distinct, segregated domains has characterized modernity, in fact, as the title of his book declares, "We have never been modern." Instead, modernity ushers in a proliferation of unacknowledged hybrids. Latour demolishes the presumed distinction between nature and society as he outlines a complex network of phenomena that stand betwixt and between. Science is always subject to social forces and ideologies, be they law, religion, economics, or politics (Latour 1993).[10]

Similar assumptions appear to be at work in progressive Christian approaches to the Bible. Like Deborah, many progressive Christians presume an original, pure text that reveals "what really happened" or that "read[ing] correctly" might unveil "the little bit of truth." The focus on historical criticism is noteworthy, as it shares certain assumptions with the scientific method. Biblical scholars are not scientists in the traditional sense, but they employ a methodology that rests on the objective analysis of evidence garnered from historical, archeological, textual, philological, and cultural studies. While they lack the requisite laboratories and equipment, their field depends on similar measures to circumvent human corruption in the form of theological intervention, personal opinion, or conjecture.

The anthropologist Webb Keane infers that the project of purification is not just about purity or originality but rather that it endorses a moral vision. This vision presupposes an autonomous self-regulating liberation from social, material, and psychological distractions (Keane 2007; cf. Elisha 2011, 19–20). Under this model, progressive Christians are seeking an authentic biblical text not just out of a desire for purity or originality but, more important, out of an ethical drive to interact with the Bible in its most accurate form. As I have shown, purification, revision, and repudiation uncover this form.

Either whittled down by attending to historical criticism, scientific empiricism, and liberal humanism or inflated through the addition of contemporary moral norms and expectations, the Bible becomes a novel entity. It is akin to what the social theorist Jean Baudrillard calls a simulacrum, an intentionally distorted representation that stands in for the real thing (Baudrillard 1994). Progressive Christians maintain the authoritative framework of Bible reading and interpretation while rejecting its message and teachings; alternatively, they allow biblical exegesis and those trained therein to assume the space of primacy. In this way, they are haunted by the Bible. Even their best attempts to move past it—by rejecting, rationalizing, or revising it—are directed by interpretive practices that originate with specialized hermeneutics to which they lack immediate access. The Bible is a text that is both an obstacle to be overcome and an artifact to be analyzed; the ambitious miner might mine its deepest crevices for truth. Like all mines, however, when it no longer yields raw resources, it must be abandoned in favor of newer ones with more easily accessible reserves.

"Jesus is different from us only in degree, not in kind," Pastor Dawn fondly reflected as she counseled the congregants at Holy Cross about the process of rejecting Jesus as a divine figure. Each time she made this declaration, she paused and waited for the statement to sink in. Newcomers often furrowed their brows, while longtime members grimaced and nodded. When I asked whether they agreed with Dawn, many pointed to other historical figures who they felt exemplify difference in degree rather than kind. These examples most often included Mother Theresa, Martin Luther King, Jr., Mahatma Gandhi, and Nelson Mandela. Occasionally, others listed parents, a kindly schoolteacher, or a clergy person. One could suggest that it is not only the Bible that undergoes simultaneous purification and hybridization. Other historical and personal figures may also be subject to similar refining.

At a dinner hosted by an older couple, Samantha and Jonathan, who attended Holy Cross, someone broached the question of the uniqueness of Jesus. Samantha began by acknowledging that she felt torn. On the one hand, because she had been Christian since childhood, Jesus was important to her understanding and experience of her faith. On the other, she felt that the church's focus on him could be considered a form of idolatry because it diverted attention from what she termed "God within us." Surprised at the evocation of God, I pursued the topic. "That's fairly traditional theological language," I responded.

Jonathan was quick to clarify, saying, "I think Spong puts it well when he says that Jesus was so imbued with God—God was so present within him—that he was such a complete human being because of that. That is what we should aspire to." Both Jonathan and Samantha used the term *God* as a nontheistic reference to a form of energy or love that humans are capable of exuding.

Jonathan went on to tell us about hearing a recent lecture in which the speaker had argued that Martin Luther King, Jr., was America's greatest prophet. Picking up the theme of prophetic figures, he continued, "I guess King would sort of be in line with Jesus because Jesus was—" Jonathan trailed off. "You know, Muslims consider Jesus the greatest prophet of all. It's interesting." Without prompting, he shifted to the topic of people who might be equated with Jesus: "And Gandhi? Gandhi once said, 'I think Christians are great, I'd like to meet one.' Or something like that. I don't know about Mandela. It's interesting. But Mandela, certainly with his Truth and Reconciliation Commissions, he took a different tactic than most people do. Most people, when they get into positions of power like that, usually wreak revenge on the people who have tormented them. He chose not to do that, which I think says a lot about him."

It is not a stretch to say that Martin Luther King, Jr., Nelson Mandela, and Mahatma Gandhi would be high on anyone's list of great religious and political leaders of the twentieth century. Of interest to this analysis is that these figures can be located in a historical context. Like Jesus and the Bible, they can be evaluated empirically and ethically. Much like the observation that the Jesus of liberal Christians is himself a liberal Christian, the Gandhi of progressive Christians holds the same ambiguities toward Christianity that progressive Christians do. Like the historical Jesus, Nelson Mandela is so purified that the core values attributed to him are all that remain. These figures can be mined with a process similar to the one that progressive Christians use elsewhere to reflect a version that serves their collective ideological purposes.

The rejection of certain tenets, passages, and traditions is not always easy. While the opportunity to expand the corpus of their tradition exists, it, too, is subject to continual reevaluation. Progressive Christians often must decide to abandon theological beliefs that they have held since childhood. They rigorously examine for inconsistencies not only the Bible or tradition but also their own sincerely held beliefs. They consider it an offense to believe what one knows to be inaccurate. This offense warrants a religious ablution, which, while gauged to be necessary, is sometimes distressing. The next chapter describes how progressive Christians might experience the rejection of traditional Christianity as painful or traumatic. It outlines the story of departure or deconversion, which yields a purified, stripped-down self. The process by which one forges a progressive Christian self bears a striking resemblance to biblical exegesis.

3

Deconversion

Progressive Christians and the Protestant Proximate Other

She stood in front of the congregation, trembling ever so slightly, looked down, closed her eyes, took a deep breath, and began: "My name is Monica James and I am a recovering Christian."

Monica invited her audience into her story, which consists of a relentless overbearing mother and a distant alcoholic father; years spent trying to fit in at an expensive Christian private school that her family could not afford; Bible college in Toronto; the perfect Christian marriage; the perfect Christian family. The day her son accepted Jesus Christ as his personal Lord and Savior was, she declared, the best day of her life. Yet Monica's story of an idyllic Christian life included insecurities and a sense that she could never measure up, could never assume the role of the perfect Christian daughter, mother, and wife.

"I would pray that my parents would divorce, that they would stay together, that I would be the greatest gospel singer in the world, that I would marry rich. I wanted to be a super-Christian. I wanted security. I spent a lot of time sitting on my hands, not asking questions," Monica said. Speaking of her deconversion, she explained, "I wish I could point my conversion to faithlessness to some sort of terminal illness or car crash, but nothing like that has happened. The universe has smiled on me. I have three wonderful children and a husband I love dearly. It really was a slow ebbing away that has occurred over the last eighteen to twenty-four months. Through conversations with my friends and family, with complete strangers, the bricks began to fall. I no longer seek salvation because I think that's archaic. And—" She paused, leaned forward, and in a barely audible whisper said, "I feel so good now!"

In a presentation titled, "Losing My Religion and Finding My Soul," Monica shared her story with a room of twenty to thirty like-minded Christians at a progressive Christian conference. Her talk incorporated tactics and insights garnered from her training as a life coach to lead the group through a conversation about loss and grief management. In Monica's view, loss of faith parallels other losses, such as the death of a loved one or the end of a marriage. Drawing from her own experiences, she highlighted the transitional nature of leaving religion behind: "It's like being a trapeze artist—you have to let go and you don't know what comes next, but you have to grab the next rung and trust that it will be there for you."

It appears that one does not convert to progressive Christianity. Rather, both scholars and practitioners of contemporary Christianity usually frame the transition to progressive Christianity as what they call a deconversion (Barbour 1994; Bielo 2009a; 2011a, 28–46; Davidman and Greil 2007; Harrold 2006; Streib et al. 2009). Deconversion is a distinct experience with some parallels to conversion but with a greater reliance on the reevaluation of one's previous religious stance. Whereas conversion narratives denote a newly found system of meaning and adherence "marked by teleology, a straight line of change from rebellion to obedience," a deconversion narrative is derived from a "cultural critique" of former beliefs and practices (Bielo 2011a, 29). In other words, a deconversion narrative is classified as such because its focus rests on the identity that the person has abandoned. Its power lies not in an initial, recognized experience but rather in the ways the individual recounts and narrates it after the fact. As the anthropologist E. Marshall Brooks indicates, such narratives should be analyzed not in terms of their accuracy or reliability but rather as a means "to understand how the people who tell them make meaning out of their own lived experiences—how they emerge from, critically reflect on, and at times speak back to the sociocultural context in which they were produced" (2018, 20).

The religious studies scholar John Barbour (1994) coined the term and explained that, like a conversion narrative, deconversion accounts chronologically organize a distinct shift in worldview, ideological commitments, or lifestyle. While conversion may point to a dramatic, public, and instantaneous transformation, as in an altar call or praying the "sinner's prayer," deconversion often is not as pronounced. The narrator reports a gradual disaffiliation accompanied by intellectual doubt, moral criticism, emotional suffering, and the loss of religious experiences (Barbour 1994; Streib et al. 2009, 22). As in the case of Monica, deconversion usually occurs during a sustained period of time, requiring intellectual and emotional effort. The narrator will often arrange the story to follow a timeline that pinpoints those instances that led to religious defection. The narrative brings together a series of events that might otherwise be "experienced as unconnected, confusing or inconclusive" (Barbour 1994, 51). Those recounting a deconversion emphasize the loss of their former self and denounce their previous religious associations. They offer a contrast between their former and current self. Monica told her audience that "the bricks began to fall." She made clear that the process was difficult but worthwhile. She concluded with relief: "I feel so good now." The narrative reifies her departure and buttresses her new religious affiliation by highlighting differences between the old and the new (cf. Stromberg 1993).[1]

Progressive Christian deconversion narratives emphasize choice and conviction. Most cite intellectual doubt or moral criticism as the primary cause of their deconversion. Here, as I showed previously, they present skepticism as an ethical imperative. Thus, for progressive Christians deconversion rests on the idea that one is morally obligated to possess sufficient evidence to account for beliefs. Deconversion becomes necessary when they no longer perceive Christianity to be intellectually viable, that is, they see it as irreconcilable with science or with biblical scholarship, or when they see Christianity as morally inadmissible, for example, when religious doctrines conflict with social norms.

This perceived necessity prompts two important questions: Why and how do progressive Christians retain a Christian identity? And what, exactly, do they think it means to be Christian? While it might seem more plausible that they would abandon Christianity and adopt secular humanism, progressive Christians hold on to the idea that they are Christians, albeit as skeptics, atheists, and heretics. As I have shown, their continual process of examination, purification, and reconstitution of the Christian faith leaves progressive Christians with little religious content with which to contend. While the task of scholars should never be to adjudicate claims to Christian identity, the means through which Christians themselves negotiate insider and outsider status is informative to the broader comparative study of Christianities (Garriott and O'Neill 2008). The anthropologist Jon Bialecki argues that there is plasticity inherent in the "constitutive elements that make up

Christianity" (2017a, 5). Different configurations of these elements yield different varieties of Christianity. For progressive Christians, their claim to the label of Christian rests in rearranging and exchanging the constitutive elements of Christianity. It is almost as if Christianity is a container or a mold into which they pour religious ingredients, adding and subtracting beliefs, practices, and authoritative assumptions as needed.

Thus, for progressive Christians, deconversion is not a matter of switching religions but rather of forging a new way of being Christian. They maintain their commitment to being Christian through comparisons with the beliefs and practices within the version of Christianity they claim to have forsaken. For this reason, the form of Christianity from which they departed influences the constitution of their new one. Resistance is the basis of this new form of Christianity. Intriguingly, while they present this other as a previous identity, in many instances, what occupies the place of the former self is an imagined rather than an experienced other. Less an account of actual events, the deconversion narrative speaks the progressive Christian self into existence.

Undoing Belief: Practice, Performance, and Proximate Others

Most scholars of religion dismiss the commonly held assumption that religion is primarily about belief. In contrast to modern individualistic models of belief as a state of mind, they corroborate Asad's observation that belief is better conceptualized as an "activity in the world" (Asad 1993, 47; cf. Callum Brown 2009; W. Smith 1978; McKinnon 2002). Whereas a previous generation of academics took for granted a narrow model wherein belief stands alongside creeds, doctrines, and institutions as defining features of religion, a recent near-consensus has exposed this paradigm to be rooted in post-Enlightenment, Christocentric categories (see, for example, Chidester 1996; Fitzgerald 2000; Martin 2010; Masuzawa 2005; McCutcheon 1997). In response, many scholars of religion incorporate practice and identity into the larger spectrum of religiosity and highlight concepts such as embodiment, performance, and affect (for example, Bell 2009; Schaffer 2015; Vásquez 2011). This new rubric provides greater insight into the lived, and at times contradictory, experiences of religious adherents. In this context, belief is examined not for what it signifies but rather for what it does.

Progressive Christianity reflects an uneasy balance between belief and identity. Its focus on social engagement and intellectual inquiry instead of dogmatism and moral regulation provides nuance to the ways progressive Christians deploy belief. For them, belief serves as a motive that generates skepticism as a form of conviction, not as a negotiation of facts. This premise is evident in the subtitle of Gretta Vosper's first book, *With or Without God: Why the Way We Live Is More Important Than What We Believe* (2009). Vosper argues that in many cases, belief impedes a full and ethical life. Not only is it unnecessary to believe in God to be a good Christian, many progressive Christians probably consider that they cannot be a good Christian if they do. Beliefs run the risk of being deemed false in the future. Since progressive Christians hold that claiming beliefs that are known to be false is disingenuous, Vosper concludes that one should remain committed to humanitarian acts and personal virtues rather than propositional beliefs.

Progressive Christians deemphasize the traditional understanding of belief. Yet, particularly when it comes to doctrines to which they no longer subscribe, progressive Christians hold belief as distinct from practice and see it as a sign of their religious affiliation (cf. Strhan 2015). The espousal of belief linked to affiliation resembles observations that the sociologist Abby Day (2010) made concerning the social and performative functions of belief. Day examines agnostic and nonreligious individuals in the United Kingdom who identified as Christian when asked about their religious affiliation for the national census. While many of her informants did not believe in God and did not actively participate in religious observances, Day found that when pressed to choose, many resorted to religion as indicative of "self-perceived family or 'ethnic' social groups" (2010, 19; see also Day 2011). She suggests that belief contributes to the performance and maintenance of identity and does not indicate propositional assent. By asking open-ended questions such as, "What do you believe in?" instead of "Do you believe in God?," Day found that her informants had recast belief to signify broader values and aspirations within their social worlds. Many of Day's interlocutors provided personal stories and anecdotes that demonstrated belief as something one does. Thus, Day concluded that belief is related to social codes and practices learned at an early age and refined during one's life (2010, 23; cf. Morgan 2010). Presented in the form of a narrative, this framework exposes a new hierarchy wherein belief involves social relationships rather than theological propositions, moral conventions, or an active engagement with Christianity (Day 2010, 21).

In conjunction with the performative model of belief as something one does, Day notes that, for some, belief carries the possibility of undoing social codes and practices. The act of affiliating oneself with Christianity despite not assenting to its premises can serve as a form of resistance and work to unsettle its more traditional versions (2010, 25–26). Similarly, Monica's deconversion testimony supports this notion that stories might undo belief and reframe its function. Monica's narrative reflects a desire to be unsettled in the context of a hierarchy of identities. In the end, losing her religion is better than losing her family. Her deconversion was as much about her experiences as a daughter, mother, and wife as it was about her inability to assent to theological beliefs. While recounting her religious loss, Monica also related the intimate story of coming to terms with the particular dynamics of her family, her own experiences, and her personal aspirations.

Here, belief is propositional in form but not in function. It both signifies Monica's identity and provides a tangible marker of her transition. Monica conceptualized religious identity and its accompanying beliefs, which she cast off, as traits of a former self from which she was recovering. In this way, the narrative creates a gap. The former Monica was subsumed in the making of her new religious self. Similar to Day's observations, the casting off of this other is a performative act of differentiation. The former self becomes an entirely different person or an other materialized through beliefs Monica no longer held. This other, which I call a Protestant proximate other, is both real and imagined. It takes the form of self and not-self. As I will show, it serves as an important figure in the larger construction of progressive Christianity precisely because accounting for its differences maintains an otherwise ambiguous link to Christianity.

The term *Protestant proximate other* echoes the *proximate other* coined by the religious studies scholar Jonathan Z. Smith. A proximate other is a prototype with which religious groups construct their identity through comparison and differentiation. According to Smith (2004), the category of otherness is always situational and based on relationships of reciprocity. Otherness is bestowed on another individual, community, or former affiliation through rhetoric and judgment. The category reveals almost nothing about the other but provides insight into those who assign and evaluate otherness. Per Smith, "a 'theory of the other' is but another way of phrasing a 'theory of the self'" (2004, 275). The *proximate other* allows a theory of self to emerge in comparison with others from one's own group or tradition.²

An advantage of the term *Protestant proximate other* is that it provides a better means to analyze the ways in which progressive Christians describe and categorize other Christians. As a classificatory model, *Protestant proximate other* makes it possible to explore the relationships between progressive Christians and other factions of contemporary Christianity without resorting to stereotypes and caricatures. The act of describing an other legitimizes a social hierarchy based on expressions of difference. It enables those defining the proximate other to place their own group at the top of this hierarchy. Something similar occurs in the context of progressive Christianity, wherein they highlight the differences between progressive Christians and their Protestant proximate others but diminish the distinctions between other varieties of Christians. In their descriptions of other Christians, progressive Christians often use terms like *evangelical, conservative, fundamentalist, charismatic*, and *right-wing* interchangeably and without nuance. The task at hand is not to determine whether their definitions of evangelicals, conservatives, or fundamentalists are correct but to discern the effects of such descriptions within progressive Christianity.

To offer just one example, I had a conversation with Alan, a retired Anglican priest, in which we discussed the rise of the religious Right in America. Alan reflected on a variety of trends he saw within this movement, including its style of worship, affluence, and popularity with young people:

> I suspect that the ultraconservatives are in fear as they see things breaking down around them. You always fight hardest just before everything collapses around you. I don't know whether that's wishful thinking or whether it's factual, but I suspect that there might be something to it. The other thing is that they seem to have an awful lot of money to spend. There's a lot of sheer entertainment value in a lot of these fundamentalist churches. The message is sort of slipped in with it. The fundamental-

ists can spend money on having really expensive production value for teenagers that the other churches don't seem to have. I'm not sure where the money is coming from. Part of it is because, in the fundamentalist church, you really are absorbed into the church: That's where you spend your money, your time, and everything else. You don't have other things going on in your life. You can just give it all to the expression. Basically, I'm holding suppositions. I really don't know, but I don't think the growth in right-wing Christianity is sustainable, and I don't think it's as strong as appearances would indicate.

Alan's comments are representative of those I encountered among progressive Christians. He switched seamlessly between *ultraconservative*, *fundamentalist*, and *right-wing Christianity* to describe religious practices that are commonplace among larger evangelical churches (cf. Chaves 2006; Elisha 2011; Hendershot 2004). Progressive Christians have a sense that conservative churches spend a lot of money on production items such as lights, music, and sound systems. They criticize this allocation of resources and see it as superficial. Progressive Christians think their conservative counterparts focus on popularity and attracting members at the expense of charitable acts or personal growth. In Alan's assessment, such trends stem from a fear of change and stand in moral contrast to progressive Christian values, although he did not elaborate on what those values might be. Alan concluded by noting that he was merely speculating and that he could not speak from personal experience. Regardless, he fused fundamentalists, conservatives, evangelicals, and the Christian Right into a single entity. While he based this fusion on real observations and descriptions, this entity, the Protestant proximate other, is ultimately a conflation existing in Alan's imagination rather than in empirical experience or observation.

Because the Protestant proximate other serves as an imagined point of departure, an exploration of the ways in which progressive Christians represent their Protestant proximate other is necessary. As I have shown, progressive Christians seek to undo belief: they reject central Christian tenets by defining themselves according to what they are not (the evangelical Christian Right) and what they do not believe (traditional Christian doctrines) rather than what they are and what they do believe. As such, their collective identity stems from an antithetical representation formed in resistance to, and in competition with, their Protestant proximate other.

Progressive Christians regularly reference the perceived failings of their Protestant proximate other. For example, as I noted earlier, the *Saving Jesus* video series used at Holy Cross included a promotional flyer that asks the would-be participant: "Ever feel that Jesus has been kidnapped by the Christian Right?" An advertisement with similar wording caused a stir in progressive Christian circles when the legal department at *Sports Illustrated* deemed the ad too "jarring" to include in the magazine.[3] Similarly, they frequently discuss conservative religious leaders such as Jerry Falwell, Pat Robinson, Joel Osteen, and Ted Haggard in conversations about the type of Christianity that progressive Christians rejected.

Through an act of undoing, progressive Christians maintain their Christianity. Many insist that the progressive theologies they now hold have saved their faith because without them they would not be Christians at all. Comparison stands as the point of origin for their identity. Not only do they persist in claiming to be Christian, but they also do so within the edifice—the symbols, the rhetoric, and even the buildings—of contemporary Christianity. Regardless of their original position, they internalize a narrative of departure, which charts their move away from conservative to progressive Christianity. Recounting this narrative reinforces their current position, which is intentionally heretical and necessarily ambiguous. This position requires continual maintenance. The focus on past experiences is highlighted by reflection on the current activities and beliefs of those varieties of Christianity from which they claim to have departed. The Protestant proximate other stands in both for their former self and as a tangible reference against which they might construct progressive Christianity.

Deconversion Narratives

In the examples that follow, Thomas, Hedy, Sandra, and Margie highlight the intellectual, emotional, ethical, and social motivations that inspired their deconversions. In narratives of continuity and disjuncture, each juxtaposed their current theological stance with what they believed before deconversion. Their recollections reveal how the new self is responsible for maintaining the former one. All made the intriguing assumption that religious identity as a category remains the same. As I have noted, the contrast between belief on one hand and affiliation on the other delineates religious identity as something that particular choices and discursive practices can add to or subtract from.

Thomas's Story—Intellectual Motivators

Thomas met me on the steps of George Street United Church. It was a bright day in early December, one of those days when the sunlight seems to cut like a knife through the cool air. I had taken a break between interviews to do some holiday shopping in Peterborough's quaint downtown. "Why don't we go to a coffee shop instead of doing this at the church?" he suggested as I walked up to meet him. "It's not too far of a walk," he added. I agreed and we headed back downtown.

It is possible that this was not the first time that I had met Thomas, although neither of us remembered or recognized the other. As a master's candidate in Kingston, Ontario, I wrote a term paper on the evangelical church that Thomas had attended as a teenager. As part of my research, I had interviewed the youth pastor, Erin, a childhood friend of mine. As we walked, Thomas and I bonded over our shared affection for Erin. Smiling, I remembered how she had been frustrated with the kids at the church for sneaking onto the roof, and I wondered whether Thomas had been among the troublemakers.

Four years later, Thomas was now an undergraduate at a local university in Peterborough. He was studying history and no longer considered himself an evangelical Christian. As we were seated in the crowded coffee shop, he told me that he grew up nominally Catholic and converted to evangelical Christianity as a teenager. Thomas spent his summers working at a Christian summer camp and was involved in various youth activities through his church. Initially, he appreciated the evangelical depiction of Jesus as a friend, whom he jokingly called "buddy Jesus." As he assessed his religious upbringing, he spoke warmly yet wistfully. His admiration for Erin and other religious mentors was clear. He highlighted the fact that they provided him with space to ask difficult questions and to consider the Bible's impact on his life.

Despite his frequent participation in church activities, Thomas told me that he began to experience doubt shortly after his conversion. I asked him to elaborate, and he struggled to find the words to make sense of when and how his skepticism emerged: "It was kind of intense in terms of making your faith your own. All these catchphrases and cool ideas of bringing your faith outside of [a Christian environment]. A lot of it wasn't making sense because I had a lot of questions. I was doubting a lot, because it had never meant anything to me beyond church. I was really playing out, 'Okay, what if ____?' I was just trying to process a lot of things and talking to my [church] leaders about it." Thomas's doubts coincided with his initial conversion. He explained that from the beginning there were parts of Christianity that did not make sense. He struggled to reconcile his faith with his life at home and school.

Further on in our conversation, Thomas revealed that the Bible was a source of both doubt and certainty: "I'd committed to following the words of Christ to the best of my ability. As my God, I guess. From there, it's just been a journey of seeing 'What does this actually mean?,' 'How do I interpret the Bible?,' and 'Does the Bible mean anything to me?'" Thomas clarified that, while at that point in his life he read the Bible literally, he was not a fundamentalist. Commenting on his departure from biblical literalism, Thomas explained:

> I'm at this stage, kind of coming out of—I don't want to call it fundamentalist, but those past years, were kind of, "Yes, the Bible's literal," let's see the meaning out of it, blah, blah, blah. Now the more that I've learned—just in an undergraduate education as a history student—the more I've thought about some of the implications of this literal [interpretation]. This is where Spong comes in, in a big way to me. He was the first person I encountered, through reading his work, who was open with his doubts. And now I know that there is definitely critical biblical scholarship, but I was just blind to it. I'd never had that be part of my reality. So it was very refreshing to hear him voicing a lot of the concerns that I was having in my heart. So, no, I don't think the Bible is literal. I think that my relationship to it is very complex.

Thomas noted that progressive Christianity is not the only place where one can encounter scholarly biblical criticism. When he was in Kingston, he sometimes attended a church that follows the emerging church model and posits itself as a place for seekers and those with doubts. Thomas is critical of this church, stating that its members position themselves as part of the emerging church without referencing specific thinkers from that movement. "They'll use Borg a bit as a catalyst for their discussion. But they never admit it," he explained.

When I asked him how he found George Street United Church, his eyes lit up. He had been church shopping for a while and was looking for a place where he could feel comfortable. Having just finished Spong's best seller, *Why Christianity Must Change or Die*, Thomas was delighted to learn that Spong would be lecturing at George Street that fall. "I was amazed and somewhat perplexed [about] why Peterborough would be hosting him," Thomas recalled. "Because I didn't think—why would he give Peterborough the time of day? Like, how did he wind up in this small town in Canada? It made me really, really happy. And it also made me think [that] there has to be something special going on here, some honesty that a lot of other Christian churches in this town won't be allowing their congregants even to think about." His affection for George Street and for the church's minister, Karen, was evident. Having never been part of a congregation that used gender-inclusive language, Thomas was especially fond of the way that Karen referred to God as "father-mother" while reading the Bible.

Thomas was the only twentysomething I interviewed and one of only a handful I encountered during my fieldwork. Although he did not attend the reading group at George Street, he made a point of finding me during Spong's visit. Thomas is a prime example of someone for whom progressive Christianity provided a means of maintaining a Christian identity. Like many young Christians his age, he had been involved in an evangelical church, and he found it challenging to reconcile Christianity with his everyday experiences. His perspective changed when he was introduced to Spong's books by a friend at their university. When we met, Thomas described himself as a "confused Christian" for whom progressive theology raised many difficult questions. He found progressive Christianity refreshing, a point that he emphasized during our interview.

> Well, I have definitely, I guess, progressed much more toward the progressive or liberal movement. And I've started to kind of internalize some of their messages. I'm at the point where I ask: "What have I lost or will I lose, if I continue on this way from my traditional background?" So I

don't know. I'm kind of torn. I'd say this is an interesting time for me because in one way I really want to stay on this Spong path, or whatever you want to call it, because, like I said, the honesty that I don't find in other institutions is what draws me to it. The ideas are very refreshing.

As he explained his attraction to progressive Christianity, Thomas reiterated that he had high esteem for evangelical Christians. "I don't know if I found that elsewhere, if I would gravitate towards their beliefs? Like Rob Bell and Mark Driscoll. These guys are pretty conservative in their theology, but they promote openness."

For Thomas, reading progressive Christian theologians and attending Spong's lectures allowed him to justify his exit from evangelical Christianity while maintaining a link to it. He was acutely aware that he was undergoing a transition that was as much a departure as it was a changing of perspective. Thomas was seeking a balance between critical discernment and the freedom to reject those components of the tradition that simply did not fit his experiences. Taking a sip of his coffee, he explained that he shared Spong's frustrations: "One thing that he once said was that he was tired of jumping through theological hoops or dealing with becoming a theological pretzel to come to all these places of understanding God." I smiled and nodded. Thomas continued: "Which I appreciate, it was one thing that I was, like, 'Yeah, you're right! I don't want to keep trying to figure out how does the Trinity work? How all these different things work?'"

Like Thomas, many progressive Christians claim to have experienced a revelation. Fellowship with other Christians with the same misgivings was transformative. Thomas's deconversion involved skepticism, doubt, and cognitive crises that emerged from his evangelical faith. Despite his young age, Thomas's exposure to progressive Christianity followed the model that many presume is normative. He began by searching for answers from his religious leaders and the Bible. Dissatisfied with the results, he turned to popular theological books by progressive authors. He then sought out a congregation that featured such books and authors. Thomas's story focused on intellectual engagement as the primary impulse. For others, however, the intellectual aspects of progressive Christianity were daunting. Instead, their personal experiences and emotional connections spurred their deconversion.

Hedy's Story—Emotional Experiences

On her almost daily walks to and from West Hill United Church, Hedy hummed the melodies of the old church hymns that she no longer felt comfortable singing. Many liberal and progressive Christian churches have banned songs like "Onward Christian Soldiers" because of their imperial style of theology. But for Hedy, the beat helped her pass the time as she walked between her tiny apartment and the church.

It was a wet and cold weekday in May. When I pulled up in the empty church parking lot, I saw Hedy's slender body bent over the garden as she pulled weeds and prepared the flowerbeds for planting in a few weeks' time. As I got out of the car, she slowly straightened up, turned to face me, and smiled. As always, her face was expressive. Her form and stance were those of an on-duty soldier, perhaps an involuntary acknowledgment of the three years she had spent in the air force during World War II.

"You don't get to be ninety without hitting a few bumps in the road," Hedy told me over a cup of tea as we sat together in the church lounge. The church had always played a central role in Hedy's life, and she had always insisted on doing church her own way. As she recounted her story, independence emerged as the predominate theme. It was an independence that she had proudly earned as the by-product of playing the role of the outsider. For much of her adult life, Hedy had felt like an impostor, which perhaps partially explained her attraction to a congregation that likewise saw itself as an outsider.

As we stirred our tea, I asked her about her religious journey. She began by tracing her family history. Hedy was born into a Methodist family in a rural town in Ontario. Her grandfather had been a minister and a proponent of the creation of the United Church of Canada, which resulted from a merger of the Methodist, Presbyterian, and Congregationalist churches in 1925. Following family tradition, her father had been a Sunday school teacher and taught young Hedy that Christianity was something that was practiced, not preached. Despite the fact that she grew up during the Great Depression, Hedy's childhood was a happy one. As she described it, church was a way of life:

> My life was pretty well centered on the church. Most of my friends went to church, not necessarily the same one, but it was a way of life in a

small village and rural community. We all had similar backgrounds and stability, even during the Depression when things were tough. Even the people that had money didn't flaunt it. We all lived in somebody's hand[ed]-down clothing and made do with what we had. We were fortunate that we lived in a situation where, despite of the fact that farming had hit a tough spot in the midthirties, when there was a drought in our county, we all still had enough to eat and we lived pretty well. I think we lived exceptionally well because our farm was beside a small lake: we swam, we skated, we had boats. When I look back now, I think we really were privileged that we had all of the advantages that we had. My dad had spent his teenage years in Montreal and chose to be a farmer. He had some college education, I don't know whether . . . (*laughs*). Anyway, he was a very clever man. He was a pretty firm disciplinarian but I guess he spoiled me. Because, now that I think of it, I had two older brothers, but when it became time for me to skate, I was the one who got new skates. I got new skis. I got a new bicycle. When I think of it now, I was the spoiled brat.

Hedy's parents encouraged her to do everything her brothers did. They instilled in her a love of reading by taking her to the library every weekend. She spent her Saturday nights with her head buried in a book, often continuing with a flashlight under blankets long after she had been sent to bed.

Like her father, Hedy pursued postsecondary education. She attended an instructional college for women that taught home economics. While she made some friends, Hedy was a tomboy and never quite fit in with her classmates. She preferred the outdoors and working the fields with her brothers to cooking and homemaking skills. On Saturday nights she and her friends would sneak out the windows of their dorm. "Those were interesting years," she told me with a wide smile and a twinkle in her eye. She elected not to disclose whatever indiscretions may have occurred, revealing instead that "lots of people knew about those windows." While her Saturday nights saw her sneaking out windows and engaging in youthful revelry, Hedy remained committed to church attendance on Sunday mornings. She accompanied her roommate to a nearby Anglican church, where she found the rote nature of the liturgy puzzling: "By the time you've done it a few times, you don't need the prayer book. You just say it. It's repetition. You don't think about it. You're probably half-asleep from being out the night before."

During her three years in the air force Hedy continued to attend Anglican chapel services, noting that they gave her a temporary reprieve from the daily grind of military service. Hedy's bewilderment at the static nature of the Anglican liturgy stuck with her. In 1990, while at an air force reunion in St. John's, Newfoundland, she attended a Sunday morning service as part of the weekend celebrations. Even though she had not been in an Anglican church for almost fifty years, Hedy was shocked to find that in the ensuing half-century, little had changed: "I sat down in the pew and opened it up right in the right page in the prayer book. I hadn't forgotten it in all those years," she said, shaking her head in disbelief.

After the war, Hedy and her husband, James, moved to work on her parents' farm. Because she loved farmwork, Hedy took over daily operations, leaving James, a mechanic, to work with the agricultural equipment. While living with her parents, Hedy drove her mother to various church functions. Because she felt out of place in the social world of women her own age, she preferred to accompany her mother and her mother's friends in the Women's Missionary Society. There she had her first encounter with book study groups. The Women's Missionary Society would read travel accounts written by overseas missionaries. These accounts opened up a whole new world to Hedy. While most women her age were interested in child-rearing and homemaking, Hedy was drawn to the wider perspectives and interests of the Women's Missionary Society.

Hedy spoke little and hesitantly about her husband. I got the sense that her marriage was difficult, and I did not push her for details. James had grown up in a large family with seven siblings. His mother was a devout Pentecostal. Though James and his siblings recognized that the church had been of great comfort to their mother, they abandoned religion as soon as they could. Hedy struggled with James's resistance to church attendance. When she did discuss her marriage, it was in reference to her daughter, Anne, with whom she was close. In 1961 the family moved to Scarborough at a time that she described as "the height of the atomic bomb scare." Anne was nine years old. At first, amid Scarborough's homogeneous, "WASPy" environment, Hedy felt out of place. "I found that it was a real culture shock to go from a small town, where I knew everybody and was involved in everything, to come to a city and be nothing! But my daughter and I found a church, and it wasn't too long before we were back being involved in everything."

Hedy described the years of Anne's childhood as a time when they "coasted along," participating in the typical activities of girlhood: Girl Scouts and Sunday school at the local United Church hall. As the years went by, Hedy became increasingly anxious about her faith. "I read a fair amount and began to be a little uncomfortable with some of the things that I was hearing. I know that things like saying the Lord's Prayer got to be so much of a rote that I could figure out what I was going to have for lunch while I was saying the Lord's Prayer. It sort of got to be meaningless." Frustrated yet again with what she perceived to be overly static religion, she went in search of a new church.

West Hill's flamboyant and charismatic minister, Fred Styles, was reason enough for Hedy to switch congregations in 1979. "I remember so well the first time I saw him come down the aisle. He wore a white robe and I think up to that time, I had never seen a United Church minister in anything but a black one," she said. "Here comes Fred up the aisle." She joined the congregation and quickly became involved in the day-to-day activities of the church. According to Hedy, the early 1980s saw a lot of changes at West Hill. The congregation instituted fresh ideas and new programs, such as a study group that examined popular books. Hedy missed the first book study group in 1981 because it was geared specifically to couples, and she knew that she would not be able to convince James to accompany her.

The following year, the book study group was open to all. Hedy joined the group in reading Scott Peck's *The Road Less Traveled* (1978) and had attended nearly every book study group since. Hedy found the highbrow nature of the group's discussions to be inspirational but at times intellectually intimidating. Participating in the book study group made her feel uncertain. It brought back familiar insecurities, and she felt the urge to withdraw and recast herself as an outsider, as she had done so many times throughout her life. This time, however, the group's accepting and inclusive spirit won her over: "I remember participating in that group and breaking down and *not* feeling that I would be excommunicated because I couldn't handle what was going on. I cannot remember what it was. But the comfort, the hands that came out to hold my hand. I can get emotional about it now. It meant so much to me." As she remembered her initial participation in the book study group, Hedy started to cry softly. Speaking earnestly, she recounted the profound effect the group's acceptance had on her:

> It meant so much, being accepted. My husband was a mechanic. All these other people, they were university graduates but they never excluded me. They included me in their lives, their groups, their homes. I got great comfort out of that because I always felt like I didn't belong. Normally, I would think to myself: "I'm just sort of on the fringe—they're accepting me because I'm willing to get in and participate and so on, but socially I'm an outsider." But I never felt that way here. I felt total acceptance from the time I walked in the door, even though I wanted to be the outsider.

In this new setting, far from the rural community in which she grew up, Hedy set aside her outsider status. She had found a place where she was finally able to be open about her insecurities.

In the ensuing thirty years, Hedy had become a quintessential insider at West Hill United Church. She participated in all aspects of the church's life and was a regular lay leader during religious services. As Hedy spoke about her transition, I thought about the first time we met. "You'll have to meet Hedy," Gretta Vosper had pronounced during my first Sunday at West Hill. It was just after the church's board had approved my application to study the congregation. Gretta was eager to introduce me to active members of the book study group. "She'll be a great resource for you," Gretta continued as she marched me up to the simply dressed, smiling woman who several months later sat across from me sharing her story.

It is fair to say that Hedy's theological perspective was representative of many from her generation. While she recounted that there had been instances when she had felt uncertain about her faith, it appeared that her primary objective was to find a welcoming congregation. She had been active in church her entire life. Her participation in book studies went back to her early twenties, when she had joined the Women's Missionary Society. For Hedy, reading books and meeting with others to discuss new concepts was part of her religious practice. In the book study group, she encountered new ideas that challenged her preconceived assumptions but not her sense of her Christian identity. Like Monica, who described herself as a recovering Christian, Hedy recounted that her transition was gradual: "We began to read Spong. And I began to think, instead of just sitting back and accepting things. To be challenged and really wonder about where I was coming from and where I was going. I don't have any problems at all. I'm not worried about whether I'm going to heaven because I have such strange beliefs. I think heaven is here. It's what we make here." As a long-standing member of West Hill, Hedy's theology had evolved alongside the church's worldview. The congregation's sense of traveling together had resolved much of her intellectual uncertainty. Hedy's story reveals something significant about those who have been actively engaged in progressive Christianity over time.

As our conversation moved to the theological shifts she had experienced, Hedy picked up her earlier critique of the rote nature of saying the Lord's Prayer. She explained that she no longer felt comfortable reciting it aloud. She fully supported West Hill's decision to remove or rewrite hymns and prayers that evoke traditional Christian language. I asked for a specific example, and she broke into song, humming the tune to the old hymn, "Jesus Christ Is Risen Today." Both of us began to laugh. "Well, come on now, I don't believe that!" she exclaimed. "I belong to a group who thinks that Christ, the man, bucked the trend two thousand years ago. He accepted women, the outcasts, and the diseased. Maybe he started our journey? But to think that he rose from the dead and ascended into heaven? I can't believe that."

Not everyone shared Hedy's affection for and commitment to West Hill. Over the years, as the church assumed a public spotlight, waves of members had left the congregation in protest of the changes. I asked Hedy about these former members, and her response was once again emotional: "What has broken my heart is that a lot of the people that I did love and still do are not here now (*starts to cry*). I don't know. I'm very awkward when I meet them. I can't accept the fact that they can't accept the fact that (*pauses to regain composure*), that some of those old hymns that they sing and so on, that I can't sing them now. And some of those creeds that they recite, I can't recite them now (*sighs*)." While deconversion narratives are personal, they emerge as stories formed through relationships with others in intimate settings.

Hedy's rejection of what, for many, is a central part of the Christian tradition reflects the larger scope of progressive Christianity. Somewhere along the line, she was transformed. This shift was dependent on her previous religious self. At one point, she could recite traditional prayers and sing the old hymns, but she no longer could. Additionally, her transition occurred alongside the transitions of other members of the congregation. The image of hands that reached out to hold hers during emotional uncertainty speaks to progressive Christianity's collective potential. It stands in contrast to the story of those former congregants who left because of a difference of theological opinion and religious practice. For Hedy, it was more than just the loss of friends at church that upset her. She mourned the loss of companions' assembling a narrative together. While many progressive Christians have undergone such deconversions in solitude, disembarking from an earlier form of Christian adherence and finding progressive Christianity in the aftermath, for others it has resulted from shared experiences. Relationships, it seems, may trigger theology.

Sandra and Margie's Stories—Shared Ethical Concerns

"Rebekka will have some wine," Sandra declared as I walked into the kitchen, answering the group's speculation as to whether it is appropriate to open a bottle or two of wine at lunchtime. Before I had a chance to respond, someone opened the bottles, and Margie, our host, began to pour wine into several glasses. Sandra nodded in approval and continued to busy herself with arranging crackers on a plate filled with cheddar, gouda, and brie.

Sandra was one of my favorite members of Holy Cross Lutheran Church because she reminded me of my mother: she was decisive, enjoyed the occasional midafternoon glass of wine, and would often stop to reflect on the beauty of a moment, such as the way the afternoon sunlight fell in her sitting room as she watched it from her rocking chair.

That day in the kitchen, Sandra and Margie shared the easy friendship that women form later in life, after their children have left home and, as was the case for both women, their marriages had ended. As someone handed me a glass of wine, I nodded appreciatively as I looked at the smiling faces of children in the pictures on the refrigerator door.

"Are these your grandchildren?" I asked. I knew her grandkids were Margie's pride and joy. As expected, her face lit up and she hurried across the kitchen to explain who was who and the context of each photograph. Sandra smiled at the children's photos, handed me a plate of pickles, and asked me to help her to make room on the already overflowing dining room table. It held a spread of breads, cheeses, salads, and cold cuts for a special meeting to discuss the church's plans for the year ahead.

Margie had grown up attending church for most of her life. Her childhood was a world of Sunday school socials and quilting bees at the local United Church hall. She loved church and she loved being involved. When she got married, her husband told her that he was not interested in church. As a child, he had attended a rigid Anglican church and had been forced to go to several services on Sundays when he would have preferred to be playing outside. "When we got married he said, 'I don't have any intention of ever setting foot in a church other than for weddings or funerals.'" Initially, Margie followed her husband's lead. "When we had our family, I said, 'I loved Sunday school and I really want the boys to have that experience.' So I started taking them on my own. But it wasn't the same because of that tension."

With her young boys in tow, Margie struggled to find a religious home. She attended a number of churches that were caught up in social conflict, which she saw as un-Christian:

> At that point we were in Kitchener, and there started a battle in the church over "I don't like this minister" and "Oh, I do." "I don't." I felt like it was a very un-Christian place to be at that moment. We moved to Newmarket and I started at [another church] here in town. Within a couple months of being there, it was exactly the same thing. One faction against the other, and everybody coming and saying, "What do you think? Don't you think he's terrible?" That's not what I want. I don't want to be involved in that kind of battle.

Margie quickly gave up and focused on community activities for her children. It was several years before the thought of church crossed her mind again.

Sandra and Margie had been friends for years. They worked together at a primary school where Sandra was the principal and Margie a teacher. One day in the teachers' lounge, each described her religious background. They reflected on growing up in a faith tradition and noted how important church had been to them. They agreed that they missed a sense of fellowship that comes from being involved in a religious community. Together they resolved to find a church. During the next several months, they attended a half-dozen churches in their quest to find one they liked.

One day, Margie saw an ad in the local paper for Holy Cross's Rethinking Christianity speaker series at the local country club. The speaker for that event was Tom Harpur. "We had both read a lot of his work, so we went to that," Margie explained to me. "Pastor Dawn had put the church's mission statement up on the screen, and they had put the brochures on the chairs. We kind of read it and looked at each other and said, 'Well, this kind of sounds interesting.'" But they were hesitant. "We didn't trust that. We went back to [hear] the second speaker and the third speaker and said, 'You know, we should go and check that church out.'" Six months later, they finally attended a service. Margie's initial hesitation, however, was quickly overcome: "I've been every Sunday since that first time, other than when I'm away."

Sandra grew up in the United States and attended a Free Methodist church during her childhood. She described her religious upbringing as "very conservative," noting that "there was no room for questioning or maneuvering." When she moved to Canada in her twenties, she joined a Baptist church. Like Margie, she found the environment distasteful and un-Christian. She was horrified by the negativity of the pastor: "Everything was bad for him! The whole world was going to hell! I'm not opposed to that kind of thinking. It has its place. But that can't be everything. I couldn't go to church and think like that."

Finding Holy Cross was a turning point for Sandra, but she struggled more than Margie did to feel at home: "The first few months I attended the church, I spoke to no one. If anyone had offered me a kind word or encouragement, I would have broken down into hysterics. I never took part in any of the rituals. I just listened to the sermons. It was like I was being reprogrammed. I had to listen carefully. Soon I began to see that everything I had been taught was wrong. It was a whole new world and I was a new person." Sandra's comparison with being reprogrammed is especially apt in this discussion of deconversion. Margie and Sandra's language concerning religious transformation is not uncommon among former evangelicals. Sandra's insistence that she needed to "listen carefully" reflects common Protestant concerns that religiosity is rooted in comprehension of beliefs. Her transformation into what she termed a new person resembles motifs popular in evangelical Christianity, wherein a new self emerges through faith in Jesus. In this case, however, the new self was made possible only through an explicit rejection of the beliefs and practices of the former self. The case of progressive Christian deconversions suggests a reversal of the "lost and found" motif within evangelical Christianity. The point of departure, the Protestant proximate other, whether it is real or imagined, retains an almost tangible status. Through certain acts of differentiation, progressive Christians undo the Protestant proximate other and move into an increasingly ambiguous religious identity.

Born Again, Again: Deconstructing Deconversion

The shift of religious identity accompanied by a focus on an other is not unique to progressive Christianity. The anthropologist Diane J. Austin (1981) studied Pentecostals in Jamaica who, despite already having been saved, participated in altar calls as a way of asserting that their religious identity emerges from experience, not instruction. The Pentecostal pastor she interviewed used this practice as a point of contrast with established mainline denominations in Jamaica, where formal study, membership, and infant baptism denoted Christian affiliation. The Jamaican Pentecostals saw established churches, such as the Anglican, Roman Catholic, and Methodist churches, frequented by wealthy elites, as complacent in political, racial, and economic systems of domination. Such congregations equated education and social status with one's spiritual state. In contrast, the Pentecostal believers emphasized the universality and egalitarianism of spiritual practices such as glossolalia and exorcism. While such practices are standard in many forms of Pentecostalism, Austin further notes that they provide a means of rejecting the social norms, authority, and material wealth held by elites at other churches (1981, 235).

Unlike material wealth, an experience is more difficult to quantify. In the case of the Jamaican Pentecostals, experience gained legitimacy through repetition. Frequent altar calls, testimonies, and public deployment of spiritual gifts provided evidence of religious capital. Despite having already been saved, the Jamaican Pentecostals revisited conversion as a means of reifying their collective identity (D. Austin 1981). In much of the anthropological literature, conversion serves as a point of return that reflects the ways that Christians locate themselves in historical moments (Harris 2006). Figuratively speaking, returning to their moment of conversion works to buttress adherents' investment in their religious identity. According to the anthropologist Simon Coleman, it allows them to situate their religious identity within a matrix of ideological positions and social relationships. Thus conversion may denote a particular experience or historical moment, but it also operates as what Coleman calls a "continuous conversion." In its recounting, the adherent carries the conversion experience into the present moment and allows it to shape their current situation (Coleman 2003).

The aforementioned literature points out that conversion is normally a protracted experience. Organized through its retelling, conversion provides meaning after the fact. The same could be said of deconversion. It might be possible to speak of a "continuous deconversion" akin to the multivalent work of conversion. Given its preoccupation with the former self as an object of critique, deconversion might be understood as preeminently reifying one's current position, a process that is all the more noteworthy among progressive Christians whose deconversion retains the category of Christian and reconceptualizes it through a description of, and differentiation from, the Protestant proximate other. It is further significant that in the case of progressive Christians, their proximity to the other rarely comes from personal experience. Instead, it requires extra knowledge obtained from outside sources to set the foundation for the identity from which they depart.

Monica's authority stemmed from her self-identification as a "recovering Christian" and an atheist. It is not surprising that she was invited to speak at the Canadian Centre for Progressive Christianity conference. As I mentioned previously, atheists, or what we might more appropriately term *strong atheists*, make up a smaller contingent within progressive Christianity alongside nontheists, skeptics, and agnostics, who are more common.[4] Those most likely to adopt an atheistic stance are often former evangelicals or recovering fundamentalists. These individuals appear to hold the most symbolic social capital and assume positions of authority within the progressive Christian church. In his autobiography, *Here I Stand* (2000), Spong writes about growing up in the American South during the 1930s. At church and elsewhere, he encountered segregation, homophobia, and fundamentalism. His intimate exposure to religious fundamentalism allowed him to assume an authoritative position within progressive Christianity.

The social theorist Pierre Bourdieu explains that the authority of a discourse does not depend on its content or style "but rather in the social conditions of production and reproduction of the distribution between the classes of the knowledge and the recognition of legitimate language" (1991, 113). It can be argued that the authority of Monica's discourse stemmed from its similarity to, and tension with, an evangelical testimony narrative. As I have shown, she deployed similar language, describing herself as lost and then found. Most important, she retained Christianity as a container. Her deconversion narrative draws upon the institutional aspects and performative language in Christianity writ large (see Bourdieu 1991 following J. Austin 1962). Thus, a conscious rejection of evangelical content is balanced by a subconscious assumption of the same linguistic mode of communication and narrative patterns. Her account works to subvert or, as Day (2010) puts it, to undo traditional Christianity.

When I began to examine progressive Christian promotional material, I mistakenly assumed that most progressive Christians would be former conservatives, evangelicals, or fundamentalists. I was surprised to learn that progressive Christians' access to their Protestant proximate other was limited. Instead, they drew their primary information about what conservative Christians do and believe from television broadcasts, media reports, films, and YouTube footage.[5] While some progressive Christians had been involved in evangelical or conservative churches as children, they had often left those congregations long before they began to frequent progressive ones. Overall, with some notable exceptions like Monica, most of my interlocutors had been previously involved in mainline churches or moderately liberal Roman Catholic ones.[6]

This observation amplifies the importance of understanding the nature of deconversion narratives within progressive Christianity. Progressive Christians emphasize that they have prevailed over a form of deception that both their Protestant proximate other and their former clerical leaders have perpetrated. Progressive Christians report that the church has concealed the truth from its members but that they have uncovered it through their engagement with popular exegetical texts and moved past a restrictive and misleading belief system. In explaining this process, many of my interlocutors emphasized that they had undergone a transformation. They related a specific type of deconversion narrative, classified as such because of its emphasis on a former or original way of being Christian in juxtaposition to a new version. Despite the fact that they claim a former affiliation aligned with the Protestant proximate other, in most cases, the progressive Christians featured in this study were not explicitly departing from it. In contrast, they maintained their institutional affiliations within mainline liberal churches. Indeed, the majority of my interlocutors are long-standing members of such denominations who undertook their deconversions therein.

If progressive Christians imagine the Protestant proximate other, it is possible that it reflects a desired, rather than an actual, competition. Throughout my fieldwork, I was often struck by the fact that progressive Christians do not direct their attention to, and critique toward, liberal Christianity but rather toward evangelicals, charismatics, and fundamentalists. As I noted earlier, while liberal Christianity is ideologically more proximate, and progressive Christians do critique its beliefs and practices, such as its use of metaphorical language, their focus is largely on evangelicals or conservatives. Returning to Jonathan Z. Smith's (2004) point that the process of othering is a rhetorical project, it can be argued that this tendency reflects a sense of proximity in terms of an imagined social field. Progressive Christians imagine evangelicals are more politically provocative and powerful than liberal Christians. Evangelicals occupy the public and discursive spaces that progressive Christians wish to engage. Also interesting, given the location of my research, is progressive Christians' focus on American, as opposed to Canadian, evangelicals, an emphasis fueled by social media and twenty-four-hour news. Again, it should be noted that American evangelicals are more prominent in the public sphere and perceived by progressive Christians to be a problem because they stand in obvious contrast to progressive Christians.[7]

Establishing themselves in competition with their Protestant proximate other, progressive Christians construct their version of Christianity as antagonistic to it. Their understanding of what being and becoming a progressive Christian means can be located in the ways that they mimic their Protestant proximate other. The examples I have used illustrate the ways in which progressive Christians adopt and adapt their language from the Protestant proximate other, even in cases where there is limited knowledge or access to that identity. Instead, progressive Christians construct the Protestant proximate other through a coalescing of personal experiences, popular misperceptions, and social imaginaries. In its imagined form, it is easily reified, subsumed, and rejected through a parallel discursive act.

Ultimately, both conversion and deconversion narratives are the story of how one got from one place to another. Conversion carries with it a sense of having, at last, arrived, while the deconversion narrative denotes a "clear point of departure," in which its animators' endpoint is ambiguous (Harrold 2006, 81).[8] While the question of from what, or where, the deconvert has turned provides the structure of deconversion narratives, there remains ambiguity concerning where progressive Christians are headed and what ideological distance they have traveled. In the case of each person I discuss in this chapter, the presumed past of the individual, the community, and Christianity is central. The past is revealed in personal experiences in a manner that mirrors the ways progressive Christians seek to uncover the history of Christianity and biblical origins.

The church historian Philip Harrold argues that when deconversion, along with its focus on the past, serves as the prevailing disposition, it sets the stage for how religious adherents voice their values, conceptualize otherness, and envision the future (2006, 80). I have demonstrated that deconversion influences progressive Christians' use of beliefs and depictions of the other. Harrold's third factor, representations of the future, warrants consideration.

Progressive Christians understand their journey as a radical transformation. Undergoing a deconversion experience creates the possibility that another equally radical one might wait on the horizon. *Progressive* explicitly suggests this possibility because the word refers to a continual motion forward. But to what end is unclear. As I showed earlier, to a certain extent, the Bible, which is inevitably present in its absence, haunts progressive Christians. Likewise, the past envelops and haunts the progressive future. The next chapter shows that progressive Christians are held in tension between the past and future, in a state of suspension that their use of eschatological adverbs (e.g., *still*, *already*, and *yet*) reveals. As a linguistic trope, these adverbs imply an expected future that is ultimately unrealized. Before exploring the ways the larger progressive Christian community imagines the future, it is worthwhile to return to Hedy, Thomas, Sandra, and Margie to unpack the way in which they envision the future.

Back to the Future: The Role of Rupture and Recollection

Hedy

At times Hedy looked past me, as if my questions were those she was posing and delivering to an invisible audience. When I asked her what she saw for Christianity in the future, she began by referring to fundamentalists. "Oh, boy," she exclaimed. "If I defined Christianity by what's going on in our fundamentalist Christians, I see a very destructive future." She sighed and continued, "I just hope and 'pray'"—she paused to draw air quotes with her fingers around the word *pray* to signal that this was not a religious use of the term—"that we don't lose it all in the long run." Hedy perceived an uncertain future for Christianity. Elaborating on the topic of fundamentalists, she outlined why she thinks they are a problem. As she spoke, she enumerated with her fingers: "They don't accept nonbelievers, they don't accept other religious faiths, they don't accept any but their own." She threw back her hands and continued emphatically, "I guess this is true of all fundamentalists. I don't know. I just hope that there are enough people who can stick it out. But sometimes we seem to be overwhelmed by the 'my way or no way' people."

Shifting the topic from Christianity in general to West Hill United Church specifically, she began, "I know what I want. I want West Hill to go on and on and on." Hedy grimaced and glanced out the window. After a lengthy pause, she reflected on a conversation she had recently had with Kevin, who appears in the introduction. For the second time in our conversation, she got emotional, pausing frequently and fighting back tears.

> I think it was just last year that Kevin said, "You know, in twenty years, there won't be any United Church." And probably West Hill will be one of the first—as a building, maybe one of the first ones—to drop off. But as a community? I hope it can survive. But you know, the buildings are (*pause*) a burden. The original churches where people just got together and—. I don't know, I don't know. I just hope that West Hill hangs in as long as I do. I don't want to think about my life without this community. If I have to go and meet with this community in a (*pause*) I don't care! I just don't want to lose this community. I want this community to survive, whether it's in this building or in some other place. What I feel for the people here? I don't want to lose it. I don't want to lose it.

Hedy and other members of West Hill foresaw a future without the United Church of Canada. She differentiated the church as a building and the parishioners who frequent it. But Hedy worried that the community would not survive with or without its building. She employed a series of repetitions to emphasize how adamant she was on this topic: "I want to see West Hill go on and on and on"; "I don't know, I don't know"; "I don't want to lose it. I don't want to lose it." The fact that she spoke so strongly, coupled with her emotional reaction to the recent departure of several members because of theological differences, suggests that Hedy *was* uncertain about the future of West Hill. For Hedy, the church had served for many years as a substitute for her family and as the central hub of her social network. It was a community in which she had found a place to ultimately overcome her notion of herself as an outsider—in part, because at West Hill, they are all outsiders, heretics, and skeptics.

Thomas

Asking a ninety-year-old about the future of Christianity and asking the same question of a twenty-year-old is, in many ways, like asking two completely different questions. Throughout my interview with Thomas, he interrupted and demanded my opinion on matters of theology and group dynamics. Thomas was the only person I interviewed who was younger than I was—though by only three or four years. When I asked him about the future of Christianity, he was critical of the progressive movement: "They're locked in a framework, just like fundamentalists." Speaking quickly, he continued, "I would hope—this is not what I actually see happening—but I would love if all denominations or all sects—progressive, traditional, conservative, it doesn't matter—were just willing to enter into a dialogue with one another. But I don't actually foresee that happening." Instead, Thomas predicted a growing division between what he calls the different factions of the church. He continued with this explanation: "Like I said earlier in the interview, I think we're still at a point where, if you sat down one on one with a lot of people and actually asked them [about the topics explored by progressive Christians], a lot of the questions that the progressive movement is trying to react to are still in the hearts of these people who are more traditional. But I think as time goes on, and the conversation isn't had between the two factions, you're going to lose those bridges." For Thomas, schism and rupture lie in the future of the church. And while he was critical of progressive Christianity, he reserved his greatest criticism for the evangelical and emerging church.

> Yeah, because I wonder if people within the emerging church, myself for a few years included, were almost tricked, you know? I mean, I think that people have all these questions, and you're going to a church, and it's really laid back and everything seems—you don't feel the tradition there at all. But if you look at it a little more closely, what your heart has problems with isn't any different from the church where they're all wearing shirts and ties.[9] I mean the evangelical church, not the progressive one. It just kind of seems like the setting in which the emerging church does their worship service is kind of like a mask to the fact that nothing has actually changed. We're just making it appear like that for reasons. I don't know why. I guess the final thing that I would add is that I'm really disheartened and pretty sad that it only seems to be in the progressive church where, well, progressive things are happening. So, like working with aboriginal communities, working to bridge the gap between the homosexual community, queer community, and the church, regardless of the morality of

it. I'm not even concerned about that right now. Social justice. I just wish that people that claim to follow Christ literally would actually have reflections of it more in their structures.

Thomas's statements here reflect the fundamental nature of the deconversion narratives. His story of departure is equally marked by critique, loss, and longing. The story of his journey to progressive Christianity was not a joyful one. It was marked by the categories of deconversion—intellectual doubt, moral criticism, emotional suffering, and disaffiliation—and ensuing struggles with, and internal conflict about, his transition, the future of the community, and his place within it.

Sandra and Margie

Like Hedy, when asked about the future of Christianity, Margie pointed to fundamentalism as a problem. She described how Christianity was part of the fabric of the social world her grandchildren were encountering in Houston. In contrast, her grandchildren in Canada were less familiar with Christianity because her son, their father, was agnostic. From time to time, Margie would take them to the Sunday school at Holy Cross, and they appeared to enjoy themselves. Commenting on her son's reaction to his children's visits to the Sunday school, Margie noted,

> He has agreed to let his kids come to Sunday school because he thinks it's important for them to make some choices themselves. But he's really listening to the kinds of things they say. They went to a summer camp at a fundamentalist church last summer with some friends and it was awful. I said to Pastor Dawn, we need to have one ourselves. There aren't enough kids, that's the problem, but I really don't want them to go back and hear that. The first thing they were told in the morning was, "You are all sinners."

Margie continued, reflecting not just on fundamentalist varieties of Christianity but on progressive Christianity as well. Building on the importance of language, Margie turned to Gretta Vosper's recent presentation at Holy Cross, where she discussed the larger arguments of her book. "I felt like she was struggling to make sure that she didn't ever say the word *God*." The night that Vosper had spoken at Holy Cross, a youth group from a nearby conservative church had been in attendance. The unexpected presence of a group of teenagers had thrown off some of the usual dynamics for speakers. "You can tell the leader was wishing that he hadn't brought that group of young people," Margie recounted. "I thought that maybe she [Gretta] was holding back."

A few days later, Margie and Sandra decided to attend a service at West Hill. Margie was measured in her assessment of the church. She told me that she wished that she had been there for a communion service because she wanted to know how West Hill deals with the Eucharistic images of the blood and body of Jesus. The evocation of blood in the Eucharist is problematic for both Margie and Sandra, one that both raised with me on several occasions. At West Hill, they had hoped to find a liturgical approach to the communion service that would allow them to resolve their discomfort with the ritual celebrated weekly at Holy Cross. I asked Margie about her impression of the service. She explained that she found it perplexing and lacking in liturgy. "I didn't dislike it," she began, noting that it was her first time in attendance so it was difficult to form a real impression. "But I thought that it appeared to be hard work [for Vosper] to stay away from [the word] God. I don't quite understand why she needs to not use that word." Moving on, she described the prayers: "There was not really a prayer, different people stood up and said, 'Oh, so-and-so hasn't been well' and whatever, but it wasn't really a prayer. The music was nothing that was religious. So it was kind of, well, I'm just not there yet and I'm not sure I want to be there." Picking up on Margie's point that she was not there yet, I asked if she thought she or Holy Cross would arrive at that point eventually. She responded that she needed more information but that she did not want Holy Cross to replicate West Hill: "I don't think so, not to that degree. Again, who knows? Maybe if I understood a little bit better what her purpose is?"

Returning to my question, I asked again where Margie saw her faith going. Her response, not unlike Hedy's, was rooted primarily in the community and the process of building a theology together. "I really, really hope that Pastor Dawn remains at Holy Cross for a long time because I feel like I really learn from her. And the speaker series just is such a great way to find what you want to read next, what you want to check next. Beyond that? I haven't got a sense." Here Margie tied the development of her faith to the larger church community and the choices that they would make concerning which books to read and which authors to invite to the speaker series. What remained important was not which book, video, or speaker was chosen but rather the act of choosing together as a community. There was a sense of shared responsibility for the path they would take together.

Finally, when asked about the future of Christianity, Sandra indicated that her thinking had changed. She explained that she was not concerned about whether the church continued as an institution. I asked her directly where she saw Christianity going, and in her reply she differentiated Christianity, the church, and religious thinking.

> I don't have a clue. I really don't have a clue. As I've said, *Christianity*, that term doesn't mean a lot to me. If you had said the church? Um, initially I would have said, not many years ago, "The church will last forever." I'm not so sure about that now. Maybe the church as an institution needs to fade. But what that would mean as far as the nurturing that comes from a religious community? To consider the notion of a former church structure, we might be better off without that hierarchy and all that goes with it. I can see where that might happen. But as far as Christianity? I don't know. I have no notion about that.

In an attempt to move past Sandra's uncertainty, I rephrased the question and asked, "That suggestion that the church might fade away, does that bother you, disappoint you, or worry you?" She gave me a confused, almost disappointed, look and responded, "No, no, no! Not in the context of—." She stopped, interrupting herself. "I'm assuming that does not mean the end of religious thought, spiritual thought, I'm making that assumption," she continued. Again, she related that while she was not certain about the logistics, she had confidence that it would work out. "But how that would all be nurtured without the institution? That would be most interesting to know. I don't know how that can happen."

Perhaps in this instance it would have been better had I asked, "What is the future of progressive Christianity?" Implicit in the answers to my questions was an overriding ambiguity—it was easier for my interlocutors to focus on the future of fundamentalism, which represents the Protestant proximate other. Each affirmed that other forms of Christianity would continue on their chosen path without any diversions. Thomas told me that they are "locked in their frameworks." Hedy predicted that their future would be destructive because they continued to endorse a "my way or no way" approach. Margie turned to a discussion of progressive Christianity but only by offering it in contrast with her grandchildren's regrettable summer camp experience. Finally, Sandra placed her former self in the position of the Protestant proximate other and reported that previously she would have replied that "the church will go on forever." None had an answer as to what the future for progressive Christianity would look like, but all were clear that it would not be able to sustain the status quo.

Of course, sustaining the status quo is not what progressive Christianity is about. As I have shown, the very ethos of progressive Christianity evokes a fluid, continuous, and unfinished evolution of beliefs, practices, and identity. Progressive Christianity emboldens the assumption of a new way of being Christian, wherein Christianity is able to hold different, interchangeable elements. As a novel form, progressive Christianity is constructed in relationship with and resistance to a Protestant proximate other whose identity and discursive tropes are at times subsumed. This antagonism is observable in the deconversion narrative. Their use of linguistically performative tropes enables progressive Christians to suspend themselves between past, present, and future, all three of which are ambiguous and inconclusive.

4

Still, Already, Yet

Imagining the End of Progressive Christianity

It was the first session of a brand-new book study group at West Hill United Church. We bustled about the room playing a get-to-know-you version of bingo as the ice breaker. The lighthearted nature of the questions on the bingo sheet set the tone for the evening. Statements such as "Find someone who can name all five Spice Girls" and "Get the name of someone who owns a Pez dispenser" were interspersed with more serious theological prompts, such as "Find someone who has answered an altar call." The point of the game was to mingle, introduce ourselves, find someone who matched the prompt in one of the boxes on the bingo sheet, and write that person's name in the corresponding box. I was more willing to declare my love for novelty candy and my familiarity with the girl-power pop sensations than to reveal my religious or spiritual leanings when asked, "Which of these statements or statements describes you?"

Eventually, someone shouted, "Bingo!" and we returned to our seats. Our facilitator for the evening, Ian, distributed the agenda for our three-hour session together. It included a short video clip, to be followed by small group discussions, a snack and social period, and a group debriefing.

"Most people come to the book study for the socializing," whispered Kevin, one of the veterans of the study group. "And wait until you see the *food*! It can get quite competitive, really," he explained proudly. Later that evening, an elaborate spread of fruits, cheeses, dips, and baked goods confirmed Kevin's assertion.

The format of the progressive Christian reading group at West Hill United Church had not varied much in its thirty-plus years of existence. Indeed, my time with the group was strikingly similar to Hedy's description of the early group meetings. The agenda Ian handed out followed a tried-and-true format—socializing, reading, small group discussions followed by larger group discussions, and friendly competitions—that the group members loved. Yet while the structure itself had not changed, the theology and the worldviews of the book study participants had transformed dramatically. Since its inception, the book study group and West Hill had assumed a public profile. No longer were they a discrete group of United Church of Canada folk who read popular theology and self-help texts in the main hall of their church; they now saw themselves as having established a model for adult education programs, one that pushed the boundaries of what many progressive Christians believed was an emerging Reformation determined to change the definitions of Christian identity, belief, and practice.

Following the bingo ice breaker, we watched two ten-minute video clips. The first introduced the New Atheist thinkers Richard Dawkins and Sam Harris. The second was a rebuttal clip featuring the American journalist Christopher Hedges. Afterward, we broke into smaller groups of six or seven to discuss our impressions.

"So, does anyone *still* believe in God?" asked Cheryl, whom our group had chosen to lead the discussion. Without waiting for a response, she paused and amended her question, "Does anyone still feel the need to believe in God? Who *isn't ready* to give up that image *yet*?"

"Do you mean like the old man in the clouds with a long-flowing beard who watches over us and answers our prayers?" another woman asked. "I certainly don't believe in *that* type of God anymore!"

"Yes," a man chimed in, "we've *already* moved far past that God concept."

The conversation proceeded. The six members collectively agreed that *we* certainly did not believe in the theistic version of God familiar to many of us from childhood. Furthermore, the group affirmed that *if* there is a God (not that they were saying there is), he (or she, most probably she) certainly does not resemble the traditional church representation of God. Ultimately, the group determined that, for progressive Christians, the best course of action would probably be to do away with this whole notion of God altogether.

Cheryl's questions: "Does anyone *still* believe in God?" and "Who *isn't ready* to give up that image *yet*?" may seem out of place in an ecclesiastical setting, but they represent familiar linguistic tropes employed in all five of the churches featured in this book. Amid the lighthearted culinary competition, members of the West Hill book study group were attempting to recast Christianity so that it can move beyond a reliance on the traditional Christian apparatus. To accomplish this task, members rejected key elements of the Christian faith, such as the Bible, conventional notions of God, and even the church as an institutional structure. Of particular interest was Cheryl's use of such temporal adverbs as *still*, *already*, and *yet*. These terms, along with the group members' identification as progressive Christians, suggest a continual, temporally oriented, and unfinished evolution.

The temporal nature of these terms lends a sense that one might outgrow certain beliefs and practices. Intriguingly, the idea that one might evolve beyond significant elements of the Christian tradition diverges from, yet emerges out of, what the anthropologist Susan Harding identifies as a normative static Christian temporality. For many Christians, especially evangelical and conservative Christians, the present may be replete with doubts and uncertainty, but there remains an abiding sense that all will be revealed at the end of time. As Harding puts it, the evangelical, or "born-again ear," understands the future as predetermined and fixed, related to the past in so far as biblical history contains prophetic inklings of God's plan (Harding 2000, 230; see also Engelke 2013, 66–67). Conservative Christians understand the future as having an eschatological end: decisions made and actions taken in the present are directed toward ensuring a favorable position in this predetermined future. Progressive Christianity must therefore be situated within a broader Christian discourse about the future, temporality, and the end of time.

Christian Eschatological Thinking

The term *eschaton*, referring to the end of the world, comes from the Greek word *eskhatos*, meaning last or end things (Frykholm 2016). For most North American Christians, biblical interpretations are the basis of their eschatological beliefs (see Crapanzano 2000; Harding 2000; Reading 2021). The Bible posits a supernatural eschaton (e.g., Christian scriptures predict the *parousia*, or Second Coming of Jesus). Given that progressive Christians do not see Jesus as a divine figure, nor do they anticipate his miraculous return, the use of the term *eschatological* might seem out of place in this analysis. However, when considered in the broader context and cultural patterns of religious endings, the term provides further nuance to an understanding of progressive Christianity. An eschatological temporality for progressive Christians likewise emerges from biblical interpretation but in an indirect manner. They predict a future culminating in atheism, one in which they will no longer be Christian. Deliberations concerning the ethics of belief most fully reveal this anticipated future. Like evangelicals and fundamentalists, progressive Christians engage in a hermeneutical process, in this case, biblical criticism. Unlike other adherents of Christianity, however, they come to reject traditional eschatological teachings. In doing so, they adopt or retain the very patterns of eschatological thought associated with the type of Christianity they have rejected.[1]

There are several problems inherent in offering a normative perspective of Christian eschatological or temporal thinking, especially given the fact that progressive Christians do not fall within—and indeed work hard to delineate themselves from—the so-called norm. However, their attempts to differentiate themselves from a perceived normative consensus, which they see as a starting point, warrant this discussion. As the anthropologist Joel Robbins notes, there is a benefit to discussing an "ideal-typical notion of Christianity," which resembles certain forms of conservative and evangelical Protestantism (2007, 10). Once scholars studying Christianity have established the model, they are able to pursue the critical task of exploring variation (2007, 16–17). Progressive Christianity represents one such variation.

An understanding of temporality as distinctively linear and irreversible is at the root of modern Christian eschatological thinking.[2] According to the Christian master narrative, time has both a beginning (creation) and an end (apocalypse), and God controls and directs both.[3] In Pauline apocalyptic thinking, true believers will be separated from the rest of humanity at the end of time, which the early church saw as imminent. Contemporary Protestantism highlights the notion that each adherent is responsible for their fate at the time of the final judgment. Evangelical Christians usually distinguish this individual responsibility by the choice to internalize Christian teachings and practices, a process wherein individual believers consciously grant God agency over them. In this schema, present actions (e.g., the choice to "be a Christian," to be baptized, to believe) directly determine a believer's place among the righteous or the damned at the end of time.

This description provides the standard, or ideal-typical, contemporary evangelical theological position wherein time culminates in an eschatological end. Because it links current actions to an eschatological endpoint, this stance has led to the prominence of premillennial dispensationalism. Current events are interpreted through a prophetic lens with the assumption that they might provide insight about the imminence of the end times. According to Harding, central to this framework is that it results not so much in a theology or a set of beliefs but rather in a narrative mode or a way of *knowing history* in which history is seen as progressing toward an ultimate end, the apocalypse (1994, 60). According to this reading, the end of time is divinely predetermined and therefore assured. God has not determined actions and events in the contemporary world, but everything will cumulate in, and indeed lead to, a specific end. As Harding explains, "Christians have no role in unfolding the events that bring about the millennium: nothing they (or anyone else) do can change the date of the Rapture, which only God knows, having set the date at the beginning of time" (1994, 61). In this scenario, premillennial dispensationalists understand themselves as lacking agency regarding the ultimate fate of humanity and the world. Similarly, Robbins notes that dispensationalists understand themselves "as living in a gap between the narratives that make up sacred history and those that they have already been foretold as structuring the future" (2001, 543). As such, this theology makes a believer's present existence meaningful through the assurance of the (apocalyptic) future. Just as dispensationalists claim to know history, there exists a parallel sense of *knowing the future*.

Among the Social Gospel roots of liberal Christianity is a similar future-oriented trope, a postmillennium view of history in which humans act as agents in their ultimate destiny. The Social Gospel adherents adopted the rhetoric of progressivism and saw themselves as participating in and expanding the kingdom of God, as described in the Gospels. Prominent in the early twentieth century, the Social Gospel movement sought to achieve collective salvation by resolving socioeconomic problems. In this view, the eschaton featuring the return of Jesus could not happen until collective human actions eliminated social evils. While there were different groups within the movement, each held an overarching, future-oriented optimism about industrial developments and the social sciences as tools for improving the conditions of human life (White, Hopkins, and Bennett 1976, xviii; for an in-depth discussion of the Social Gospel movement, see Dorrien 1995 and 2009; Evans 2017). In his 1907 book, *Christianity and the Social Crisis*, the great Social Gospel thinker Walter Rauschenbusch wrote optimistically that the goal of a just society was possible but that it remained indefinitely in the imminent future:

> In asking for faith in the possibility of a new social order, we ask for no Utopian delusion. We know well that there is no perfection for man in this life: there is only growth toward perfection. . . . We make it a duty to seek what is unattainable. We have the same paradox in the perfectibility of society. We shall never have a perfect social life, yet we must seek it with faith. We shall never abolish suffering. . . . At best there is always but an approximation to a perfect social order. The kingdom of God is always but coming. (1913, 420–21)

Those in the Social Gospel movement understood temporality as suspended: always progressing but never reaching its conclusion.

While there is no genealogical relationship between early twentieth-century Social Gospel adherents and the contemporary progressive Christian communities featured in this book, many of the beliefs and practices of the Social Gospel shaped the face of liberal Protestantism in North America.[4] For liberal Protestants, investment in the future (i.e., the bringing about of the kingdom of God or creating a more just society) requires engaging in activities with this end in mind. They share with evangelicals and conservatives a belief that the future might direct the present. While evangelicals see the future as assured, predicted future events (i.e., the Apocalypse, the Rapture) play a vital role in directing actions in the present. Both liberals and conservatives discuss the immediate present in anticipation of the future. At first glance, this orientation does not depart from the secular understanding of linear time. In everyday life, people save for retirement in the hope of securing financial stability and vote for political candidates they believe will promote the best interests of the nation. Such anticipation becomes nuanced, however, in a Christian context when considered alongside the eschatological expectation of a future rupture that might occur through divine intervention.

Temporal Language of Intervention

Across the Atlantic Ocean lies the quiet and picturesque Scottish fishing village of Gamrie. With a population of about seven hundred people, Gamrie is somewhat of a religious anomaly. In his ethnographic exploration of the town, the anthropologist Joseph Webster found that while the rest of the United Kingdom appeared to be abandoning its Protestant roots, the residents of this seaside Aberdeenshire village were steadfast in their work to sustain six fundamentalist churches with only subtle denominational differences (2013, 50–51). Though they are contemporaneous and perhaps even, in part, distantly descended from the same Presbyterian forebears, at first glance, the fundamentalist Christians of the northern Scottish coast bear little resemblance to the suburban North American progressive Christians featured in this book. Closer examination, however, reveals that both groups share an ambiguity toward the future that is revealed through strikingly similar assumptions about how language works.

Webster's research illustrates how religion and social context are intertwined. Demographic changes and economic challenges in Gamrie have resulted in social instability. Fishing restrictions from the European Union alongside certain technological innovations have made the entry-level fishing vessel much more expensive than previously. As a result, traditional small fishing operations have shut down. While the total time spent fishing has decreased because larger vessels are going farther out to sea and netting more fish, the intervals that crews spend away from home have increased. While many of the town's young men moved away to work in the oil industry or found employment in large urban centers, those who remained in the fishing industry were able to earn large sums of money for only six to eight weeks of labor. Because of the seasonal nature of this work, many were spending their extra earnings on luxury items and other distractions, such as new cars and drugs (2013, 61–63). Meanwhile, wealthy English families were moving up from the city to find a better quality of life in the Scottish countryside (2013, 54).

These developments were distressing to the staunchly religious older citizens of Gamrie, many of whom turned to the church for guidance. Foundational to their variety of Christianity was the belief that God and the devil were actively engaged in a struggle for human souls. In their personal lives, the older Gamrie residents remained on the alert not only for evidence of God's providence in answered prayers and unexpected blessings but also for signs of demonic intervention, which might be as benign as accidentally falling asleep during a church service or as severe as pain and discomfort caused by demonic possession (2013, 164–65). The evangelical view of divine providence perceives a war between good and evil playing out on the world stage through international entities such as the State of Israel and the European Union (2013, 185–93). According to this view, this struggle between good and evil will eventually result in the second coming of Jesus and the end times. The older Scottish Gamrie residents believed that these end times were drawing ever nearer and that the signs of this were everywhere. For example, "homosexual ministers in the Kirk, the Scottish banking crisis, [and] the spread of Islam" indicated that they were living in the last of days (2013, 177).

Such a perspective results in an orientation toward the future wherein "all questions about the future, no matter how mundane, need to be qualified eschatologically" (2013, 174). In the case of Webster's research, this perspective manifested itself in the daily lives of his interlocutors, such as when one man stood up to announce the upcoming weekly activities at the church but paused to note that while they made these announcements every week, they were eschatologically contingent on whether or not "the Lord might have returned to take us home" (2013, 176). While signs abound in the immediate present, the actual instance of divine intervention is understood as impossible to foresee. As a result, they remained suspended in a present that pointed toward an inevitable future without ever actualizing it.

In his analysis, Webster draws from the theoretical work of the anthropologist Jane Guyer (2007), who distinguishes between two futures, understood according to their temporal proximity: the near (proximate) future and the ideal (distant) future. According to Guyer's assessment, the near future is a time of political action, a point in time when human agency is activated and results produced. While one might presume that the near future is the standard orientation for most people, Guyer observes shifts in focus away from the near to an ideal and distant future. Guyer compares macroeconomic theory directed toward long-term forecasts with evangelical premillennial dispensationalism. Guyer argues that in the current postmodern turn, our understanding of time has shifted so that the "ultimate origins and distant horizons were both reinvigorated, whereas what fell between them was attenuating into airy thinness, on both 'sides' (past and future) of the 'reduction to the present'" (2007, 410). As Guyer shows, focus on an ideal distant future comes at the expense of action or agency in the near future. In this process, she identifies a "symmetrical evacuation" of both the near future and the near past that prohibits meaningful political or social activity concerning either (2007, 410).

Likewise, in the case of the fundamentalist Christians in Gamrie, their eschatological expectations coalesced in such a way that even plans for the upcoming week were conditional—at least at a discursive level. While they remained steadfast in their eschatological expectations for the future, such contingencies—and, more important, verbalizing such contingencies—provided a buffer in the face of ongoing economic problems and social issues in their near past and near future.[5]

In considering discursive and temporal orientations, Webster's analysis of the Gamrie Christians provides a salient comparison with the progressive Christians featured in this book, whose focus on the distant past of Christian origins by way of biblical criticism is linked to a discourse about belief that orients them to the distant future. Cheryl's question and the group's insistence that the best course of action—that is, the moral course of action—would be to do away with the notion of God altogether introduces essential questions about how progressive Christians position themselves along a theological trajectory. Just as the Gamrie fundamentalists use language that posits a contingency on whether or not they are present on Earth, the language of progressive Christians presumes a future in which they are no longer Christian. Thus, a theology directed toward the distant future does so at the expense of the near future and perhaps without ever reaching its anticipated eschatological end.

Still Christian?

While Guyer contrasts the near future with an ideal future, the term *eschatological* fits better than *ideal* with the theological temporality that progressive Christians employ. For many of the progressive Christians featured in this book, the ultimate end in atheism is not necessarily an ideal. In private conversations, many speak apologetically or mournfully about their future position as atheists. Cheryl's question regarding whether anyone *still* believes in God speaks to the fact that, for some, disbelief is a challenging prospect. Despite their discomfort, most progressive Christians indicate that they are resigned to their fate of becoming atheists because they see it as the most rational and honest end for Christianity. Many of them evoke John Shelby Spong's analogy of a sacrifice for the greater good. Spong's allusion to sacrifice intentionally replicates themes of atonement, martyrdom, and the crucifixion of Jesus. This focus on eschatological temporality further reflects underlying despair about the present that many progressive Christians share with liberal and mainline traditions in regard to the steady decline of their congregations and a perceived loss of relevancy within society.

Their use of the adverb *still* further articulates an ethical dimension to giving up certain beliefs. The suggestion that elements of Christian narrative and doctrine might *still* be believed hints at the possibility that there will be a point when such beliefs are no longer held. Moreover, it suggests that this endpoint is a desirable one. Think, for example, of the term's use in social and political settings (e.g., "there are still places in the world where women are unable to vote" or "racism is still a problem in twenty-first-century America"). Among mainline liberal Protestants, *still* reflects the tenuous and fluid nature of theological thought. For example, in 2004, the United Church of Christ adopted the motto God Is Still Speaking as part of a more extensive campaign to promote inclusivity and to highlight the relevance of the denomination.[6] The "still speaking" campaign evokes temporal language, using the image of a large comma accompanied by the words "never place a period where God has placed a comma" in its promotional material as if to capture the unfinished nature or uncertainty regarding those things about which God is "still speaking." The video ads for the campaign, which were released over the internet, feature an array of individuals of different ages, genders, abilities, sexual orientations, and ethnicities.

In a similar advertising campaign, West Hill United Church's website featured a series of ads employing a similar trope that played on the congregation's name "West Hill" (WE st'ill) to indicate what the church *still* thinks, feels, or believes. For example, the church's home page regularly featured an ad stating, "West'ill get together every Sunday! Join us!" Other word plays using West Hill/We Still included, "Even though it's hot, we still think church is cool" (used in the summertime); "We still got rhythm" (advertising a benefit concert featuring one of the church's members); "We still gather in Scarborough, but you're virtually everywhere" (a message directed at online followers who participated in worship services at West Hill through podcasts). Although presumably intended for their marketing impact rather than a significant theological decree, these two examples illustrate the term's rhetorical saliency within progressive Christian churches.

The term becomes more interesting when examining individuals' use of it to demarcate their beliefs in comparison with others' within a given congregation. At various points in life, Jodi, a member of St. Matthias Anglican Church, flirted with atheism. She held on to Christianity because she initially saw it as an ideal venue for charitable acts and community service. It was not clear to her how people could be inspired to do good works without the agency of the church and the promise of reward for the individual. For many years, she retained a Christian identity to participate in acts of altruism. In finding progressive Christianity, she also found a community in which she could not only be open about her beliefs but encourage others to adopt her worldview.

Such opportunities were essential to Jodi because, in her view, any hope for justice or ethical behavior required that the entire community (the collective) adopt and share her theological perspective and beliefs. Jodi explained that she was "more theologically advanced" than other members of her community, some of whom "still" believed in God or a higher power. As she explained,

> I call myself an atheist to the Anglican Church. But when I get more specific, I say that I don't believe in anything that I can call God. I think we need to get rid of that word. It's a stumbling block.[7] I mean, if I say I

believe in God, that doesn't communicate to people what I want to communicate. It communicates to me the standard view of a God that fixes things. I don't really think there's anything in control of all this. I think that it's a mystery. I'm fine with mystery. And for a long time I have been [saying], "We don't know and we won't know." I'm fine leaving it like that. So often, when people say they believe in God, then they will get busy telling you what God thinks and what God wants. I don't think we can say that. I don't think we can be so sure. I just think that we have a collective responsibility, and as a people, as humanity, we can inspire each other to do good things and great things instead of being disruptive. That power was in all of us, to do that. We don't need to rely on something external that is going to punish you if you don't and reward you if you do.

For Jodi, belief in God was not only uncertain but also unethical because it gets in the way of what she imagined to be the more authentic goal of altruism and inspiring others. Within her congregation, Jodi understood she was on the margins or the fringes in terms of her belief system. Her husband, for example, explained to me that he "was not as far along" as his wife, primarily because he "had not thought things through" as much as she had.

Throughout our conversation, Jodi expressed impatience toward others in her church who were not yet atheists. She found herself exasperated with those who desire to hear theistic language in the prayers. Jodi saw herself as a forerunner, or an early adopter, of atheism. This self-depiction is especially interesting when examining her use of personal pronouns in what she said about being an atheist. Jodi began by positioning herself as an atheist ("I call myself an atheist") and explained her disbelief in God ("I don't believe in anything that I can call God"). She went on to assert that the word should be jettisoned ("I think we need to get rid of that word") and that she was comfortable doing so ("I'm fine leaving it like that"). Jodi's language here began with the personal ("I") and then shifted to the inclusive ("we"). Once Jodi adopted the pronoun *we*, she was able to speak about activities and events located in the ideal future. Jodi assumed that if the entire community (the we) adopted her atheism, they could achieve a "collective responsibility" to "inspire each other to do good things,"—that is, "the power . . . in all of us."

Of course, Jodi's community did not wholeheartedly adopt an atheistic worldview—some members "still believed" and continued to use God language even though it was a stumbling block that did not accurately communicate meaning. Such individuals included Jodi's husband, who indicated that he retained Christian beliefs and language because he had not engaged in the intellectual reasoning required to jettison them. He did not believe his wife was wrong, just further along the path to atheism than he was. He had the capability to get there; he just had to do the intellectual work. From Jodi's perspective, those members who retained aspects of Christian beliefs, practices, and traditions were delaying the onset of an inevitable future in which all will espouse atheist beliefs and engender an inspirational, justice-oriented community.

As I have already noted, a rupture was created at West Hill United Church when several members opted to transfer to another local United Church congregation because they felt that the West Hill community had "gone too far" in its rejection of traditional Christian practices and language. I also described Hedy's confusion about the decision of the members to leave West Hill United Church because of the use of language—she did not comprehend their inability to understand why she could not sing certain hymns or recite certain creeds. Disagreements about the integrity of language led to a split in the community. Hedy was unable to reconcile her beliefs with traditional language, to the point that she could not share worship space with individuals who used the language of traditional prayers, hymns, and creeds.

Later in our conversation, Hedy outlined that she *still* enjoyed traditional hymns but felt that they have no place in a church service: "If I want to sing the old hymns? If I want to sing 'Onward Christian Soldiers'? I can do it when I'm tramping up and down the street because it's got a good [beat]—I like the music when I'm walking." For Hedy and other progressive Christians, this song is a problem because it valorizes the colonial practice of forced conversion of other cultures to Christianity. While the song had a place in Hedy's memory as one that she grew up singing, and it resonated with her during her time in the air force, she was clear that it could no longer be admissible within a Christian liturgical setting or worship service. Like the Bible, which was rarely read at West Hill because the community was trying to provide space for other texts and other voices, the song was relegated to either the private sphere or the past. Many in this community conceded that they would accept individuals who still read the Bible at home but that they thought it was unfair to allocate to the Bible a prominent place within the church.

Here it becomes apparent that progressive Christians understand their church as a public space. Theological discussions emphasized the collective rather than the individual and the need to establish a community that was inclusive and hospitable. There was a clear divide between the collective space of the church service and the private space of the individual adherents' beliefs, practices, and opinions. They debated, amended, and rejected in the collective space texts, traditions, and doctrines from the past, whereas individuals acknowledged that they still held on to certain traditions such as reading the Bible, celebrating the nativity, or singing the old hymns in the private sphere—a point that raises the question of in which space were they being authentic?

Two weeks before her ninetieth birthday, Hedy revealed that she often contemplated her death and plans for her funeral. For the most part, the progressive Christians featured in this book were ambiguous—although not anxious—about death and dying.[8] Since Hedy did not believe in an afterlife, she did not want a traditional funeral, which she viewed as overly ritualistic, but she did want a memorial service for her friends: "I have a favorite psalm, [or] hymn, that I have said I want sung at my funeral. Well, I don't want a funeral because there is not going to be anybody here, but I would like people to get together and have a good time."[9] When I asked her what the song was, she could not remember at first, but then she began to hum, and I identified it as "On Eagles' Wings," a popular funeral song in mainline Christianity.[10]

The song is not overly theistic in that it does not presume doctrines of substitutionary or sacrificial atonement,[11] born-again experiences, or other tenets held by conservative Christians. It does, however, suggest a relational and interventionist deity upon which humanity is entirely reliant for protection. The song posits a relationship of dependence between God and the believer, who is assured of shining "like the sun" and being held "in the palm of His hand" in exchange for a declaration of faith ("Say to the Lord, 'my refuge, my rock in whom I trust!'"). Thus, the underlying theology of this song is not unlike that which caused the rift in the church through which Hedy lost friendships.

While Jodi and Hedy employed *still* to contrast themselves with other members of their congregations, others evoked the adverbs *already* and *not yet* to denote how they had undergone processes of revision throughout their lifetime. It is in these terms that Guyer's argument about the foreclosure of agency in the immediate future is most relevant. As they place themselves on a trajectory between Christian and atheist, progressive Christians remain suspended between actions and beliefs that are deemed *already* and *not yet*. At the beginning of this discussion, Cheryl posed the question: "Does anyone still feel the need to believe in God? Who *isn't ready* to give up that image *yet*?" The group debated her use of the word *image*. One woman declared that she did not believe in a God that resembles an old man with a long beard who is seated on a cloud and responds to human prayers. A man in the group affirmed this point, concurring, "We've *already* moved far past that God concept." Implicit in this conversation is an undefined space between a traditional heavenly vision of an interventionist God and the complete nonexistence of God. It is a space, or perhaps a series of spaces, between *already* and *not yet*, where each progressive Christian or each congregation might rest in different stages of *still*.

Already and *Not Yet*

The evocation of temporal language such as *already* and *not yet* is not novel to progressive Christianity. The terms echo Jesus's description of the Kingdom of God as at times in process and at other times forthcoming. The anthropologist Jon Bialecki explores the use of *already* and *not yet* among charismatic Christians in the Vineyard tradition, where the terms are combined as "already/not-yet" to denote an inaugurated eschatology. According to Bialecki, the terms reference "an indeterminacy in eschatological time that the Vineyard believers identify in the biblical narrative" (2017a, 37). This viewpoint hinges on the idea that the life, death, and resurrection of Jesus initiated the eschaton (already), but the soteriological cycle is not completed until the Second Coming (not yet) (2017a, 37–38). In Bialecki's assessment, this theological view allows those who hold it to explain why miraculous interventions that God promised do not always occur. Bialecki explains that they serve as a kink in time wherein the present divides into both the past and the future (2017a, 46).

In addition to the theological properties of *already* and *not yet*, Bialecki notes that they are used to promote future-oriented political rhetoric (2009, 116). In his fieldwork with Vineyard Church members in Southern California, Bialecki was surprised to learn that, despite their conservative evangelical theologies, many promoted liberal social justice activities. The subjects of his study understood themselves as partly responsible for bringing about the political actions necessary to establish a new political order. As such, they affirmed their backing of leftist social justice causes, such as immigration reform, democracy in the developing world, and civil unions for same-sex couples. However, their belief that transformation must accompany the return of Christ limited their actual contributions to such causes. Despite the stated intention of Vineyard believers to bring about social change, Bialecki notes that because of their understanding of Christian temporality as "fundamentally discontinuous" (2009, 120), they were instead constrained by the present moment that oriented them toward an assured but inaccessible future directed by a divine entity defined by its alterity (2009, 116).

Bialecki's use of the term *progressive Christian* is not synonymous with the progressive Christians featured in this book. While my interlocutors shared political and social justice commitments with Bialecki's, as well as with leftist evangelical leaders who sometimes label themselves progressive Christians (such as Jim Wallis, Tony Campolo, and Shane Claiborne), there is little knowledge of, or interaction between, these movements. On several occasions, my interlocutors reported that they were much more comfortable collaborating politically with atheists and liberal members of other religions than they were with evangelical or charismatic Christians. The reason was usually a perceived closed-mindedness on the part of theologically conservative Christians, specifically related to their understanding of Jesus, atonement, and salvation. However, while progressive Christians take different theological and ontological stances and hold an even more divergent worldview than the theological conservatives', progressive Christians similarly endorse a specifically eschatologically oriented conception of their faith and what it means to be Christian.

Unlike Bialecki's subjects, the progressive Christians in this book were constrained by neither alterity nor divine immanence of any sort. Instead, they looked forward to a time when theological beliefs would be dispensed with and no longer necessary. Nevertheless, similarities rest in the ways that they deploy *already* and *not yet* that obfuscate their final goal. Among progressive Christians, this final goal anticipates a future in which they will "no longer" be Christians. While typically the trajectory of one's religious journey consists of private considerations marked by personal experiences and sentiments rather than prescribed declaration, on one occasion, a leader of the book study group at West Hill encouraged participants to complete a survey to determine their most comfortable religious affiliation.

During one book study session, Suzan led another member of the community, Stewart, through an online survey posted on the popular religion website Beliefnet.com, while the rest of the group watched. The point of the multiple choice survey was to determine or recommend within which religious community the survey taker would feel most comfortable or which religious affiliation was best suited to their worldview. The survey, Belief-O-Matic, was available in the Entertainment section of the Beliefnet.com website. It began with the following introduction and disclaimer:

> Even if YOU don't know what faith you are, Belief-O-Matic™ knows. Answer 20 questions about your concept of God, the afterlife, human nature, and more, and Belief-O-Matic™ will tell you what religion (if any) you practice . . . or ought to consider practicing.
>
> Warning: Belief-O-Matic™ assumes no legal liability for the ultimate fate of your soul.[12]

The Belief-O-Matic survey was intentionally lighthearted, as was the community's interaction with it.

Stewart's final results suggested, not surprisingly, that he should be a secular humanist. I met with Stewart the next day, and our conversation naturally gravitated toward his answers to the survey. Stewart reported that he had completed the survey several times in recent years. Reflecting on his transitions, he explained, "The first time I came through as 'mainline liberal.' And then I sort of moved towards the 'neo-pagan' and another group they called the 'Advanced Quaker group'? I can't exactly remember what they call it. I was moving this way (*motions to the left*). The secular-humanist part didn't really start to show up until about two years ago." Stewart's shifting religious affiliation followed a trajectory that is similar to many progressive Christians' as they distinguish themselves from both their former selves and other varieties of Christianity. The lengthy transcript of our conversation that follows shows this process at work.

> REBEKKA: Now on the Belief-O-Matic survey last night, you said that you don't believe in God, that you don't believe in any sort of divine incarnation, you don't believe in heaven or hell. These are fairly radical views for someone in a church community.
>
> STEWART: Yes.
>
> REBEKKA: Do you think that most people at West Hill hold the same views, or do you consider yourself to be sort of at one extreme?
>
> STEWART: Umm. I'm probably a bit more radical than some.
>
> REBEKKA: Okay.
>
> STEWART: But I would say that the answers that I gave—and I answered only nineteen of the twenty questions because, for the one, there just wasn't an answer that I could give—I would say that if you were to ask (*pause*) seventy percent of the congregation, they would probably answer similarly to me for about eighty percent of the answers.
>
> REBEKKA: Okay.
>
> STEWART: We have some people who attend with their spouse, who still believe that there will be a judgment day, et cetera, et cetera. They're quite happy to attend because they love the fellowship in the church and the fact that their spouse is fed. There aren't too many, but there are some.
>
> REBEKKA: Now, do you have—do you want to qualify your answer to whether or not you believe in God? I know a lot of progressive Christians—while they'll say they don't believe in God—they do have a sense of something they could call God. Do you have any?
>
> STEWART: I used to.
>
> REBEKKA: You used to, okay.
>
> STEWART: I haven't been able to find it recently. I can't really understand how the laws of the universe together are controlled by a supreme power. If they are!? I have a hard time believing that there would be a God. More the—how things have developed through natural selection. I'm sure that's it.

REBEKKA: Okay.
STEWART: And I'm guessing that thirty-five or fifty billion years ago, there's a lot of things happening. Well, now the origin of them? I have no idea. I have no idea whatsoever.
REBEKKA: Are you concerned about it? About the origin of things?
STEWART: Umm, no, other than realizing that you can't destroy matter, you can change matter or its form. You know? How it happened or where it came from. I'm not worried about that.
REBEKKA: Umm.
STEWART: Give me a few more years.
REBEKKA: (laughs). A few more years? Okay. Often when I tell people about my research, and I'm explaining about West Hill and what they believe, people say: "Well, they're not Christian; it's very obvious." Especially my students, when I tell my students about West Hill, they'll say, "It's very obvious that they're *not* Christians." How do you respond to this accusation?
STEWART: I don't consider myself a Christian.
REBEKKA: Okay.
STEWART: But I realize that being a part of an organization such as the United Church of Canada allows the group to move forward and (*pause*) umm, gives some sort of authenticity. I don't know if I want it. I'm not sure about that. I don't want to think of us—I've heard Baptists described as a group that multiplies by division.
REBEKKA: (*laughs*). Okay.
STEWART: You've probably heard that before.
REBEKKA: I have (*laughs*).
STEWART: So, um, I think, ah, the chance of um, ah, people coming to a point where they are loving their neighbor—a community such as West Hill is [one] which has ties that can recognize it. That's why I feel that we should be [Christian].

In this discussion, Stewart identified several principal characteristics of progressive Christianity: a rejection of traditional Christian beliefs, a desire for authentic community, and an emphasis on scientific explanations regarding the origins of the universe. He temporally positioned himself with regard to his beliefs: he "used to" believe in a God-like force, but he "hasn't been able to find it lately" and has "a hard time believing that there would be a God." Stewart also temporally juxtaposed himself with other congregants who "still" believe for various reasons. Moreover, Stewart pointed out that, while he was not Christian, West Hill was part of the United Church of Canada. He indicated that, while it was not ideal, West Hill's affiliation within the denomination was preferable to the sectarian approach that he equated with Baptists—who, as the Protestant proximate other, have chosen an undesirable path.

Stewart typified a religiosity that holds belief as the primary category of Christian identity.[13] Interestingly, he simultaneously rejected traditional Christian beliefs in his own determination of what is necessary to be Christian. Stewart's beliefs, or his inability to believe, served as the core marker of his religious identity. He held assumptions about belief that are closely related to overarching Protestant ones about interiority and sincerity. Ultimately for Stewart, the question of what he believes, or rather what he stated he believes, becomes an ethical one.

Ethics of Belief

The ethical dimensions of belief or believing can be situated within the study of the anthropology of ethics (Faubion 2011; Lambek 2010; Zigon 2007). An anthropological approach to ethics departs from the abstract or hypothetical nature of a philosophical approach and allows for examining specific instances of ethics as they are practiced or lived. This focus evokes the recent turn toward ordinary or everyday ethics as a category of ethnographic investigation. The anthropologist Michael Lambek situates the study of ordinary ethics within the realm of practice rather than knowledge. A systematic study of ethics cannot account for inconsistencies and complexities. For Lambek, the study of everyday ethics makes it possible to understand the process of discernment or judgment employed in assigning value to certain practices over others (2010, 23). While everyday ethics can be examined in many fields of human activity, the linguistic realm remains one of its primary locales (Keane 2010).[14]

In the context of progressive Christianity, the ethics of belief are a core concern. As I have shown, many progressive Christians struggle to accept the Christian narrative's claims of miracles.[15] This struggle is depicted primarily as a moral one in which intellectual honesty and Christian tradition vie for precedence (see Livingston 1974). Many contemporary Christians conflate belief and ethics. They have a sense that an examination of an individual adherent's deeply held beliefs provides insight into their interior self and moral character (Elisha 2008; see also chap. 3). For progressive Christians, rejecting certain beliefs, or stipulating that they will reject certain beliefs in the future, likewise provides insight into moral character. This position rests on the idea that it is unethical to hold beliefs that are scientifically implausible, historically inaccurate, or incoherent to a modern liberal worldview. Thus, according to these qualifications, they regard as unethical or weak someone who claims to believe something they know to be false.

Perhaps what is most intriguing when examining such conclusions is the presumption that spoken words are a manifestation of an individual's character. Anthropologists of contemporary Christianity who are interested in religious discourse have brought to light evidence of the ways that specific Protestant subjectivities shape, and are shaped by, religious language. For example, Simon Coleman (2006) shows how words can stand in place of, or as evidence for, the transcendent. Peter Stromberg (1993) explores how religiously derived language reconstitutes the identity of both the listener and the speaker (cf. Harding 2000). Most pertinent to this discussion of progressive Christianity is Webb Keane (2007), who argues that Protestant assumptions of a sincere interior self reflect a language ideology that privileges spontaneous speech as referential, thus revealing something about the speaker's ethical character (cf. Crapanzano 2000).

Such studies highlight two critical characteristics of contemporary Protestant linguistic practices. First, evangelicals exemplify and prefer a subjective or personalized religiosity that they juxtapose with mainline Christianity, which they see as static, overly routinized, and irrelevant (Keane 2007, 1–2; Shoaps 2002, 35; C. Smith 1998; Wolfe 2003, 22). The evangelical critiques of mainline Protestant churches resemble those levied by progressive Christians. For both evangelical and progressive Christians, criticism of mainline worship provides a means of differentiation from other varieties of Christianity. Second, as Keane's work makes clear, Protestants understand language in moral terms. In this model, spontaneity and sincerity are bound together. A normative Protestant perspective assumes that the act of speaking reveals something about the speaker's character. According to Keane, modern Christians can determine the character of an individual (or community) by considering their spontaneous language (Keane 2007). For example, if someone prays for the safety of soldiers, one might conclude the person is patriotic. Within a religious community where patriotism is understood to be a moral virtue mandated by God, this person can be seen as both an ethical person and an authentic Christian. In this case, the authority and authenticity of language point to the authority and authenticity of the speaking subject.

A similar impulse exists among progressive Christians. Although the language their services use lacks the spontaneity that Keane describes as core to contemporary Protestantism, the assumption that language is referential and thus provides insight into the inner thoughts and character of a speaker is prevalent. At West Hill United Church, for example, referential language served as the primary indicator of the ethics of belief. The members wanted the liturgical texts that they recited and the hymns they sang during the services to reflect their actual beliefs. This view contrasts with liberal Christianity, which often evokes the idea that religious language is metaphorical (Frei 1974; McFague 1982; Frye 1982, 1991; Funk 1996; Borg 2001, 2003). As Gretta Vosper explained to me in an interview early in the formation of the Canadian Centre for Progressive Christianity, the metaphorical understanding of Christianity poses a problem for progressive Christians. It is especially problematic when explaining their theology to newcomers. As Vosper put it, "If somebody walks in off the street who hasn't been indoctrinated into that new metaphorical understanding of everything, they'll still just think, 'Oh my God! Do they really believe this? Do I have to believe it? Do I have to come to believe it in order to be part of this community?'" (King 2005, 49). In her eyes, making statements during a religious service that do not reflect the beliefs, experiences, and worldview of that particular congregation is disingenuous.

This approach, shared by progressive Christians and some conservative forms of Christianity, promotes a view that language corrupts and must always be carefully considered and reconsidered in an attempt to communicate the most accurate message. Whereas a metaphorical approach determines that there is no antidote to the problems inherent in language, and therefore the real or pure intention of the communicative act is located somewhere beyond language, the referential approach favored by progressive Christians seeks to refine language to a point where it can communicate essential truths in a nonmetaphorical manner. Proponents of the metaphorical approach to religious language advocate a reading of scripture and liturgy that sees historical and scientific inaccuracies and supernatural content as an attempt by the authors to express sentiments and experiences that transcend human descriptive categories. For these thinkers, the liturgical language used in worship services should be understood not as describing a historical event but rather as communicating something too important to be expressed in descriptive language (see Aitken 1991; Denham 2003). However, from Vosper's perspective, this model requires specialized knowledge of the tradition, something that her would-be adherent would not have.

The referential language ideology presumes that what one says is more important than how one says something. Implicit in this assumption is the idea that language is interactive. Vosper's would-be adherent from the street locates the authority of spoken words in each individual speaker, whom the adherent perceives as "a distinct and self-possessed self" responsible for their verbal speech act (Keane 2002, 75). This would-be adherent can evaluate not only the inner character of the individuals in the congregation but also the prerequisites for membership based on their collective and public recitation of prayers and hymns. When Vosper imagines the would-be adherent's asking: "Do they really believe this?" and, more interestingly, "Do I have to come to believe it in order to be part of this community?," she assumes that the would-be adherent will share her skepticism regarding the claims about miracles and nonempirical tenets of traditional church liturgy. Many progressive Christians point out that in a secular post-Christian multicultural society, theological language and allegories no longer possess the same currency that they might have in a homogeneous Christian society. Vosper's reference to someone coming off the street into her church reflects the multicultural realities of the church's location in Scarborough, a highly diverse area that was home to many recent immigrants to Canada with a variety of different religious and cultural backgrounds.

Interestingly, there is no consideration that membership might transform the would-be adherent from the street. An evangelical perspective anticipates a radical transformation of the would-be adherent through the born-again experience. It is through this transformation that one gains access to Christian membership and comes to understand religious language. This notion is absent within progressive Christian communities. Instead, progressive Christians posit that theirs is a way of being Christian that is entirely rational and transparent to the nonbeliever and that no inner transformation is required for progressive Christianity to make sense to an outsider. Indeed, it is often former evangelicals and conservatives who undergo an inner transformation or, as I showed earlier, a deconversion upon encountering progressive Christianity. This deconversion allows them to align their inner beliefs and spoken words with a religious perspective rooted in scientific facts, historical evidence, and liberal humanism.

While individual progressive Christians understand themselves as moving toward a revised version of Christianity and ultimately atheism, the means through which they make revisions is a collective and gradual process. For example, some progressive churches rarely read the Bible during services and prefer to engage with more secular texts in their book studies, but others maintain a closer connection to theological and biblical content. These groups often identify some progressive Christians as having gone too far or indicate that they are not willing to give up certain aspects of the Christian tradition. As one man, Stephen, half-jokingly explained: "I understand that the miraculous birth of Jesus didn't happen—there was no Bethlehem, no stables, no wise men, no shepherds-watch-their-flocks-by-night, no heavenly chorus of angels—but can I at least keep the camels?"

Collective Liturgical Revisions

Stephen's question, "Can I at least keep the camels?," points to the importance placed on continuous refinement and revision of belief and practice. In the space between Christian and atheist, progressive Christian churches find themselves on a trajectory in which they evaluate and reevaluate different traditions through the lenses of biblical criticism, scientific empiricism, and liberal humanism and classify them as either *already* extraneous, *no longer* relevant, or *still* necessary. To illustrate this process of classification, it is helpful to examine how progressive Christians encounter liturgical statements and doctrinal creeds. As a sign of their evolving theologies, many progressive churches have rewritten prayers and hymns to exclude patriarchal language, atonement theology, or references to Jesus and God. Prayers, religious songs, and creeds are usually understood as reflections of group ideology that serve as an "(observable) domain of religious practice" (Shoaps 2002, 34). Traditionally, the collective uses them to regulate beliefs. When all congregants recite the same statements of belief continuously, one may assume that they share a common theology and worldview. For this reason, progressive Christians have eliminated or altered the language of prayers, hymns, and creeds that no longer accurately represent their beliefs.

In mainline Christianity, the Lord's Prayer plays an important role by unifying the congregation. Nevertheless, some progressive Christians see it as problematic for several reasons: it presupposes a heavenly realm, an interventionalist deity, and a system of bartering in which God forgives people based on acts of reconciliation with other humans. An example is West Hill's replacement of the Lord's Prayer with a revised version of the Prayer of St. Francis of Assisi called the Children's Prayer. Rather than attending to the collective body in the Lord's Prayer, this version of the Prayer of St. Francis focused upon individual agency and personal character, and it lacked any references to God's nature or intervention in the world.

CHILDREN'S PRAYER
As I live every day,
I want to be a channel for peace.
May I bring love where there is hatred
and healing where there is hurt,
joy where there is sadness
and hope where there is fear.
I pray that I may always try
to understand and comfort other people
as well as seeking comfort and understanding from them.
Wherever possible, may I choose to be
a light in the darkness,
a help in times of need,
and a caring, honest friend,
And may justice, kindness, and peace
flow from my heart forever,
Amen

West Hill United Church had emended the prayer on several occasions. In contrast, the traditional Prayer of St. Francis begins with a request to God that the supplicant be "a channel of [the Lord's] peace."

Other congregations have also emended traditional Christian prayers. A common practice is to substitute the word *mother* for *father* in prayer. Most have eliminated the creeds and prayers or hymns that refer to a relational deity. Holy Cross Lutheran Church retained its liturgical frame, but each week Pastor Dawn reworked the language to more accurately reflect the congregation's developing theology. As one congregant, a retired Lutheran pastor himself, explained: "The pastor wears vestments, there is an altar, there is a baptismal font, there is liturgy. I think the liturgy follows the traditional form of Lutheran liturgy. But the pastor rewrites everything [so] that [it] is beyond inclusive; it's inclusive-inclusive! That's not typical. Most people would not put the time and energy in that she does; they would just accept the book as the book. . . . But Dawn goes beyond that and cleans up the language even more, so in that sense, it would be untypical."

As with other progressive congregations, at Holy Cross the spoken word occupied a primary space. Christian practice was subordinate to belief and verbal expressions of faith. This structure meant that members could maintain traditional frameworks of the liturgy because words are the most significant component, where the real power lies. In other words, the vestments, the altar, and the font were subordinate to the liturgy, and, as such, it was the liturgy to which Pastor Dawn turned her attention to ensure that it corresponded with the identified beliefs of the community (in this instance, the emphasis was on ensuring that the wording was inclusive).

The continued revision of language is an essential component of progressive Christianity. In my conversation with Judith, the Presbyterian who had recently returned to the church, she explained that while she valued tradition, one of the first steps in articulating a progressive Christian theology is rewriting traditional prayers to correspond with a liberal and empirical worldview. As Judith made clear, this initial revision is temporary and further emendments may be required in the future:

> There are very few times in our daily lives that we join with other people to participate and experience exactly the same thing. The caution would be:

Let's understand what we're saying and let's understand why we're saying it. So, let's not just say the Lord's Prayer because the Lord's Prayer has been said since the beginning of time. Let's have a study group on the Lord's Prayer. Let's figure out what it means for us. So, when we're saying, "Our Father who art in heaven," what do we mean by that? And what does it mean for us? And maybe we've decided we can't say, "Our Father who art in heaven." Maybe we have to say, "The divine presence which is all around us and in us." These are things that need to be decided and discussed. While we can't throw the baby out with the bathwater, we have to examine everything that we're doing to see whether it fits with our current understanding of the world. . . . Twenty-five years from now, the people may be saying: "Why are we saying, 'the divine presence that is around us all'? That's ridiculous! What are we trying to say here? We're trying to say that we're all connected." They'll create some other saying that gets that across.

While Judith's imagined prayer was fluid, the intention was to capture the actual beliefs and worldview of the present community. Judith had no desire to maintain a connection to the past through words, only to create a potential connection with the future. When Judith envisioned her church in the future, she imagined that the congregation would struggle with her version of the Lord's Prayer for precisely the same reasons that she struggled with the traditional one. Judith posited that the church of the future would understand prayers and creeds as performative statements of assent and that, like her, the members would construe the recitation of creeds or prayers as an ethical or moral act. Judith's two-part process of studying the prayer's content and articulating new language that rejects a previously determined stance is common within progressive Christianity. The present is a tentative location, one that progressive Christians perceive to be subject to revisions and elimination in the future.

What is most interesting is that while the churches featured in this book did not retain the traditional prayers or creeds of the Christian tradition (e.g., the Apostles' Creed), they preserved the perceived function of prayers and creeds as performative statements of assent. As Keane explains, "The impact of the creed as a paradigm lies, in part, in the more ordinary domain of semiotic practices" (2007, 70). In examining the Apostles' Creed, he points out that the creed involves propositional phrases ("I believe") and subsequently appears to place the speaker "in an exterior third-person relationship to her own beliefs, as that of a subject to an object world" (2007, 71). Among the congregations featured in this book, I did not encounter any creedal statements focusing on the first-person singular (although the aforementioned Children's Prayer at West Hill did use first-person singular). While some prayers begin with statements such as "We believe," most depart from statements of belief altogether. Instead, they focus on a desire for cohesion within the congregation, Christianity, or the world in general.

At some point, one might wonder why progressive Christians bother with the continued revisions to prayers and other collective statements and songs. If they forecast an atheist stance as their ultimate end, the smaller steps to get there might seem futile. The ethic of belief, and its focus on individual agency and transparency, accompanies an equal emphasis on the collective. Thus, they employ liturgical language to endorse and generate a sense of community. Even more important, the process of revising prayers and hymns usually occurs as a collective effort in an attempt to maintain community loyalty. The practice of rejecting traditional prayers in favor of new models is crucial to progressive Christians. Doing so allows them to position themselves in opposition to a normative version of Christianity. This other, exemplified by evangelicals and liberals, enables progressive Christians to construct an imagined community.

As I noted earlier, many progressive Christians understand their theology as in a continuous state of transformation. Indeed, they consider this the point rather than an anomaly. Even between progressive Christian congregations, there is disagreement about what theological and ritualistic constructs to include or reject. Other churches I have studied consider West Hill United Church to be the most extreme. On more than one occasion in interviews and group discussions, individuals at these other churches indicated that they were not *as far along* as Vosper or West Hill. Moreover, in some cases, traditional theological language *still* resonated with them or they acknowledged that they weren't *ready* to give up certain symbols or rituals *yet*. While particular churches might be seen as further along in this "evolutionary process" than others, they were all more or less understood to be heading in the same direction, which they perceived to be a forward-oriented path to ultimately abandoning their Christianity in favor of atheism.

In many progressive churches, the tenuous space between believer and atheist creates a divide between an inner and outer circle of adherents. For some, while they attend church services regularly, the presence of those few who "still believe" can be a source of discomfort. They often feel more authentic in book study and discussion groups. The members of the reading and discussion groups often distinguish themselves from those in their churches who do not participate in the reading or discussion groups through their self-perception of being more theologically advanced. As the discussion of the Theological Studies Group at George Street United Church showed, Jerry criticized other congregants who still needed to "sing some of the hymns that we sing, [the ones] that really give you the yippies."[16] Jerry understood the church as fulfilling a role for those who "are very happy with their faith and the stories in the Bible," but he was grateful for others, like himself, "who are really restless." While Jerry still found weekly services to be meaningful in some ways, he lamented that he felt forced to "turn off stuff that I don't relate to." The progressive Christians who continued to attend more liturgically traditional churches did so because they trusted that the rest of the church would eventually embrace their perspective. In the meantime, the book study and discussion groups provided a venue in which they could practice their religious commitments in a way that they viewed as more authentic.

Future Uncertainty

Once they have dispersed, what such modern, yet closed communities leave behind them is not the past but the future.
—Boris Groys

Progressive Christians, as their name suggests, see themselves as moving forward, yet they do so by focusing on both the past and the future.[17] And while they look to the future and the past, they are suspended in the present. Theirs is a gaze that is likewise fixed on the activities and presence of their Protestant proximate other. This gaze holds them between the past and the future and between devotion and atheism. The regular examination and rewriting of performative statements—such as prayers, creeds, and hymns—mirrors their approach to the Bible. The inability of progressive Christians to access what they identify as the authentic biblical narrative resembles their inability to access the desired end of Christian beliefs. While progressive Christians point to atheism as their ultimate end, and some members of their communities—like Judith, Stewart, and Jodi—have assumed this viewpoint, other members contemplate Cheryl's questions: "Who isn't ready to give that up yet?" and "Who still feels the need to believe in God?"

The continuous revision of theology is vital to the progressive Christian community. Their narrative is always unfinished. Just as Judith believed that future generations ultimately will reject the "divine presence that is around us all," the discussion group deemed the possibility of using "Share" as a commandment to be too ambiguous and open to misinterpretation. Some members of Hedy's congregation departed because of the absence of specific prayers and songs, but Stephen accepted that his days of celebrating Christmas with a traditional nativity scene were numbered. In each instance, progressive Christians pointed to an ethical imperative that drove their theology: Hedy could not sing the songs or recite the creeds because they *were no longer reflective of reality*; Stephen would "give up" the nativity because *it is not historically accurate anymore*; Jodi's husband eventually would share her perspective *once he had put the time into thinking about it*.

The progressive Christian use of specific phrases such as "believers in exile," "intellectual integrity," and "church alumni association," as well as their understanding of their theology as observably developing and progressing forward—as evidenced in such statements as "Does anyone *still* believe in God?" and "Can I *at least* keep the camels?"—situates them within an imagined community. Furthermore, these signifying phrases and temporal positions represent progressive Christians in opposition to their Protestant proximate other—evangelical, conservative, and traditional forms of Christianity—as both Christian and atheist. This process is both informed by a rejection of this other and is simultaneously encompassed by it. Unconsciously, progressive Christians have adopted the eschatologically oriented temporal position of their Protestant proximate other and its cognitive frameworks. Progressive Christians remain rhetorically suspended in a belief system in which they "still hold certain traditional tenets," "have already given up other beliefs," and are "not yet ready to reject particular components of the Christian narrative."

Not yet—and perhaps not ever.

Conclusion

"We Are All Heretics Now"

In his 1979 book, *The Heretical Imperative*, the sociologist of religion Peter Berger famously argued that "we are all heretics now." Though it might conjure images of early church squabbles about the incarnational substance of Jesus or medieval so-called infidels burned at the stake, Berger used the term *heretic* to denote something uniquely modern and further contended that modernity is a period defined by the shift from fate to choice (Berger 1979, 11). Whereas an individual's lot in life once was determined at birth, with few opportunities for upward mobility, Berger saw modernity as increasingly marked by choices of occupation, lifestyle, marriage, consumer and leisure practices, and, of course, religion. In regard to religion, it was not just that people could choose their religious affiliations and traditions but that choice had indeed become necessary or imperative.

At the crux of Berger's argument lies the etymology of the English word *heresy*, from the Greek word *hairesis*, meaning to choose. From it, Berger charted an inevitable and antiauthoritarian trajectory set in opposition to a more powerful orthodoxy. Originating in Paul's earliest epistles, where the term *heretic* denotes dissenting factions or groups, and continuing through the ecclesiastical structures of European domination to the present day, evidence of a heretical impulse—a *choosing against*—can be identified throughout Christian history. Protestantism was the paradigm for understanding this religious impulse, according to Berger. In his assessment, choice is a virtue. His work enumerates several varieties of religious choosing, all of which betray a considerable Protestant bias to which many of Berger's critics have attested (see, for example, Douglas 1982; Dorrien 2001; Wuthnow 1986; cf. Hjelm 2019). In each instance, the chooser or heretic chooses against the dominant orthodox leadership and therefore is perceived as dangerous to the status quo (Berlinerblau 2001,

351). Such danger is thought to prevail precisely because the heretic remains entangled in the tradition and thus demands a response from it (Coser 1964, 70; Kurtz 1983, 1087–88).

As I have shown, choice is fundamental to progressive Christianity. It is an informed choice. Progressive Christians weigh historical, scientific, and ethical evidence to determine those components of Christianity they wish to retain and those they will jettison. Buttressed by scholarly fields (history and science) and an overarching moral humanism, progressive Christians allow secular frameworks to shape their religiosity. Even more interesting is that they do so with the awareness that new information and data might transform taken-for-granted conclusions. This final chapter looks at choice as a marker of progressive Christianity specifically and lived secularity more generally.

What to Read?

This book has sought to reveal the diversity of belief and belonging in progressive Christianity. Amid long-standing debates about serious religious and ontological positions, ostensibly everyday or worldly concerns are equally critical to constructing a progressive Christian identity. Thus, difficult theological questions stand side by side with the seemingly mundane. For instance, a progressive Christian might ask: Should one adopt a theistic, nontheistic, or atheistic view of God? What do the words used in liturgy, music, and prayer reveal about a community's ethical stance? What is the place of Bible reading in postcolonial contexts? These theological questions often are accompanied by less weighty queries such as, Should we open a bottle of wine with lunch? Who will connect with questions about Pez dispensers in a get-to-know-you ice breaker? Can we at least keep the camels that appear in a nativity play? I have attempted to animate the stories of the progressive Christians featured in this book so that you, the readers, might feel as though you attended the discussions and debates. In this way, you have been privy to moments of consensus and disagreements. You have sat with different members of these communities as they have weighed the evidence, explored the historical data, and considered the moral consequences of their decisions. Now, in conclusion, I want to turn to one final question posed by every book study group: What to read?

After two years of participating in the West Hill United Church study group, I attended my last book study session during the week following Easter. An unusual heatwave had hit the previous week. Something about the rapid transition from winter to summer weather felt awry; the requisite anticipation that accompanies the spring season had passed Scarborough by, and there was a sense that Toronto had already transitioned into the lazy glut of summer.

I entered the church and quickly made my way into the lounge, where forty or so chairs were arranged in a circle. While attendance had often waned over the weeks and months, particularly on cold snowy nights, we were expecting a larger turnout than normal for that night's meeting. This last session was much anticipated because the current book study group members would choose next year's study text. Several church members were eagerly clutching books they hoped the group would choose. One member, in particular, Jon, had an armful of books. I had been present for this session the previous year, so I was excited to see what the evening would bring. The meeting the year before had consisted of multiple rounds of voting, ardent defenses of certain books, impassioned speeches, and jabs at each other's literary expertise and choices.

I knew better than to join in the voting and debate that night. At the previous year's final session, one of the members had tried to have my votes stricken from the record out of concern that I would not attend the following year's study group. Only after I swore that I would indeed be present was I allowed to participate in the voting (I should note that her objections were all for naught, as neither her favorite nor mine was the final selection). These objections—which at the time seemed nitpicky since no one else was asked to commit to attending a book study group scheduled for nine months hence—reflected some of the more significant concerns around intellectual integrity and group membership that animate progressive Christianity. The notion that one's words (in this case, my vote) and one's actions (participation in the book study group) must align applies to the purpose of the book group itself.

As Suzan called the group to order, I sat down next to Jon and glanced at the books he planned to suggest. Jon had brought quite a collection: three books by the popular author and journalist Chris Hedges: *War Is a Force That Gives Us Meaning* (2002), *American Fascists: The Christian*

Right and the War on America (2006), and *The Empire of Illusion: The End of Literacy and the Triumph of Spectacle* (2009). Additionally, Jon held a compilation of fictionalized essays by Barbara Kingsolver, *Small Wonder* (2002).

The room turned its attention to Suzan, who welcomed everyone to the final book study session of the year. "This is the only time we ever come to fists at book study," she joked. Everyone chuckled, and with that Suzan explained the format for the evening. First, each person who had brought a book for consideration would have a few minutes to extol the virtues of their suggestion. After a period of discussion and debate, we would take a snack break, and then the voting would begin. As usual, the voting format followed the exhaustive ballot system and included several rounds. After each round, those books that received the fewest votes would be eliminated until a winner finally emerged. During the first round of voting, everyone was to rank their first, second, and third choice (an individual's first choice would receive three votes, the second would receive two votes, and the third choice would receive one vote). The second round counted only first and second choices, and voters had only one choice in the final round.

After explaining the logistics, Suzan looked around and asked, "Does anyone have any questions?" The majority of the people in the room shook their heads, indicating that they were ready to commence the first round of presentations, debates, and voting.

"Wait a minute," Kevin interrupted. "I think we should take a step back and discuss some of the larger issues that affect the book study. I want to talk about where we are in the evolution of the book study."

Several people leaned forward in their seats and shifted their bodies to face Kevin more directly. Kevin was well known for taking time to reflect and consider points that others might overlook. For example, as I noted in the introduction, Kevin expressed concern about the suggestion of beginning a commandment with "Share" because it was not clear enough to be used in the truncated six commandments. While he sometimes called for consideration of issues or concerns that others might view as trivial, most church members appreciated his reflective temperament.

"Was John Ralston Saul's *A Fair Country* (2008) the right kind of book for us?" Kevin asked, referring to the book we had studied most recently.

Kevin's question was a good one. On more than one occasion, the members of the book study group had complained both publicly and privately that the philosophical nature of the text had been too complicated. Others complained that Saul's historical and political commentary on the construction of Canadian identity was too far removed from the interests and knowledge base of a church book study group. As a result, many arrived for book study, week after week, without bothering to read the book or after giving up midway through the week's assigned selection.

Summarizing these and other concerns, Kevin continued judiciously: "*A Fair Country* was a very political book, which to me was very relevant. But five, six, seven years ago, we would have had a very different type of book. We would have chosen a 'faith journey' type book. So is this where we want to go?"

Kevin's wife, Nancy, jumped in. "I found the book hard to get into. As it went along, it became more relevant; I struggled with the first half, and then gradually it became easier."

Several people nodded in agreement. Suzan, however, disagreed: "I found the first part better because I enjoyed the history, which I was familiar with."

Picking up on Kevin's point, Jon returned to the question of the direction of the book study group and the perceived problem of participants who did not complete the assigned readings. "I've been giving thought to Kevin's point," Jon said. "There were several times I heard people say they hadn't read the chapter." Recalling the sessions about *With or Without God*, written by the church's minister, Gretta Vosper, Jon continued: "When we read Gretta's book, everyone read it. The conversation was really active and exciting. People aren't doing the readings now. I don't want people to not do the readings or to feel like it's a pain! We need to choose a book that is meaningful. One that people want to read."

"That's right," another woman chimed in. "We are a book club! We are readers!"

Nodding in agreement, Kevin returned to Jon's point, saying, "I want a book that is accessible and also represents something that we are passionate about."

It was not surprising that Kevin and others expected the book study group members to be passionate about reading. As I have shown, the book study group at West Hill United Church was foundational to the church's identity. This passion hit its maximum potential when one of their own wrote a book. The community received Vosper's book as theirs—something that they could lay claim to and boast about in the larger progressive Christian community. Jon's memory of studying this book was similar to what I recorded in my field notes. Compared with the more recent book studied, the discussions about Vosper's book far more closely engaged its arguments and ideas. The group eagerly worked through the extensive study guide that a congregation member had prepared and seamlessly tied their own experiences to the arguments that Vosper raised in *With or Without God*. In contrast, Saul's florid writing style and unfamiliar terminology had proved too much for several members.

At this point in the conversation, a couple of different members interjected that they, too, wanted something more accessible. Audrey explained, "I found it [Saul's book] hard to read. I had to look up terms, which was difficult [to do]. Vocab-wise and idea-wise, it was slow. You had to stop reading and think." Perhaps because she did not want to appear negligent, Audrey continued: "I didn't read all of the book, but I'll get to it this summer."

Following a similar line of thought, Caroline, who was in her midforties and therefore younger than many participants, acknowledged that she, too, had not read most of the book but did not see it as a deterrent to her participation in the discussion. "I want a book that I can just skim through. But I'm also looking for a book that will challenge me. I enjoyed the discussion even having not read the book."

"There is a false dichotomy in the air," Jon interrupted, "that there are hard-to-read books that are meaningful and easy ones that are not [meaningful]." A chorus of no's resounded in response to Jon's suggestion. However, he continued, "we want a book that reads easily and is challenging."

Another man, Pat, offered the following opinion: "The history and politics are very important to me. I had two books that I had thought about bringing tonight. One was small, based on a true story. But it didn't have anything to do with religion, so I didn't bring it. I also had a friend who used it for a different book study, and he said it didn't work for his group."

"What was the book?" a couple of members inquired.

"*Tuesdays with Morrie.*"

A chorus of "I love that book!" and "That's a great one!" filled the room.

Pat then made a case for his second suggestion. "The other was a trilogy, *The Vatican Trilogy*. But it's about Catholics, uh-oh, who wants to read about that here?"

A couple of members of the book study group smiled and chuckled.

Trying to return the conversation to the question of the direction of the book study, Jon summarized the key points. "It sounds like we are saying that this last book wasn't a success—there were people who didn't read it."

Suzan challenged Jon's assertion. "I don't think we can say whether someone read the book is a measure of success," she argued.

Offering an alternative way of evaluating success, Kevin proposed that the measure should be whether the group felt challenged. Some other members agreed with this qualification, and the conversation turned to how *A Fair Country* affected them as a church book study group.

The question, Caroline proposed, "is what are we wrestling with? The roots of our faith?"

Another woman agreed: "I'd like to think about what we could look at that might revive the church. People are leaving the church. We should be thinking about what will bring them back."

"Through the book study?" Pat asked.

"Yes," the woman continued. "How can the book help us revive the church?"

Throughout the conversation, I had been scribbling rapidly in my field journal. Taking note of what I was doing, Kevin drew the room's attention to my presence. "Let's say that Rebekka's project is about how the book study at West Hill leads the way." Picking up on the content of a book about ethical eating that they had read a few years earlier, he noted, "The latest thing we cared about was food." After the group read that book, the church adopted new food practices and encouraged members of the congregation to eat locally and purchase fair trade products. Additionally, the church began to offer vegetarian cooking classes to motivate members to decrease their meat consumption. In several interviews with congregants, many identified this book study as one of the most meaningful and relevant to their community.

"Are we still looking for that kind of book?" Kevin asked. "West Hill is progressing as a community and as a church group. We need to ask ourselves whether the book study is related to our progress as a community in the church. I would like to establish whether this is the ground rule of what we study." Kevin's reference here was to the idea that book study group members believe that they are partially responsible for shaping the direction of the church as a whole.

A moment of silence ensued. Then, looking puzzled, Caroline responded to Kevin's question. "The only requirement is no fiction," she said. "We tried that, and it didn't really work in our format because the chapters didn't stand alone."

Another member responded, "We have a core group who come every year. But some people come because of the book. This year, some people didn't come because the book was political."

"Each person is able to stretch the group," Jon interjected.

Audrey agreed and described how at times she felt as if she was stretched in unexpected ways: "Each book has an ah-ha moment. It flips a switch. Then something changes my way of thinking. Sometimes it comes out of the discussion and not the book itself. It just needs one thing and then everything is different."

Seeing this moment as her opportunity to redirect the group to the assigned task for the evening, Suzan took the floor and pointed out that the group was limited by what people suggested. "I've found, year after year, that, if the choice is one of the books that I didn't recommend, that I would never have read the book. I would have missed it," she concluded. And with that, Suzan directed our attention to the task at hand and asked each member who had brought a text to describe it.

Since Jon had multiple books, Suzan asked him to go first. Jon began by describing his admiration for Chris Hedges and offered a brief rundown of his career. Next, he gave a synopsis of the three books he had brought with him. Concerning *American Fascists*, which outlines the politics of the Christian Right in America, he asserted, "I think it is important to know what the enemy is up to. You want to know what is going on in the name of Christianity." Then he hastily added, "Some of us are innocent to all that."

Despite Jon's enthusiasm for Hedges, his other suggestion, *Small Wonder* by Barbara Kingsolver, generated the most discussion. Jon was similarly enthusiastic about this option. He explained that Kingsolver's book is a collection of about twenty short essays, several of which are about nature. Part of the appeal of this book for Jon was that he saw Kingsolver as a noncelebrity, someone to whom he and the other members of the book study group could relate. As evidence, Jon turned to the second chapter of the book and read the first two paragraphs from a selection titled "Lily's Chickens":

> My daughter is in love. She's only five years old, but this is real. Her beau is shorter than she is, by a wide margin, and she couldn't care less. He has dark eyes, a loud voice, and a tendency to crow. He also has five girlfriends, but Lily doesn't care about that, either. She loves them all: Mr. Doodle, Jess, Bess, Mrs. Zebra, Pixie, and Kiwi. They're chickens. Lily likes to sit on an overturned bucket and sing to them in the afternoons. She has them eating out of her hand.
>
> It began with coveting our neighbor's chickens. Lily would volunteer to collect the eggs, and then she offered to move in with them. Not the neighbors, the chickens. She said if she could have some of her own, she would be the happiest girl on earth. What parent could resist this bait? Our life style could accommodate a laying flock; my husband and I had kept poultry before, so we knew it was a project we could manage, and a responsibility Lily could handle largely by herself. I understood how much that meant to her when I heard her tell her grandmother, "They're going to be just my chickens, Grandma. Not even one of them will be my sister's." To be five years old and have some other life form entirely under your control—not counting goldfish or parents—is a majestic state of affairs. (Kingsolver 2002, 109–10)

"How would that work with using that book as a study?" Kevin asked when Jon finished reading.

"Each chapter is discrete," Jon replied. "I'm not sure this is the best for the discussion group, but I think everybody would get a lot out of this book."

"I could see us relating it to our lives," Suzan agreed. "There are a lot of groups that prefer fiction," she continued. Returning to the earlier question about the purpose of the book study group, she amended her comment: "This group needs a question, a problem to wrestle with. It isn't a problem to deal with beautiful literature. It just isn't the habit of this group." Having drawn this conclusion, Suzan invited other members to offer their proposed texts.

Next up was Nancy, who proposed Thomas Lippman's *Understanding Islam* (1995). Like Jon, she thought that it was vital for the book study group to understand contemporary religion. She wanted to learn about Islam because it is the fastest-growing religion globally and especially relevant in the multicultural context of Scarborough, where the church is located. Caroline followed and recommended two options by the journalist and activist Raj Patel. Next was Suzan's suggestion, *Half the Sky: Turning Oppression of Women into Opportunity* (2009), by Nicholas Kristof and Sheryl WuDunn. Suzan described it as both hopeful and heartbreaking. *Half the Sky* outlines the many challenges women face in the developing world, such as sexual enslavement, poverty, violence, and war. The book includes personal stories of women overcoming these and other forms of oppression and argues that providing women access to ever-important resources will change the world. "I think there would be a lot of head nodding, but I think there would be a lot of head scratching, too," Suzan explained in justifying her choice.

After Suzan, another member offered Greg Mortenson and David Oliver Relin's *Three Cups of Tea* (2007) and its sequel, *Stones into Schools* (2009). These books build upon similar themes in advocating for education and humanitarian initiatives in the developing world. This suggestion was not a popular choice, primarily because many of the book study group members already had read one or both. The final suggestion from a man named Tom, which was equally unpopular, was to simultaneously read one fiction and one nonfiction book on the same topic. The two books, Giles Milton's *Paradise Lost, Smyrna 1922* (2008) and Louis de Bernières's *Birds without Wings* (2004), portray life in Turkey following World War I. This option did not garner much response, perhaps in part because the group had disliked the historical dimensions of the previous study book.

After each member had described the books they were proposing, we took a short snack break and then returned to the lounge to vote. Suzan wrote the titles of each book on a flip chart. Everyone was instructed to write their first, second, and third choices on slips of paper. Since I had already stated that I would not be voting, I volunteered to distribute and collect the ballots. There were three rounds of voting, and the results appear in table C.1. Although it did not win the majority, Jon's suggestion of Kingsolver's *Small Wonder* eventually won the runoff vote and became the group's choice for the following year.

TABLE C.1.

Author, Title	Suggested by	Round 1	Round 2	Round 3
1 Chris Hedges, *War Is a Force That Gives Us Meaning*	Jon	1	—	—
2 Chris Hedges, *American Fascists*	Jon	4	—	—
3 Chris Hedges, *The Empire of Illusion*	Jon	6	6	5
4 Barbara Kingsolver, *Small Wonder*	**Jon**	**10**	**8**	**7**
5 Thomas Lippman, *Understanding Islam*	Nancy	8	7	6
6 Raj Patel, *Stuffed and Starved*	Caroline	6	3	—
7 Raj Patel, *The Value of Nothing*	Caroline	7	5	—
8 Nicholas Kristof and Sheryl WuDunn, *Half the Sky*	Suzan	6	4	—
9 Greg Mortenson and David O. Relin, *Three Cups of Tea* and *Stones into Schools*	Francis	2	—	—
10 John Milton, *Paradise Lost*, and Louis de Bernières, *Birds without Wings*	Tom	2	—	—

Number of Votes

I was surprised by the group's selection, and I suspect that readers of this book about progressive Christianity might be as well. A close reader of the third chapter would probably assume—as I did—that the group would select one of the books by Chris Hedges, particularly one that focuses on the problem of political engagement on the part of the Christian Right. However, they had read his *I Don't Believe in Atheists* (2008) two years earlier and had found his portrayal of liberal Christianity to be condescending and unfair. For example, in his introduction to *I Don't Believe in Atheists*, Hedges writes:

> The liberal church, attacked by atheists as ineffectual "moderate" religion and by fundamentalists as a "nominal" form of Christianity, is, as its critics point out, a largely vapid and irrelevant force. . . . The liberal church is a largely middle-class, bourgeois phenomenon, filled with many people who have profited from industrialization, the American empire, and global capitalism. They often seem to think that if "we" can be nice and

inclusive, everything will work out. The liberal church also usually buys into the myth that we can morally progress as a species.... It is this naïve belief in our goodness and decency—this inability to face the dark reality of human nature, our capacity for evil and the morally neutral universe we inhabit—that is the most disturbing aspect of all these belief systems. There is nothing in human nature or human history to support the idea that we are morally advancing as a species or that we will overcome the flaws of human nature. We progress technologically and scientifically, but not morally. (Hedges 2008, 4–5)

While progressive Christians often differentiate themselves from liberal Christianity, in the book study group's reading of Hedges, they clearly—and I think accurately—saw themselves as part of the cohort that Hedges critiques. They positioned themselves as the objects of his criticisms because they believed in the goodness of human nature and the possibility of moral progress. Many of the book study group members objected to his criticism of this ethical standpoint.

The act of discerning this parallel between themselves and liberal Christianity reveals much about the tension and fuzziness that emerges when articulating what progressive Christianity is. In this case, progressive Christians align with one of their proximate others to defend liberal Christians against what they perceive to be unfair criticism. A particular ethic at work presents liberal Christian belief in the goodness of human nature and moral progress as a higher good. To defend it, progressive Christians take on or embody the label of liberal Christianity.

That night, as I watched Jon passionately plead his case for works by Hedges and then again for something completely different with *Small Wonder*, I was struck by the dissimilarities of the two options. Even though he had prevailed, Jon seemed disappointed that the group had not chosen one of the Hedges books. My impression of the conversation that night was that the book study group wanted something lighter and less politically driven. While the book study group did not explicitly discuss it, the church as a whole was still reeling from the departure of several longtime members of the congregation and some financial difficulties. Jon and I discussed the group's selection a few months later over drinks one Sunday afternoon at a local pub. Jon explained that he wanted the group to read the Hedges books and begin to "think in that direction," but he understood that Hedges was not for everyone. "Besides," Jon pointed out, "I can always read things like that on my own. I don't need the study group for that."

Jon's statement that he does not *need* the study group did not initially resonate with me. As a graduate student, I understood the benefits of reading and studying with others in various settings. But I am acutely aware that solitary reading practices are usually the normative mode of reading for most North Americans and are often the most rewarding. Readers can get what they need out of the text without bearing any responsibility for other readers in terms of evaluation or explanation. But if Jon did not *need* the study group, why was he there? Moreover, why, when I began to study the development of progressive Christianity, was I directed to the book study and adult education groups as the place where progressive Christianity was happening?

Further questions emerged. Why did Barry choose to attend the speaker series, adult education programming, and church services at Holy Cross Lutheran Church after all those years of happily participating in online discussion forums? Why did the notion that West Hill United Church might not outlive ninety-year-old Hedy bring her to tears? Why did Kevin—who on my first night at West Hill told me that most people come to the book study group for the socializing and food—insist that the group take the time to discuss where the book study group was heading? Finally, why was it considered a problem when I, as the ethnographer, participated in the voting to select the next year's book?

Participation in progressive Christianity is not about *need* but about *choice*. In this way, the collective reading practices of progressive Christians take on ethical significance. Progressive Christians do not need the study group. They choose to participate in it to make a direct statement about the theological, ideological, and political directions in which progressive Christianity is heading. Furthermore, they choose to do so because they believe it is the right thing to do. They choose to do so in a collective setting because they share a sense of responsibility for one another. Linking religious activity to moral choice extends Berger's argument that all contemporary religious agents are heretics by virtue of their participation. According to Berger (1979), we live with a "heretical imperative," which for progressive Christians is not only a side effect of modern religious life but the defining feature of what it means to be simultaneously Christian and secular.

Ultimately, it seems that the book study and discussion groups are about being together with each other's questions—that is, gathering physically around a text to discuss and debate. They have a sense that with whom they choose to do so will affect the development of progressive Christianity. For this book, I spent time with five congregations. They were all aware of each other. Indeed, I found them through each other. I first met Pastor Dawn during Spong's visit to George Street United Church. A member of Holy Cross Lutheran Church drew my attention to St. Matthias Anglican Church, and I met a member of the book study group from St. Peter's in the lunch line at Holy Cross during a special weekend lecture series featuring John Dominic Crossan. West Hill United Church was by far the best known because of its public profile, but its congregants were also more insular regarding awareness of other progressive Christian communities in the region. This lack of awareness may be a result of hosting the Canadian Centre for Progressive Christianity and promoting progressive Christianity to national and international audiences. The congregants knew the other churches as places where Vosper had visited as a speaker, but they had little knowledge of the other churches' interests and styles of services. For example, when I explained to one of the members of the book study group at West Hill that the discussion group at Holy Cross Lutheran Church met over drinks in a pub and began its sessions by singing folk songs together, he expressed a longing to participate in that session, which to him "sounded a lot more fun."

In contrast, representatives of each of the other churches had attended services at West Hill and reported on the sermon, music, and style of the services. Many of these members of the other churches saw West Hill as further along the continuum of progressive Christianity. They were quick to point out that this position at the head of the pack was not necessarily a good thing. They worried that Vosper and her congregation were "moving too quickly" and "throwing the baby out with the bathwater." As Eileen, a member of the Theological Study Group at George Street, confided in me about Vosper after reading *With or Without God*, "I thought, 'She's spun off, right out into outer space.'" When I asked her for clarification, she explained that she felt that the book was too cerebral and vague about the day-to-day workings of progressive Christianity: "The critique is necessary. And it's true, but then after the critique, where are we? What was her last conclusion? I don't think she recognizes that we're just human beings grounded in this earth, maybe needing meeting places. I'm not sure what kind of an ideal world—a real world, I mean a *real world* [Vosper depicts]. There were some vague (to me) descriptions of an ideal world and an ideal faith community. But where's the coffee? If we were just ethereal? But we're so Earth-bound. And I think that's the limit." Indeed, the answer to Eileen's question, "Where is the coffee?" (or steeped tea, beer, peanut-free snack, or afternoon glass of wine), is different at each of the communities as each tries to negotiate what progressive Christianity means to them. What they share is an understanding of congregational dynamics, which are directed from the bottom up. Deciding to participate in a book study or discussion group means that one can and should expect to actively participate in shaping the direction of the congregation as a whole.

Further Considerations: Lived Secularity

Locating lived secularity among progressive Christians, who self-consciously understand and define themselves as secular, is straightforward. Ultimately, their rejection of religion and privileging of secularism comes through a tripartite critique wherein Christianity is deemed to be somehow deficient compared with history, science, and ethics. As this book has revealed, the response to such critiques for progressive Christians has been skepticism of traditional religion. The defining impulse of progressive Christians has been to follow the logic of their skepticism and uncover a more amenable version of Christianity.

By way of a conclusion, I would like to highlight opportunities for comparative analysis using other religious groups that undertake similar evaluation processes. It is helpful to draw briefly on recent case studies wherein a certain privileging of the perceived secular or secularity serves as a defining framework. In what follows, I offer brief reflections on three additional potential venues for analysis: Christian creationism (Bielo 2018; Stevenson 2013; Trollinger and Trollinger 2016), Islamic apostasy (Cottee 2015; Vliek 2019, 2021), and the nones (Drescher 2016; Thiessen and Wilkins-Laflamme 2020).

The first is perhaps the most prominent example, the recently constructed Creation Museum, located in Petersburg, Kentucky. The museum's mandate is to demonstrate scientifically that the account described in the book of Genesis—that is, six twenty-four-hour days of creation occurring six thousand years ago—provides an accurate and factual explanation for the origins of existence (Stevenson 2013, 128–61; Trollinger and Trollinger 2016; Watkins 2014). Often conceptualized as located squarely within the world of Christian fundamentalisms, popular depictions of the Creation Museum and its parent organization, Answers in Genesis, have viewed it as the most recent extension of long-standing embattled critiques of secular culture, which originate with the Scopes Monkey Trial in 1925 (Harding 2000) and continue through the rise of the religious Right as a political institution in the United States (Dochuk 2011).

The Creation Museum, however, seeks to reverse the preconceived notions that depict evangelicals as closed-minded and rigid and instead paints evolutionists that way. Its exhibitions invite visitors to contrast what the Bible says with what science says and even to consider whether legends about dragons provide insight into a lost history of human-dinosaur coexistence (Bielo 2016). The Creation Museum presents its Young Earth science, or Creation, alongside evolutionary science. The exhibits contrast "God's Word" (e.g., Creationism) with "Man's Word" (e.g., evolutionary science), directing visitors to decide for themselves. For example, the fossil exhibit features explanations from both a Creation paleontologist and an evolutionary paleontologist of their assessment of the same fossils (Trollinger and Trollinger 2016, 37). As the performance theory and theater scholar Jill Stevenson describes it, such contrasts allow the museum to offer a view of "creationists as insightful, inquisitive thinkers who actively seek knowledge" in contrast to an evolutionist who "blindly follows a 'theory' as if it were unquestionable truth" (Stevenson 2013, 139). Alongside empowering their visitors to make use of scientific evidence, the museum encourages visitors to rely on common sense or the plain sense of scripture, not its interpretation (Trollinger and Trollinger 2016, 112, 138).

The infamous 2014 CNN debate between the popular science educator Bill Nye and Ken Ham, president of Answers in Genesis, centered on the relevance of creationism as a scientific model. Ham explicitly evoked scientific frameworks and theories as a means of bolstering his argument. As the communication and rhetoric scholar Susan Trollinger and the historian William Trollinger, Jr., argue, Ham and other creationists could easily remain committed to a framework based on faith and the authority of scripture. Their attention to science instead of a faith-based argument could even be understood as undermining traditional evangelical conceptions of faith beyond reason. Ham's tactic allows him to address a culture that equates science and truth while simultaneously redefining the scientific method and conceptions of evidence for his own use (Trollinger and Trollinger 2016, 66–69). This strategy is successful because it relies on what James Bielo calls "creationist poetics," which rely on rhetorical performances and interactive stances to gain legitimacy (Bielo 2020). In this context, lived secularity takes the lead in imposing skepticism as a necessary element in the equation. It is particularly noteworthy that Answers in Genesis's skepticism is directed at evolution, not science, which they go to great lengths to differentiate (Trollinger and Trollinger 2016, 67–73). Indeed, while progressive Christians are working with different conceptions of scientific evidence, their privileging of science and evidence as secular categories that operate vis-à-vis skepticism is not unlike the approach of Answers in Genesis and the Creation Museum.

A second case study allows for an examination of how to further explore, in the context of lived secularity, ethical conceptions that bring religious affiliations and secular modalities into conversation with each other. The criminologist Simon Cottee's work on apostasy in Islam (2015) is an intervention in the reception of larger politicized discourses about Islam in the West. Cottee's work explores the ways that ex-Muslims position themselves in regard to Islam by considering their descriptions of losing their faith and the decisions they made to disclose (or not) their loss of religious beliefs. Many of his respondents reported that their rejection of religion resulted from such factors as greater study of the Quran, political events, spiritual alienation, or being influenced by popular atheist thinkers (such as Richard Dawkins and Christopher Hitchens). In addition, Cottee's work finds ethical concerns—both personal and social—to be the primary impetus for their rejection of religiosity (2015, 31–42, 60).

Cottee's introductory description of his interlocutor, Irtaza Hussein, who tragically took his own life one year after being interviewed, is an emotional example of ethics driving skepticism about religious traditions (Cottee 2015, xi–xiii). While Cottee's other interlocutors cite examples of what they deem hypocrisy or injustice in the Quran, hadiths, or social regulations (particularly, those directed at women) as ethical conundrums that ultimately led to their rejection of Islam, Irtaza was troubled by a double standard in his immediate social world of Muslim relatives and friends. Analyzing Irtaza's online posts, Cottee highlights the ways that Irtaza appeared to be distressed by indifference and alienation. His renunciation of Islam rests on his inability to figure out "why it would be a good thing to call [himself] a Muslim" (2015, xii). In a manner akin to progressive Christianity, there appears to be an ethic attached to the identity itself.

Cottee's work lacks a strong theoretical lens. Its focus is the task of understanding the motivations and experiences of Muslim apostates. The religious studies scholar Maria Vliek offers insight into the intersections of religious and secular identities. Vliek's fieldwork in the United Kingdom and the Netherlands explores experiences of leaving Islam and pushes back against the assumption that it is easy to designate boundaries between the secular and religious (Vliek 2021). In Vliek's assessment, most scholars studying deconversion have neglected the everyday when considering the reasons for religious disaffiliation. In contrast with Cottee's interlocutors, many of Vliek's subjects left the tradition because they felt it did not align with their daily lives and secular worldviews. For example, one of her interlocutors, Yedder, became less religious as he became more engaged in political activism. Another slowly separated from Islam as she made friends with non-Muslims and wanted to engage in activities of which her parents disapproved (Vliek 2019).

These examples dovetail with the main modalities through which progressive Christians locate their own religious identities as they are subsumed by what are perceived to be public and secular realms: science, history, and ethics. The private world of religion (e.g., family and tradition) contrasts with them. In these cases, conceptions identified as secular emerge as the driving force of affiliation (or lack thereof) with a religious tradition.

In this way, there are parallels between progressive Christians and a third and final case study: the recently categorized "nones." In the United States, the term *nones* emerged in the wake of the 2014 Religious

Landscape Study by the Pew Research Center, which noted an increase in the religiously unaffiliated, particularly among the millennial generation (Cooperman, Smith, and Cornibert 2015). More recent surveys have shown that approximately a quarter of the US population claims to have no religious affiliation (Thiessen and Wilkens-Laflamme 2020, 7). In their recent overview of the nones in North America, the sociologists Joel Thiessen and Sarah Wilkins-LaFlamme identify a framework of stages of decline as the reason for the perceived increase in this cohort. In particular, they highlight common explanations such as "rationalization, improved material conditions, pluralism, individualism, and declining authority of religion in the public sphere" alongside ongoing political polarization and the increased acceptability of having no religion (2020, 18).

One of the first people to study this group, Elizabeth Drescher, who holds a doctoral degree in Christian spirituality, offers a useful insight into the organizational strategies of the nones. She aims to uncover latent spirituality within the classification. Drescher notes that many critics characterize nones as spiritually eclectic and idiosyncratic after experiencing a loss of faith and developing an interest in commercialized religious practices (2016, 3).[1] Drescher argues that this characterization of nones lacks nuance because it primarily sees religion as derived from belief rather than practice (2016, 7–8). Furthermore, it generalizes their identity as generated by a narrative of departure from an organized or institutional form of religion. In her assessment, Drescher refocuses attention on practices that have elements of religion attached to them (e.g., practicing yoga, reading poetry, preparing traditional family meals, volunteering in the community, finding spirituality in nature, listening to self-help tapes). Drescher sees spiritual significance in the fact that at the heart of such activities is their social nature. As she notes, "Even when people are asked about their *individual* spirituality or religiosity, their narratives consistently draw in many others" (2016, 120).

In this final example, the category retains an emphasis that privileges religious or spiritual activities as revealing one's true or more authentic self. Doing so misses the opportunity to rethink the frameworks with which scholars of religion approach our subject. It forces religious adherents and movements into prescribed categories rather than those familiar to our interlocutors. Think, for example, of a composite figure of a thirty-five-year-old woman who describes herself as not religious but who feels especially connected to her grandmother on the rare occasions that she bakes challah with her children. Alternatively, consider the fifty-year-old avowed atheist who has recently taken up yoga to help him stay fit and alleviate stress. Though he does not see it as spiritual, he has found that the moments of calm in his daily yoga practice are so meaningful that he cannot help but invite all of his friends and colleagues to join him. While there may be merit in classifying them within the categories of "spiritual but not religious," "lived religion," or "nones," to do so artificially imposes religion as the point of departure, lending it a form of a priori authority.

While these practices might appear religious to scholars trained to identify religion everywhere, the nones take their authority from their secular, not their spiritual, status. As Thiessen and Wilkens-Laflamme show, a significant portion of the nones were raised in nonreligious settings and have limited exposure to religious practices (2020, 39–40). It may be disingenuous to ascribe underlying religiosity to them. Instead of focusing on those instances in which "religion-like" practices or beliefs emerge despite their lack of religion, it would be beneficial to think about how they are appended to an overarching secularity.

Remaining Christian Heretics

As I have shown, progressive Christians allow insights from the so-called secular realms of scientific empiricism, historical analysis, and liberal humanism to direct their religious beliefs and practices. They often see the process through which they engage and evaluate their data as more important than the new frameworks they develop. It is the ethical imperative of reconsidering and choosing the most accurate framework that matters most. Everything is up for reevaluation in the future.

Indeed, the future is ever present in progressive Christian discourse. Over and over again, the progressive Christians featured in this book spoke of "the end." They postulated different scenarios concerning the end of Christianity and the ultimate demise of their own churches. Hedy's worries that the church would not be around even for as long as she would be suggest the possibility that the community would not survive for another decade. This concern was echoed frequently with regard to both social and economic realities. Many progressive Christians were apprehensive about the lack of young people in their congregations and the sustainability of their movement.

Few spoke explicitly of their own end or death. These conversations frequently were filled with ambiguity concerning the possibility of life after death and the process of dying. When they did address the topic, it sometimes felt as if it was for my benefit rather than their own; their tone was often gentle and reassuring. For example, in my conversation with Deborah—the woman who wondered about the degree to which they could mine biblical texts before they needed a better resource—she spoke positively about death as a next step and hypothesized about the possibility of reincarnation, but she ultimately turned her attention to me and the fact that death did not seem as immediate for someone my age.

Initially, Deborah employed the analogy of a garden. She explained the abundance of spirituality she finds in her garden, a place where she and Mother Nature share the responsibility and the workload.

> I find a lot of spirituality in the garden. I love to garden and it's not a very organized garden. I do about half or less and Mother Nature the rest. Just watching things grow. You plant that little carrot seed and a carrot comes every time. It doesn't come up as a beet or anything else. It's a carrot. You look at the flower, watch the bees humming around, their saddlebags full of pollen, and flying. The world is just humming around us: activities and things to watch and see. We're part of something so big that I'm just in awe when I'm out there.

Picking up on Deborah's theme of being part of something big, I asked her what something big looks like. She paused for a moment and mused about the possibility of reincarnation. She quickly pointed out that while she knew there is no evidence for reincarnation, she found it to be a compelling explanation for unspeakable injustices, such as a sick or dying child. "It was the only thing that ever made any sense to me when a child was ill in a way that was life-threatening and crippled for life. There's no justice in that. The only thing would be if you have many lives." She explained that she saw it as similar to advancing through grades in school: "You go through different grades, and you have to do certain things. If you get it, you move on. If you don't, you go back and repeat the grade."

I nodded lest I interrupt the flow of Deborah's thinking. She paused as if recalling an old memory and continued:

> Sixty years ago, I watched a three-year-old play an organ one time. She was known in the community. We went to her home and all you had to do was start humming something. And this was a three-year-old, she would just pick it up and play it. She couldn't touch the pedals at all. She was too small. It was just amazing to watch her hands. How did that happen to her? I could never learn to play like that. You watch a real musician play and think, "How did they get there?" There are some people [who] have these special talents, and you think they have to have come with them. They didn't have to study or anything. So it's always something. When I came across this reincarnation thing, I thought, "Who knows?" When I don't get to do something I really wanted to do, I say, "Oh, well, that's on my list for my next life, next time around."

At this point, Deborah turned the interview around and asked me why I was interested in studying religion. I told her about a book about world religions that had belonged to my grandmother and had always fascinated me as a child. I described how, on rainy Saturday afternoons, I would take it down off the shelf and pore over the pictures of Shinto temple dancers, Hasidic men reading Torah, and Michelangelo's famous depiction of God on the ceiling of the Sistine Chapel. I explained how my grandmother had years earlier filled the book with dried maple leaves that she had for some reason spray-painted gold and how reading her book about religion made me feel closer to her, even though she had died before I was born.

"So, if reincarnation is true, you were probably in your past a Celtic woman leader," Deborah concluded. While the reasons for her classification were unclear to me, I accepted it without question. Deborah returned to the themes of choice, the jettisoning of outdated beliefs, and the future.

> Jesus said, "I came to make you free!" And yet, the Christian church said, "Oh, there are all these other rules: meatless Fridays and church every

Sunday." You know, just all kinds of things. We're meant to be free, to make up our minds to choose wisely but to be free to choose.

That angry God is going, gone. It's very hard after half a century of believing something to change how you pray. Or do you pray? Do you just be joyous and awe-filled? I don't know. It will be interesting. I keep saying, "Wouldn't it be nice to be here fifty years from now and see what happens?" You'll be here, but I won't. Anyway, it should be fun for you.

The contrast here in Deborah's criticism of the church, which has wrongfully promoted an angry God, and the nonchalant nature with which she discussed spirituality in the garden and the possibility of reincarnation is especially telling of progressive Christian representations of temporality. A conversation about what comes next quickly becomes a conversation about the past. Deborah remembered witnessing a little girl play the organ sixty years earlier, but she now imagined that the little girl may have been a musician in a past life. When I explained my interest in studying religion (which I also resolved by telling a story about my own links and connection to the past through a text), Deborah concluded that my interest in that field of study is related to a past life. Concerning the church's future, Deborah knew only that she would not be around to witness what comes next.

Others featured in this study did not share Deborah's optimism that I will be there to record something fun. They were not worried that their message might be irrelevant but rather their method of distributing it would be. For example, one of my interlocutors spoke of a future in which the congregation would drop the word *church* from its name because the term carries too much baggage. Others worried that the high costs of maintaining church buildings and programming would eventually be too much for their congregation to support. Many saw themselves as coming to a natural fork in the road but were uncertain what would lie ahead, if anything at all.

Here Eileen's question, "Where is the coffee?," resounds again. The juxtaposition of progressive Christianity as a distinctively articulated theological movement—in which questions of what books to read and how they affect the development of progressive Christianity predominate—and the social nature of a book study group that people attend to socialize and consume food has been a central theme through this book. Within progressive Christianity, religion is as much a leisure activity as it is a space of theological construction and articulation. "We are Christian because we have always been Christian," I was told over and over again when I asked how one could be a Christian without believing in God, Jesus, or the Bible.

"I was born a Christian and I will die a Christian," one of my interlocutors emphatically exclaimed. "A very different type of Christian," she continued, "but Christian nonetheless." She smiled as she made this statement and then paused and took another sip of her tea. Before I could respond or ask for clarification, she began to enthusiastically describe how she had changed and what books and thinkers had promoted this change, one that she hoped to see spread widely throughout the church.

Suddenly, she was up and reaching for the top shelf of her bookcase, asking, "Have you read this book?"

Epilogue

There Will Be Cake and Dancing

There will be cake! Inviting any in the vicinity to join us @WestHillUC this Sunday for cake & happy dancing! We'll also be reaffirming the importance of the work we & @UnitedChurchCda do in this rapidly changing world.
—Tweet from Gretta Vosper, November 8, 2018

Anthropologists are often called back to their fieldwork in unexpected ways—whether physically through follow-up visits or emotionally through recounting and recollecting (Beatty 2012; Leggett and Leggett 2021). In my case, it was a literal call. In the early fall of 2017, I received a phone call from a Toronto-based lawyer specializing in labor and employment law. While there was no formal legal case against Gretta Vosper, she had retained legal counsel in light of an upcoming review by the General Council of the United Church of Canada concerning her suitability to serve as a minister. My name had been provided as a potential expert witness. I was then living in Tennessee but had followed with interest the Canadian media reports of what was being dubbed "a heresy trial" against Vosper, although I had not grasped the severity of her circumstances. Vosper had been featured in national media as a controversial figure for almost two decades at that point. Calls for her defrocking were not new, and as my research revealed, Vosper's controversial disbelief was not unique but rather representative of a growing mass within progressive Christianity.

This time, however, the stakes were higher. Vosper was no longer just the subject of newspaper opinion columns, right-wing radio call-in shows, or vitriolic online comments sections. Now the General Council of the United Church of Canada was debating and reviewing Vosper's suitability to perform her role as a minister in the church. In my eyes, it was a surprising development. While belief in God is certainly part of the doctrine of the United Church of Canada, many ministers and theologians within the church assign leeway to its interpretation, preferring a metaphorical one. In a 2015 article published in the *United Church Observer* (now known as *Broadview*), the United Church of Canada's publication, the journalist Mike Milne quotes Reverend Bill Steadman, chair of the General Council's theology and interchurch interfaith committee, on whether ministers should be subject to tests of faith. Steadman notes that the church does not have a clear definition of heresy: "Lots of people, I think, express what we traditionally call an agnostic viewpoint, which is, 'I'm not sure I have all the answers about this.' Well, is that heresy or honesty?" (Milne 2015).

Of course, as this book reveals, honesty and heresy are two sides of the same coin for progressive Christians. In January 2015, Vosper published an open letter to Gary Paterson, moderator of the United Church of Canada, in which she expressed deep concern about a prayer posted on the United Church's website that had been written in reaction to the religiously motivated shootings at the Charlie Hebdo offices in Paris. In Vosper's assessment, the prayer addressed to "Gracious God" represented an unwelcome intrusion of religious beliefs into the public sphere. Criticizing its assumption of "a supernatural being whose purposes can be divined" by humans, Vosper urged Paterson to "lead our church toward freedom from such idolatrous belief." Just as the church had pressed for freedom from social, sexual, and environmental injustices, so, too, should it move toward freedom from religion (Vosper 2015). In the days that followed, calls for Vosper to resign flooded in. Reverend David Ewart, a retired United Church of Canada minister, wrote on his blog that Vosper's ideas were "juvenile and unbelievable." Ewart equated her calls for freedom from religion with nonreligious ideologies such as those held by "Hitler, Mussolini, Lenin, Stalin, Mao, Pol Pot, Amin. Mugabe [sic], and too many others" whose ideological stances have led to "war, genocide, and mass starvation" (Ewart 2015). Petitions for Vosper to leave the ministry attracted notice in the Canadian media, especially from Douglas Todd, religion writer for the *Vancouver Sun*; John Longhurst, religion reporter and columnist for the *Winnipeg Free Press*; and Andy Oudman, a controversial talk radio host in London, Ontario.

In May 2015, the Toronto Conference of the United Church of Canada announced plans to review Vosper's place in the church. While the open letter to Paterson may have served as the impetus for this review, its justification stemmed from Vosper's public and explicit use of the term *atheist* (as opposed to *nontheist*) to describe her religious beliefs, starting in 2013.[1] According to church regulations, unless there is evidence of criminal or other misconduct, a minister can be reviewed only for allegations of ineffectiveness or insubordination. The general secretary of the United Church was asked to investigate whether there were grounds for reviewing Vosper's fitness for ministry. Ultimately, she concluded that effectiveness could be linked to suitability. Because ministers are asked to answer questions regarding their belief in God at their ordination, the unprecedented act of again asking the ordination questions first posed to Vosper in 1993 could be a means of determining her suitability and therefore effectiveness. In another *Broadview* article, Milne notes that the church had never required a minister to revisit ordination vows (Milne 2016a). Because Vosper's congregation supported her and did not find her ineffective, the question of the review's legitimacy was even more debatable.

In September 2016, the Toronto Conference released a thirty-nine-page report concluding that Vosper was not suitable to continue in ordained ministry based on her disbelief in "God, Jesus Christ, or the Holy Spirit" (Dempsey and Rankin 2016). Vosper's congregation and supporters across the country rallied around her. She retained a Toronto-based law firm specializing in labor and employment law. Her supporters started a GoFundMe account to help pay her legal fees amounting to more than Can$80,000.

Following many appeals and delays, the case—or the "heresy trial" as Vosper's supporters framed it—went to the General Council of the national church for a final decision in late fall 2018. Though they were expected to take several weeks, the initial meetings with the national church took an unexpected turn. Three teams of lawyers, Vosper, the West Hill United Church board chair, and officials from the Toronto Conference met behind closed doors for arbitration. They reached a settlement, and the Toronto Conference announced that Vosper was to remain in ordained ministry (Adler 2018; Milne 2019; Porter 2019).

Few other details regarding the settlement were released. The next day, the United Church of Canada posted an announcement on its website stating, "This does not alter in any way the belief of The United Church of Canada" (Porter 2019). Regardless, it was clear that Vosper and her supporters felt that the end of the heresy trial was a victory for West Hill and the United Church of Canada. Vosper invited her supporters to join the West Hill congregation for a celebratory Sunday service following the ruling. "There will be cake!" she wrote enthusiastically in a tweet the day after the verdict. Cake and "happy dancing," she added.

Vosper thanked her supporters and her congregation for their ongoing encouragement in a Facebook post on the West Hill United Church's Facebook page:

> I cannot say how central your support, love, expressions of empathy, and constancy has meant to me over these three and a half years (plus one day!). It has strewn this difficult path with wisdom, late night and early morning insights, en-coeur-agements, letters of support, of outrage and sorrow, perspective, cups of tea, space for the expressions of anger or heartbreak, shoulders braced against the wall. You persevered and this story has been told. In the telling, in the hearing, we have been affirmed. The first denomination to allow an atheist, whose heart and mind, leadership, and theology, formed by that church's own hand, to continue unobstructed in their ministry. Might I even say "celebrated"? It is a new day in the Christian world. And I am so grateful for your presence by my side.

While most of the comments communicated encouragement, several replies to her post expressed disapproval and expectations that church members would experience punishment from God—perhaps an empty threat to a congregation that no longer believes in God. Rosie DiManno, a journalist who had attended the celebration service, also levied criticism. In an opinion piece published in the *Toronto Star*, she described the service's celebratory nature as part and parcel of "the cult of Gretta Vosper." Noting that the removal of God from religion is inherently an irreligious act, DiManno questioned why Vosper did not join the Unitarian Church (DiManno 2018).

Both DiManno's rejection of Vosper's legitimacy and Vosper's suggestion that it is a "new day in the Christian world" warrant more complete consideration. As this book has shown, progressive Christians intentionally retain their Christian identity. When asked why they do not join

Unitarian-Universalist congregations or humanist associations, they respond that they are Christian because they have always been Christian. Religious belonging, it seems, plays multiple roles. On the one hand, it is a place for communal gatherings: to drink coffee or beer, to read and debate books, to laugh and cry, to eat cake and dance. In other words, to undertake the everyday activities of friendship and folly in an increasingly isolated world (Putnam 2000; see also Bibby 2017, 88–93).

On the other hand, a lingering appeal to heritage among progressive Christians may shed light not only on contemporary Christianity but also on intersections of religion and broader social imaginaries. To a certain extent, the appeal to cultural heritage shares discursive tropes with those seeking to retain Christian symbols in public and political spaces. For example, there have been attempts in Quebec to redefine Roman Catholic symbols as Francophone heritage markers in order to preserve their place in public buildings despite Quebec *laïcité* regulations restricting religious symbols in public spaces (Zubrzycki 2016; see also Kaell 2017; Seljak 2000). Likewise, understanding progressive Christians' insistence of their legitimacy within Christianity and their dedication to rectifying perceived falsehoods might help us to understand the ways that Christian nationalism serves as an orienting framework for American evangelicals' perspectives "on national identity, belonging, and social hierarchies" (Whitehead and Perry 2020, x; see also Delehanty, Edgell, and Stewart 2019; Marti 2020).

Finally, for scholars of religion, progressive Christianity illuminates ongoing debates concerning the prominence of belief in defining religion. A rich body of scholarship has challenged the insistence that religion is a universal, sui generis category, showing how it stems from certain historical anachronisms, Western colonial tactics, and political ideologies (Barton and Boyarin 2016; Chidester 2013; Dubuisson 2003; Fitzgerald 2000; Masuzawa 2005; Nongbri 2013; Storm 2012). Likewise, the field has stepped back from the idea that belief is the primary marker of religion or the representation of religion as derived from belief (Bell 2002; Lopez 1998; O'Neill 2012). Popular definitions, however, have not kept pace with scholarly ones. The example of progressive Christians generally, and rhetoric surrounding Vosper's "heresy trial" specifically, allow scholars of religion to linger a little longer on the nature of belief and believing.

In his ethnographic study of the British secular humanists, Matthew Engelke suggests that atheists are more than merely nonbelievers. Based on their understanding of religion, derived primarily from Western Christian frameworks, the secular humanists concluded that "to be religious is to be a believer, and to be a believer is to be a certain kind of person who brackets off as separate a set of truths not explicable in scientific or naturalistic terms" (Engelke 2014, S299). In so doing, they have exchanged belief for knowledge. This distinction is all the more relevant when considering the differences between *believing* and *knowing*.

Something similar is at work among the progressive Christians featured in this book. When Vosper shifted her self-identifying label from nontheist to atheist, she signaled a break from more than the tenets of church doctrine. She was no longer adding nuance or metaphor to theism; instead, she discursively and irreversibly cut ties, not with God (whom she abandoned long ago) but with belief. Her rupture pertained to the practice of belief, or the *believing*. Indeed, Vosper and other progressive Christians have replaced faith with skepticism as their principal religious modality. As I have shown, the motivations for this shift are primarily ethical: progressive Christians maintain the conviction that it is immoral to claim something is true that they know not to be. Evidence from historical research, scientific and empirical knowledge, and an overarching liberal humanist worldview buttress this moral imperative.

In so doing, progressive Christians forge a novel variety of Christianity—but a variety of Christianity nonetheless. As Vosper terms it, it is "a new day in the Christian world." Like all new days, no matter how auspicious or ordinary, it is temporary. The sum of the days that have preceded it, this day like all days, endures until it is eventually eclipsed by tomorrow.

ACKNOWLEDGMENTS

This book is dedicated to heretics everywhere—those who have stood up against oppression, inequality, and absurdity. The world needs more heretics.

This project would not exist if not for the members of the five congregations who welcomed me into their churches, homes, and lives. In many ways, they are coauthors of this book. While there are too many individuals to name, I do want to note my deep gratitude to both John Shelby Spong and "Hedy," may their memories live on as an inspiration to those whose lives they touched. I especially wish to thank the ministers of the five congregations featured in this book, Dawn, Elizabeth, Karen, Gretta, "Mary-Ellen" and "Stan," for their hospitality, wisdom, and compassion. Along with an understanding of progressive Christianity, they provided insight into what makes a good teacher, leader, and community member.

In part this book explores the ways that religious people make sense of their origins. I am fortunate to trace my own academic genealogy to Michele Murray, Harvey White, and Bruce Gilbert at Bishop's University and Bill James, supervisor for my master's thesis at Queen's University. From them, I gained a strong foundation in the academic study of religion, and their guidance allowed me to begin to imagine a project that would examine historical Jesus studies in contemporary society. I am so grateful for their continued encouragement long after I was their student.

I remain indebted to the scholarly community I found at the University of Toronto. Pamela Klassen was an exemplary mentor in every way imaginable. She is a dynamic scholar, and I have been privileged to receive her guidance and friendship. Simon Coleman nurtured my development as an anthropologist and a scholar. His constructive criticism kept me grounded in the writing process and encouraged me to return to this project after I had given up on it. Phyllis Airhart brought to life historical forerunners of progressive Christianity and reminded me to engage them throughout my ethnographic research. I owe a debt of gratitude to Joseph Bryant, who first saw the value of this project and championed it (and me) along the way. I would also like to thank John Kloppenborg and John Marshall for helping me navigate the complexities of the contemporary reception of historical biblical criticism, Stephen Scharper for insight into roles of popular theology in the public sphere, and Brian Walsh for regularly reminding me of the significance of my research to not only academic circles but also faith communities. If it is possible to emend the famous final lines from the 1986 film, *Stand by Me*, I would say that "I never had any friends later on like the ones I had when I was in graduate school." Thank you to Rebecca Bartel, Ian Brown, Chipamong Chowhurdy, Jenn Cianca, Brian Carwana, Nicholas Dion, Amy Fisher, Matthew King, Sarah Kleeb, Eva Mroczek, Sarah Rollens, Justin Stein, Laurel Zwissler, and so many others.

Several mentors and colleagues motivated me at key junctures along the way. Paul Bramadat has offered extraordinary support over the years and has made me a better researcher, teacher, and person. Craig Martin and Sean McCloud have helped me navigate and demystify academia, offering sustained encouragement and out of the blue text messages that always appeared at just the right time. I would also like to thank my academic colleagues from near and far who have offered feedback and relevant insight in ways they may not even know. Thanks especially to Richard Ascough, Jon Bialecki, James Bielo, Sophie Bjork-James, James Crossley, Omri Elisha, Matthew Engelke, David Feltmate (my conference bestie), Paul Gareau, Naomi Haynes, Titus Hjelm, Eric Hoenes del Pinal, Brian Howell, Hillary Kaell, Keven Lewis, Ellen Ott Marshall, Ruth Marshall, Mandy McMichael, Amira Mittermaier, Kevin O'Neill, Kristian Petersen, Joel Robbins, Martha Roberts, Jennifer Selby, and David Seljak.

At Middle Tennessee State University, I want to give a special thanks to John Vile and Philip Phillips, and the rest of the Honors College community for providing a space and support for me to complete this book. I am also grateful for the encouragement of my faculty colleagues, especially Roberta Chevrette, LaToya Eaves, Kathryn Fenton, Lisa Gasson-Gardner, Jenna Gray-Hildenbrand, Jamil Grimes, Ryan Korstange, Mary Magada-Ward, Ashleigh McKinzie, and Andrew Polk. And, of course, to my students at MTSU—I am critically aware of how lucky I am to be your teacher. You have taught me much and I do not take it nor you for granted.

To anyone still reading these acknowledgments, I am pleased to report that everything you have heard about working with Jennifer Hammer at New York University Press is true. Her editorial acumen, superhuman patience, and dedication to the field are beyond admirable. I count myself fortunate to have worked with her and the entire team at NYUP. I am especially grateful to Polly Kummel, whose editorial eye has transformed this manuscript into a book. Thank you also to the anonymous reviewers of the manuscript who pushed me to think about the larger picture and impact of this work.

Many dear friends provided respite and reassurance along the way. There are too many people to thank. Know that I am grateful, even if your name is not here, but I do want to pause and recognize the ongoing support of my extended family, especially, Jack and Ann Barkley, Karl Bernhardt, and Wendy Gibb and my dearest friends, Catherine Chafe, Adleen Crapo, Chris Miller, Melody Morgan, Melissa McCosh Sohrabi, and Jeff Strain. Thank you to each of you for all you do. Additionally, this book would not have been possible without the support of my therapists Brianne Fox and Brynda Quinn. I name them here both out of sincere gratitude and in hopes of contributing to ongoing efforts to destigmatize mental health treatment in academia and beyond.

Finally, as educators, my parents, Brenda and David King, instilled in me a love of reading, a respect for learning, and a deep commitment to community engagement that has sustained me in so many ways. In a world where many are lonely, I am so grateful for your unwavering support and love. Further thanks for indulging my interest in religion, which began with the big book of world religions, transitioned to a teenage rebellion, and eventually became my profession and my passion. Thank you for sharing this journey with me.

APPENDIX

The Eight Points (American and Canadian Versions)

The Center for Progressive Christianity (2003 Version)

By calling ourselves progressive, we mean we are Christians who . . .

1. Have found an approach to God through the life and teachings of Jesus.
2. Recognize the faithfulness of other people who have other names for the way to God's realm, and acknowledge that their ways are true for them, as our ways are true for us.
3. Understand the sharing of bread and wine in Jesus's name to be a representation of an ancient vision of God's feast for all peoples.
4. Invite all people to participate in our community and worship life without insisting that they become like us in order to be acceptable (including but not limited to): believers and agnostics, conventional Christians and questioning skeptics, women and men, those of all sexual orientations and gender identities, those of all races and cultures, those of all classes and abilities, those who hope for a better world and those who have lost hope.
5. Know that the way we behave toward one another and toward other people is the fullest expression of what we believe.
6. Find more grace in the search for understanding than we do in dogmatic certainty—more value in questioning than in absolutes.
7. Form ourselves into communities dedicated to equipping one another for the work we feel called to do: striving for peace and justice among all people, protecting and restoring the integrity of all God's creation, and bringing hope to those Jesus called the least of his sisters and brothers.
8. Recognize that being followers of Jesus is costly, and entails selfless love, conscientious resistance to evil, and renunciation of privilege.

Canadian Centre for Progressive Christianity (2004 Version)

By calling ourselves "progressive" we mean that we:

1. Centre our faith on values that affirm the sacredness and interconnectedness of all life, the inherent and equal worth of all persons, and the supremacy of love expressed actively in our lives as compassion and social justice.
2. Engage in a search that has roots in our Christian heritage and traditions.
3. Embrace the freedom and responsibility to examine traditionally held Christian beliefs and practices, acknowledging the human construction of religion, and in the light of conscience and contemporary learning, adjust our views and practices accordingly.
4. Draw from diverse sources of wisdom, regarding all as fallible human expressions open to our evaluation of their potential contribution to our individual and communal lives.
5. Find more meaning in the search for understanding than in the arrival at certainty; in the questions than the answers.
6. Encourage inclusive, non-discriminatory, non-hierarchical community where our common humanity is honoured in a trusting atmosphere of mutual respect and support.
7. Promote forms of individual and community celebration, study, and prayer that use understandable, inclusive, non-dogmatic, value-based language by which people of religious, skeptical, or secular backgrounds may be nurtured and challenged.
8. Commit to journeying together, our ongoing growth characterized by honesty, integrity, openness, respect, intellectual rigour, courage, creativity, and balance.

NOTES

INTRODUCTION

1 Richard Dawkins is an evolutionary biologist and author, who is best known in scientific circles for having coined the term *meme* to describe how behavioral concepts might be viewed akin to genes according to Darwinian principles. Dawkins is also a prominent figure within the New Atheist movement as an outspoken critic of creationism, intelligent design, and religious belief in general (for an overview of New Atheists see Amarasingam 2010). Jerry Falwell was a Baptist pastor and televangelist who founded Liberty University. He was a well-known conservative activist, credited as the co-founder of the Moral Majority (see Harding 1991; Sutton 2012).

2 The closest thing that West Hill United Church had to a creedal statement was a document called "VisionWorks" that was first compiled in 2004 and then was rewritten in 2009, 2015, and 2021. In this document, the church explains that it holds a diverse approach to textual sources. The most recent version of this document is available on the church's website, www.westhill.net.

3 Ralph Young argues that while dissent often is seen as un-American, it encapsulates the American experience, religious and otherwise. Dissent contributes to larger political and social modes of protest, conflict, and change (Young 2015).

4 In the conclusion I address nonreligion in conversation with the work of the sociologists Joel Thiessen and Sarah Wilkins-LaFlamme (2020). For progressive Christians, retaining their Christian identity alongside their nonbelief in traditional Christian tenets is at the crux of their religious identity. For this reason, this book does not present them under the rubric of nonreligion, despite their shared atheist beliefs, secular worldviews, and, in some cases, similar experiences departing from more traditional or conservative religious communities.

5 By focusing on skepticism rather than secularization, I do not intend to imply that secularization has not occurred within the North American religious landscape or the Western world. A more nuanced understanding of secularization points to a correlation of many different historical influences, from inside and outside institutional religion. Indeed, as some historians note, religious adherents often were the authors of secularizing trends and practices (see C. Smith 2003; cf. Cook 1985; Marshall 1992). In some cases, secularization accompanied a reevaluation of what it meant to be and to become a Christian (Clarke 1996). The shift I advocate in this book offers a fuller picture of the ways that people generate and enact religious and nonreligious identities.

6 This ethnography focuses on the Canadian wing of progressive Christianity and churches affiliated with the Canadian Centre for Progressive Christianity. The center understands itself as departing theologically from the larger American Center for Progressive Christianity and related organizations because its American counterpart is too Christocentric. In the United Kingdom, the term *post-Christian* is more prevalent. Post-Christians are often associated with the Sea of Faith Network, which takes its name from the BBC program featuring the "atheist priest" Don Cupitt, former dean of Emmanuel College, Cambridge. Cupitt promotes a theology of nonrealism, which resembles Christian humanism and sees God as a moral symbol (see Thiselton 1995, 81–117; White 1994; Ward 1997, 588–90). This movement represents Christianity as an evolutionary faith. The point is to evolve beyond Christocentric religion (not beyond religion itself). Both progressive Christianity and the Sea of Faith Network have chapters in Australia and New Zealand. While there are noteworthy differences, these different movements share certain commonalties. Central to my research is the authority granted to the process of intellectual discernment through popular theological texts that question or dismiss the divinity or existence of Jesus and other traditional doctrines and beliefs.

7 When progressive Christians discuss why they or others might leave the church, they usually perceive exclusion and irreconcilable beliefs as the primary reason for departure. Research by the sociologist Joel Thiessen on the significance of religion in people's lives reveals that a dwindling demand for religion is more frequently the cause (Thiessen 2015).

8 Noting, of course, that both "Christian Right" and "Christian Left" are misnomers, Edles further clarifies that there are two major political and theological axes that are pertinent to Protestantism: race and evangelism (2013, 5).

9 The separation of church and state was never official policy in Canada. The notion that religion remains outside the scope of Canadian public life emerged gradually alongside federal policies related to multiculturalism and privacy laws (Noll 2006). Such standards are perhaps encapsulated most succinctly in the words of the former prime minister Pierre Elliott Trudeau, who famously declared that "the state has no place in the bedrooms of the nation."

10 The historian Molly Worthen charts a similar trajectory amid evangelicals for whom questions concerning "how to reconcile faith and reason; how to know Jesus; and how to act publicly on faith after the rupture of Christendom" (Worthen 2014, 6) have striking parallels with those posed by progressive Christians.

11 *Entextualization* refers to the "process of rendering a given instance of discourse as text, detachable from its local context" (Urban 1996, 21). As an anthropological framework, it allows scholars to better understand the interplay between oral and written texts and the institutional arrangements and human strategies that enable their circulation (Barber 2007, 22–29). For a discussion of religious language and entextualization, see Shoaps (2002).

12 Russell McCutcheon offers several challenges to the lived religion model specifically and its use of the term *religion* more generally. Too often its approach to

religion reinscribes and privileges assumptions about the category of religion as a sui generis entity as opposed to a contested social domain (McCutcheon 1997). He also reminds scholars that religious adherents themselves are not as concerned with such systems of classification. As McCutcheon explains, "*It is highly unlikely that, in the midst of being religious, a religious person perceives themselves as being religious*" (McCutcheon 2015, 6, emphasis in the original). Recent scholarship on lived religion has called for development of a more theoretical orientation in conversation with scholarship attending to "the emergence and deployment of religion as a category" (Knibbe and Kupari 2020, 166; see also Ammerman 2016).

13 Taylor proposes distinguishing between three varieties of secularity: secularity 1 (decline of religion in public life), secularity 2 (decline of religious belief and practice), and secularity 3 (new conditions of belief). His analysis primarily charts the historical and philosophical developments and cultural impetus in which this third variety of secularity emerges (Taylor 2007).

14 The anthropologist Matthew Engelke observes a similar tactic in his fieldwork with the British Humanist Association. Members of the association's office in central London objected to language referencing "Acts of God" in their organization's insurance policy. Despite the fact that the term is a legal one used to denote earthquakes or other uncontrollable natural forces, they found the terminology objectionable and sought to change the language to "acts of nature" (Engelke 2014, S292–93).

15 It may appear counterintuitive to describe progressive Christians as mainstream. Yet despite their so-called heretical beliefs, progressive Christians can be classified under the umbrella of mainline and liberal Protestantism. For the most part, they are middle class and white and assume related cultural logics and social practices. Their social location positions them in the mainstream. This book offers a direct response to Hann's call for anthropological studies of mainstream Christianity (Hann 2007).

16 Agape is a Greek term found throughout the Christian Bible and is often translated as love.

CHAPTER 1. "NOT CHRISTIAN LIKE THAT"

1 In Canada, progressive Christianity is most prominent within the United Church of Canada. The United Church of Canada was formed in 1925 by a merger of the Methodist and Congregationalist churches, along with half of the Presbyterian churches in Canada. It is often described as a grand experiment in Christian ecumenism. After a long journey toward church union, the United Church positioned itself as an inclusive community that welcomes and encourages a variety of theological perspectives (see, for example, Airhart 2013; Airhart and Hutchinson 1996; King 2010).

2 The Evangelical Lutheran Church in Canada is the largest body of Lutherans in the country. It was formed in 1986 with the merger of the Evangelical Lutheran Church of Canada and the three Canadian synods of the Lutheran Church in America.

Despite its name, the church is not typically evangelical. The term refers to the German word for Protestant. In 2001, the Evangelical Lutheran Church in Canada entered into full communion with the Anglican Church of Canada. The two churches are similar in terms of doctrines and liturgical practices, although they differ significantly in institutional organization. Lutheranism in Canada places importance on heritage and is often conceptualized as an ethnic church, although such classifications are becoming deemphasized, as the religious studies scholar William C. James notes. Discussing ethnicity at St. Mark's Lutheran Church in Kingston, Ontario, James writes that the community retains its German and Danish heritage as much as the local Presbyterian Church retains its Scottish identity (James 2011, 256; cf. Hillis 2008). For more information about the history of the Lutheran Church in Canada, see Threinen (2006) and Hande and Schultz (1990).

3   While sometimes seen as a niche market, fair trade refers to a socially aware business model in which consumers purchase certified fair trade goods, often from developing countries, at a higher price in order to support environmental sustainability and more equitable labor practices. Early proponents of the fair trade movement included Christian-based organizations such as the Mennonite Central Committee and Oxfam Trading. The first company to offer fair trade coffee in Canada, Bridgehead Trading, was founded by two United Church of Canada ministers and two social activists working with farmers in Nicaragua during the civil war and the US trade embargo. Popular fair trade commodities include coffee, tea, chocolate, fruits, and handicrafts (see Fridell 2007; Low and Davenport 2005).

4   In his study of secular humanists, Matthew Engelke likewise found that many of his interlocutors listed like-mindedness as a motivation for participation in humanist networks and events (2014, S298).

5   The United Church of Canada distinguishes between members, full members, and adherents. According to *The Manual* of the United Church of Canada, an adherent refers to someone who is actively involved in the church, attends regularly, and even donates substantially, however, they have not taken formal steps toward membership. Members of the congregation usually denotes children of full members or children who have been baptized but have not yet become full members. Full members are those individuals who are named as members on the congregational role and are permitted to vote at congregational meetings. There are a number of paths to full membership, depending on one's circumstances and if they have been baptized or not. Unbaptized adults undergo a service of baptism and profession of faith. Someone who was baptized as a child can become a full member through confirmation, reaffirmation of faith, or certificate of transfer of member from another church. The service is not particularly elaborate and usually involves brief prayers at the front of the church and words of welcome from the rest of the congregation (see United Church of Canada 2021).

6   The Anglican Church of Canada's history parallels the colonial history of the British Empire in North America (Fletcher 2016). Initially the colonial outpost of the

Church of England, it achieved self-government in the mid-nineteenth century. Currently, it is the third largest religious body in Canada, after the Roman Catholic Church and the United Church of Canada. Theologically the church is diverse and runs a spectrum of affiliations including, conservative, liberal, charismatic, evangelical, Anglo-Catholic, and progressive (Hayes 2004). Its recent history has been shaped by the revelation in the 1990s of the church's role in government established residential schools in which Indigenous children were forcibly removed from their homes, suffered extensive physical, sexual, and psychological abuse, and denied the opportunity to learn their languages and cultural practices. A second recent issue within the Anglican Church of Canada has been its response to equal or same-sex marriage. An issue which resulted in the departure of a few conservative congregations from the national church (Hayes 2013). For more information about the history of the Anglican Church of Canada, see Katerberg (2001), Knowles (2008), and Westfall (1989).
7 Living the Questions is a video- and web-based curriculum that many progressive Christian churches use for biblical and theological studies. It is often presented as an alternative to the evangelical educational program known as Alpha, which offers an introduction to Christianity through prescribed programs that involve videos, discussion modules, and reflective biblical study.
8 I have changed the name of this church to protect the privacy of its congregants.
9 This notion that the exchange of knowledge in a collective setting generates and is generated by a kind of habitus is not unique to progressive Christianity. In a similar fashion, the scholar of religion Brian Carwana (2021) argues for an evangelical habitus that coalesces around conservative Christian lobby groups and their representations of traditional family values regarding issues such as sex, marriage, and childrearing. According to Carwana, evangelical lobbies advance certain orientations to traditional values in such a way that they extend beyond mere "cognitive coherence by promoting a home life whose repertoire of practices and routines instantiate habits of thinking, feeling and comportment that cultivate an evangelical ethos . . . or evangelical habitus" (Carwana 2021, 216).

CHAPTER 2. TO MINE THE TEXT
1 Webb Keane links Protestant referential language ideologies to the clear distinction that Calvinism draws between ideas and matter. For Calvin, it is language, rather than objects, that conveys and mediates the divine. According to Keane, the "theological purification of language" added a moral dimension to projects that sought to "reinforce the separation of material objects from the world of meanings and of agents" (2007, 66–67).
2 Sociolinguistic studies of reading practices that view reading as an event show that reading encompasses much more than simply reading to gather information. Texts precondition and shape readers before, during, and after reading (Darnton 2002, 21). Reading and reading events also function as spaces for social interactions, status assertion, or control (Bloome and Theodorou 1985, 24; see also Castanheira et al. 2000).

3   The progressive Christian reading groups featured in this book reflect a form of lived religion that exemplifies a "text-based cosmology" (Klassen 2006, 814). The use of texts to differentiate themselves from other forms of Christianity is not a new tactic for liberal Protestants. In examining early twentieth-century liberal Protestants and their use of texts to access therapeutic culture, Pamela Klassen shows that texts provided a venue for liberal Protestants to "challenge their tradition and each other," thereby advocating a form of rationality that aligns with historical biblical exegesis and scientific objectivity (2006, 816). As a result, they were able to view their model of therapeutic culture as superior to other forms of Christianity.

4   This observation about the social nature of church studies resembles Eva Keller's findings in her ethnographic study of Seventh-Day Adventists in Madagascar. Keller observed that her interlocutors took a Socratic approach to reading the Bible in which they regarded study as an active "reflection and dialogue" rather than the consumption of "ready-made doctrine" (Keller 2005, 114).

5   In her study of a Unitarian Universalist reading group, Erin A. Smith argues that the group's interpretations of Elaine Pagels's *Beyond Belief: The Secret Gospel of Thomas* (2003) and Dan Brown's *The Da Vinci Code* (2003) provided "a usable religious past," through which they differentiated themselves both spiritually and politically from evangelicals (Smith 2015, 277).

6   The Jesus Seminar is housed at the Westar Institute, a nonprofit organization at Willamette University in Oregon that is dedicated to fostering research in religious studies and promoting biblical literacy. The organization's mission statement claims no religious affiliation and does not promote a specific theological perspective; however, many of its supporters and members of the board of directors can be classified as liberal and progressive Christians. Furthermore, early publications of the seminar position their work in contrast to conservative denominations, which they describe as "Latter-day inquisitors among Southern Baptists and Lutheran groups" on a witch-hunt (Funk, Hoover, and the Jesus Seminar 1993, 35).

7   Many members of the Jesus Seminar have also published popular texts for a lay audience (e.g., Funk 1996; Hoover et al. 2004).

8   Spong's title, *Sins of Scripture*, bears a striking resemblance to feminist biblical scholar Phyllis Trible's foundational work, *Texts of Terror* (1984), which examines biblical narratives depicting violence toward and exploitation of women. While Spong does not explicitly reference Trible's work in *Sins of Scripture*, he acknowledges her contributions to his thinking about women's experiences within scripture in his earlier work, *Born of a Woman: A Bishop Rethinks the Birth of Jesus* (1992, xii). Trible limits her use of "texts of terror" to those that directly engage the experiences of women, however, other scholars have extended the category in a manner similar to Spong (for a recent discussion of the ongoing impact of Trible's work in the field of feminist criticism see Graybill 2021).

9   Drawing from ancient sources such as Celsus's second-century anti-Christian polemics, the feminist biblical scholar Jane Schaberg has revitalized the theory of

Mary's rape (1987, 165–69). Biblical scholars usually locate the virgin birth in the context of Greco-Roman antiquity. While academic arguments support Spong's omission of the birth narratives as a whole, what is more telling is his substitution of the orthodox narrative with an unorthodox version that he supports with gnostic, extracanonical texts and an appeal to therapeutic importance.

The virgin birth plays an important role in the development of progressive Christian perspectives and is one of the most frequently referenced examples of the necessity for scholarly hermeneutics. One could argue that it serves as a litmus test for progressive Christian beliefs. In short, progressive Christians follow scholars who note that the Gospel of Matthew's use of the term *virgin* in reference to Isaiah 7:14 (Matt. 1:23) is a mistranslation that occurred during the compilation of the Septuagint. Whereas in the King James Bible Isaiah 7:14 reads, "Therefore the Lord himself shall give you a sign; Behold, a virgin shall conceive, and bear a son, and shall call his name Immanuel," the New Revised Standard Version, preferred by progressive Christians, states, "Therefore the Lord himself shall give you a sign. Behold a young woman shall conceive and bear a son and shall call his name Immanuel."

10 A thorough discussion of the dialectical relationship between Latour's concepts of purification and hybridity as it applies to modern Protestant frameworks is found in Webb Keane's *Christian Moderns* (2007).

CHAPTER 3. DECONVERSION

1 In his work on postevangelicals in the American South, Terry Shoemaker explores how sports serve as a vehicle that former evangelicals use to navigate their deconversion from the pervasive Christian culture: sports link them to the social world from which they departed. Like Monica, Shoemaker's interlocutors report their departure from religion as therapeutic or, as Shoemaker terms it, possessing a quality of "rehabilitative hope." Central to their deconversion narrative is a focus on sports as a marker of southern identity that is conceptually adjacent to religious identities. By framing their narrative in this manner, former evangelicals are able to identify a starting point for their initial questioning of religious affiliation, retain a connection to otherwise fractured familial relationships, and imagine possibilities for social engagement through athletic activism (Shoemaker 2019).

2 As Jonathan Z. Smith explains, the delineation of a proximate other is embedded in the foundations of Christianity. The writings of the apostle Paul point to the early origins of the category, and Christians have bestowed otherness on other Christians, or, on some occasions, presumed near-neighbors, such as Judaism and Islam, which are often grouped together with Christianity under the umbrella of Abrahamic faiths (Smith 2004, 276; see Hughes 2013 for a discussion of the problematics of the category, Abrahamic religions).

3 Living the Questions, "LtQ's Jesus Jars Sports Illustrated, Angers Portland Radio Listeners," January 28, 2011, http://livingthequestionsonline.wordpress.com.

4   Strong atheism, also known as positive or explicit atheism, refers to an atheist who has made a conscious decision to reject theism.

5   For example, one of the book study sessions at West Hill featured clips from the documentary *Jesus Camp* (2006), a film that follows children who attend a charismatic Pentecostal summer camp. Book study group members were horrified at the theology and political activism of the documentary's subjects, especially the inclusion of children in antiabortion activism and proselytizing. While the film contains some misconceptions (it looks at a specific brand of charismatic Christianity and implies that it is representative of American evangelism writ large), it contributes to views that many progressive Christians hold about their Protestant proximate other.

6   The fact that the majority of the participants in this study originated from mainline or Roman Catholic churches can be attributed to the fact that this research was conducted in Canada, which by and large has fewer evangelical and conservative Christian churches than the United States. The practice of defining oneself in opposition to, and competition with, another religious community has a long historical precedent, especially in the province of Ontario where historically Francophone Roman Catholics and Anglophone Protestants struggled for cultural dominance and recognition. The construction of a Protestant proximate other is prevalent, perhaps even more so, within American progressive Christianity. It appears that the progressive Christians in this study have followed suit, despite their location in Canada, where a Protestant-Catholic divide might be expected in place of a conservative-liberal or evangelical-mainline one. The churches featured in this book used materials that came from American sources, and the majority of the authors that progressive Christians read are American. Thus, the churches featured in this study have inherited from these sources a discursive framework that assumes a divide between progressive and conservative Christianity.

7   Anglo-Canadians often define themselves in contrast to Americans. Within the Canadian political landscape is anxiety that American-style evangelicalism could emerge from the grassroots of the Reform Party and the Canadian Alliance, two now-defunct, right-wing populist political parties. Marci McDonald's *The Armageddon Factor: The Rise of Christian Nationalism in Canada* (2010) calls attention to these fears. While evangelicals in Canada share theological and ethical attitudes with their American counterparts, the Canadians engage in political and public discourses in a less overt manner and lack influence within Canadian politics (see Bean 2014; cf. Reimer 2003).

8   The emerging church movement offers an interesting point of comparison. Critiques by adherents of this movement often focus upon the beliefs and practices of the evangelical church. As Harrold explains, the desire for "a more authentic ontology [is] expressed in reaction to an ecclesial context deemed inauthentic" because of its engagement with, and accommodation to, consumer culture and the complacency of a middle-class lifestyle (2006, 82). In terms of deconversion, the emerging church appears to be deconverting from the organizational struc-

tures, worship styles, and modernist worldviews of the evangelical church in favor of what emerging church adherents deem to be a postmodernist, organic form of Christianity. For example, the Christian author, Shane Claiborne (well known for his book *Jesus for President*, and the subsequent documentary film of the same name) criticizes the evangelical church not for its doctrines of biblical literacy but its refusal to take what he sees as Jesus's message of radical love literally. This example suggests that the criticism directed at origins is also aimed at the recent past, that is, the previous generation of evangelicals.

For progressive Christians an interest in origins has entailed a focus on biblical criticism. They are less likely to critique past generations of mainline Protestantism. Rather, their criticism is of the early and medieval church, along with critiques directed at the contemporary Christian Right. At times progressive Christians do express personal anger at specific authoritative figures in their own lives: ministers, Sunday school teachers, parental figures, and former spouses.

9 At the progressive Christian churches featured in this book, few people wore what might traditionally be considered Sunday best. The dress code was casual but well put together.

CHAPTER 4. *STILL, ALREADY, YET*

1 For an in-depth discussion of contemporary evangelical eschatological and apocalyptic thought, see Boyer (1992), Frykholm (2004), Moorhead (1999), and Sutton (2014).

2 While people often assume the universality of linear time, anthropologists have challenged it since Durkheim's work on aboriginal Australians. For example, a study by Aleksandar Janca and Clothilde Bullen (2003) revealed that Australian aboriginals understand time as multidimensional and inseparable. Likewise, the Assyriologist Stefan F. Maul (2008) offers a convincing argument that the ancient Mesopotamians saw themselves as "backing into the future" so that they moved through time with their focus on the distant past. Contemporary political depictions of time as linear emerge along with modern Western conceptions of the nation, which provides an identity rooted in the past while simultaneously progressing (see Anderson 1983; Hobsbawm and Ranger 1983).

3 The insistence on God's agency accounts for the ongoing controversy surrounding evolution among fundamentalist Christians. To question God's exclusive role in creation implicitly threatens temporal assumptions concerning the incarnation and the apocalypse (see Bialecki 2009, 111). Suggestions that creation occurred apart from the hand of God challenge the likelihood that God will direct the end times. As many scholars of conservative and fundamentalist Christianity (e.g., Frykholm 2004; Boyer 1992; Moorhead 1999) have shown, beliefs about the end time are directly related to the ways that contemporary Christians position themselves socially, economically, and politically in the world (see Harding 1994; Redding 2021).

4 Likewise, prophetic rhetoric informed the civil rights movement (see Chappell 2004). Many members of the progressive Christian communities participated in the civil rights movement, attending protest marches and other cultural efforts of the 1960s and 1970s.

5 A similar observation has been made with regard to the dismissal of climate change on the part of evangelical Christians who anticipate that the Rapture, or end times, is imminent (see, for example, Barker and Bearce 2013; Jones, Cox, and Navarro-Rivera 2014; Veldman 2019; Zaleha and Szasz 2015).

6 The United Church of Christ should not be confused with the United Church of Canada, which is discussed frequently in this book. Both George Street and West Hill are congregations within the United Church of Canada. The United Church of Christ is based in the United States. It was founded in 1957 through the merger of the Congregational Christian Church and the Evangelical and Reformed Church (see Gunneman 1977; Walker 2005; Zikmund 1987). The denomination defines itself as "united and uniting," meaning that it focuses its energies on ecumenism, multiculturalism, accessibility, affirmation for the LGBTQ+ community, and justice (Cavalcanti 2010, 2). The "still speaking" campaign does not presume that God speaks literally through scripture.

7 Conservative and evangelical traditions frequently use *stumbling block* to refer to people or activities that might lead one into sin. The origin of the term is biblical. In the book of Ezekiel, for example, idols are identified as stumbling blocks that condemn those who worship them (see Ezek. 3:20, 14:3–7). In the Gospel of Matthew, Jesus identifies as a stumbling block Peter's attempt to rebuke Jesus for his explanation of his impending crucifixion (see Matt. 16:23). In several of his letters, Paul admonishes Christians to be careful that they do not themselves serve as a stumbling block to other believers or potential ones (see Rom. 11:9 and 14:3; 1 Cor. 1:23 and 8:8; and 2 Cor. 6:3).

8 Spong's publication *Eternal Life: A New Vision—Beyond Religion, Beyond Theism, Beyond Heaven and Hell* (2009) is an exception and addresses questions concerning what happens after death. Although Spong visited Holy Cross Lutheran Church in 2010 and spent a weekend lecturing on the material from *Eternal Life*, few members of that congregation, and no one in any of the other congregations I studied, had read the book. Several confided to me that they found Spong's work on this topic to be difficult to follow and not relevant to their day-to-day lives. One member reported that he found the text—even though it claims to move "beyond theism"—to be too theistic in its understanding of life and death.

9 Hedy's reference to the fact that there will not "be anybody here" concerned her disbelief in life after death; she did not want a traditional funeral in which the dead person transitions through ritual to the afterlife. In September 2021, Hedy passed away peacefully at the age of 101. Her obituary notes that she lived independently right up to the end and donated her body to science. She remained an active member of West Hill United Church and supported Gretta Vosper throughout her "heresy trial" (see the epilogue).

10 The liturgical theologian Michael Joncas, a Catholic priest, wrote "On Eagles' Wings" in 1979. The lyrics are based roughly on Psalm 91 and Isaiah 40:31. The song is a popular choice for funerals in Roman Catholic, mainline Protestant, and evangelical communities. It was performed at many of the funerals and memorial services for the victims of the September 11, 2001, attacks on the World Trade Center in New York.

11 Substitutionary atonement or vicarious atonement points to Jesus's death as a substitution for the otherwise mandated deaths of Christian adherents. Rooted in Paul's letters and theological elaboration on the part of Anselm of Canterbury, this model of salvation emphasizes the impossibility of humans to make reparation to God because of their sinfulness and, as a result, the inevitable damnation of all humans. In this model, humans can escape punishment through Jesus who is both God and human and alone is able to pay human debts. In its contemporary form, this model is often called penal substitution an envisioned in legal terms with God as a righteous judge who must seek punishment when his law is broken (see Beilby and Eddy 2006, 14–18). The penal substitutionary view is the common view of salvation among Reformed and Calvinist Christianity or the "heart and soul of an evangelical view of atonement" (Schreiner 2006, 67).

12 The wording has since been updated and now reads: "Ever wondered what religion you are? Are you sure your faith is the best choice for you? Take our religion quiz to find out! Answer 20 questions about your concept of God, the afterlife, human nature, and more, and Belief-O-Matic® will tell you what religion or spiritual path (if any) best suits your beliefs." To access the Belief-O-Matic survey, go to http://www.beliefnet.com.

13 The religion scholar Wilfred Cantwell Smith's books, *Belief and History* (1977) and *Faith and Belief* (1979), remain influential genealogical and etymological analyses of belief in the Western world. According to Smith, both literalism and an overarching uncertainty concerning the accuracy of a belief statement taint the understanding of belief, such that belief refers to a conviction, as in "the holding of certain ideas," that can then be judged true or false, for example, the belief that Earth is flat (see W. Smith 1979, 12).

In Christian theology, belief often corresponds with ultimate questions about the existence of God or miraculous events. In this schema, belief is proffered as the means through which one acquires salvation (access to heaven), an understanding promoted by Pascal's infamous wager (see Lopez 1998, 23). Smith asserts that the presumption that belief indicates something held to be true is a more recent development. Initially, *to believe* meant "to hold dear," a term originating from the medieval Anglo-Saxon *leof* or *liof* (dear). This definition is retained when one compares *believe* to a similar English word *beloved*, which stems from *lufu* (love) (Smith 1979, 105–106; Lopez 1998, 22). In a similar vein, Smith locates the Latin word *credo* as derived from the root *cor* or *cordis* (heart), and translates it as "I set my heart on" or "I give my heart to." In Smith's eyes, creedal statements originally served as declarations of affiliation or allegiance rather than propositional belief (Smith 1979: 76).

Many of the authors read by progressive Christians have popularized Smith's ideas. Conversations and sermons delivered at progressive churches often reference the idea that absolute assent to Christian tenets is a corruption.

14 Several influential anthropologists of Christianity have taken up a far more developed and theoretically nuanced discussion of the anthropology of ethics and applications to the study of religion. See, for example, Robbins 2012, 2016, 2018; Daswani 2013, 2016, 2019; and Bialecki 2016, 2017b).

15 Certain passages of scripture are especially unpopular among progressive Christians, in particular those that do not conform to modern, liberal, or inclusive moral perspectives (e.g., passages that appear to reprimand homosexuality, condone war, support violence against women and children, or advocate anti-semitism). For an in-depth popular discussion of these types of texts, see the 2005 book by Spong, *The Sins of Scripture: Exposing the Bible's Texts of Hate to Reveal God's Love*.

16 The context of our conversation and Jerry's tone suggested that yippies is a repulsive rather than pleasurable experience. I interpreted his use of this word as an alternative expression of the uncomfortable nervousness associated with heebie-jeebies.

17 In "Back from the Future," Groys outlines how contemporary postcommunist artistic movements in eastern Europe sought—not unlike progressive Christians—to delineate the identity of an other (Groys 2003, 327).

CONCLUSION

1 While in this initial description, Drescher does not explicitly provide an example of how critics see the nones as engaged in commercialized religious practices, elsewhere in her book she describes popular religious and spiritual books and the therapeutic impact of the Oprah Winfrey phenomenon as epitomes of commercialism and religious consumer culture (Drescher 2016, 57–58; see also Lofton 2011; Carrette and King 2005).

EPILOGUE

1 Vosper was not the only United Church of Canada minister to make such declarations around this time. In 2012, Ken Gallinger, a retired United Church minister, gave up his ministerial credentials. A year later, Bob Ripley, another retired United Church minister, published *Life beyond Belief: A Preacher's Deconversion* (2014), which detailed his loss of faith. He was asked to give up his status as a minister. No longer permitted to use the term *retired*, Ripley, who had served for decades, must state he is a "former minister" (see Krotz 2016; Milne 2016b).

REFERENCES

Adams, James R. 1996. *So You Think You're Not Religious?: A Thinking Person's Guide to the Church*. Cambridge, MA: Cowley.
Adler, Mike. 2018. "Atheist Minister Gretta Vosper Is Free to Continue Her West Hill Work: United Church Announcement Cancels Looming 'Heresy Trial.'" *Toronto.com*, November 23. www.toronto.com.
Aitken, Johan. 1991. "Northrop Frye: An Appreciation." In Northrop Frye, *The Double Vision: Language and Meaning in Religion*, xi–xvi. Toronto: University of Toronto Press.
Airhart, Phyllis D. 2013. *A Church with the Soul of a Nation: Making and Remaking the United Church of Canada*. Montreal-Kingston: McGill-Queen's University Press.
Airhart, Phyllis D., and Roger C. Hutchinson. 1996. *Christianizing the Social Order: A Founding Vision of the United Church of Canada*. Waterloo, ON: Wilfred Laurier University Press.
Albanese, Catherine. 2007. *A Republic of Mind and Spirit: A Cultural History of American Metaphysical Religion*. New Haven, CT: Yale University Press.
Alumkal, Antony. 2017. *Paranoid Science: The Christian Right's War on Reality*. New York: New York University Press.
Amarasingam, Amarnath, ed. 2010. *Religion and the New Atheism: A Critical Appraisal*. Leiden: Brill.
Ammerman, Nancy T. 2016. "Lived Religion as an Emerging Field: An Assessment of Its Contours and Frontiers." *Nordic Journal of Religion and Society* 29 (2): 83–99.
Anderson, Benedict. 1983. *Imagined Communities: Reflections on the Origin and Spread of Nationalism*. London: Verso.
Arnal, William. 2005. *The Symbolic Jesus: Historical Scholarship, Judaism and the Construction of Contemporary Identity*. London: Equinox.
Asad, Talal. 1993. *Genealogies of Religion: Discipline and Reasons of Power in Christianity and Islam*. Baltimore: John Hopkins University Press.
Asad, Talal. 2003. *Formations of the Secular: Christianity, Islam, Modernity*. Stanford, CA: Stanford University Press.
Austin, Diane J. 1981. "Born Again . . . and Again and Again: Communitas and Social Change among Jamaican Pentecostalists." *Journal of Anthropological Research* 37 (3): 226–46.
Austin, J. L. 1962. *How to Do Things with Words*. New York: Oxford University Press.
Baggett, Jerome P. 2019. *The Varieties of Nonreligious Experience: Atheism in American Culture*. New York: New York University Press.

Baker, Joseph O., and Buster G. Smith. 2015. *American Secularism: Cultural Contours of Nonreligious Belief Systems*. New York: New York University Press.

Barber, Karin. 2007. *The Anthropology of Texts, Persons and Publics: Oral and Written Culture in Africa and Beyond*. New York: Cambridge University Press.

Barbour, John D. 1994. *Versions of Deconversion: Autobiography and the Loss of Faith*. Charlottesville: University of Virginia Press.

Barker, David C., and David H. Bearce. 2013. "End-Times Theology, the Shadow of the Future, and Public Resistance to Addressing Global Climate Change." *Political Research Quarterly* 66 (2): 267–79.

Bartel, Rebecca C. 2016. "Giving Is Believing: Credit and Christmas in Colombia." *Journal of the American Academy of Religion* 84 (4): 1006–28.

Barton, Carlin A., and Daniel Boyarin. 2016. *Imagine No Religion: How Modern Abstractions Hide Ancient Realities*. New York: Fordham University Press.

Baudrillard, Jean. 1994 [1978]. *Simulacra and Simulation*. Ann Arbor: University of Michigan Press.

Bayart, Jean-François. 2005. *The Illusion of Cultural Identity*. Translated by Steven Rendall, Janet Roitman, Cynthia Schoch, and Jonathan Derrick. Chicago: University of Chicago Press.

Beaman, Lori G., and Steven Tomlins, eds. 2015. *Atheist Identities: Spaces and Social Contexts*. New York: Springer.

Bean, Lydia. 2014. *The Politics of Evangelical Identity: Local Churches and Partisan Divides in the United States and Canada*. Princeton, NJ: Princeton University Press.

Beatty, Andrew. 2012. "Return to the Field." *Anthropology of This Century*, no. 4 (May). http://aotcpress.com.

Bebbington, David W. 1989. *Evangelicalism in Modern Britain: A History from the 1730s to the 1980s*. London: Unwin Hyman.

Beilby, James K., and Paul R. Eddy. 2006. "The Atonement: An Introduction." In *The Nature of the Atonement: Four Views*, edited by James K. Beilby and Paul R. Eddy, 9–21. Downers Grove, IL: InterVarsity Press.

Bell, Catherine M. 2002. "'The Chinese Believe in Spirits': Belief and Believing in the Study of Religion." In *Radical Interpretation in Religion*, edited by Nancy K. Frankenberry, 100–16. New York: Cambridge University Press.

Bell, Catherine. 2009. *Ritual Theory, Ritual Practice*. New York: Oxford University Press.

Bender, Courtney. 2010. *The New Metaphysicals: Spirituality and the American Religious Imagination*. Chicago: University of Chicago Press.

Bender, Courtney. 2012. "Practicing Religions." In *The Cambridge Companion to Religious Studies*, edited by Robert A. Orsi, 273–95. Cambridge: Cambridge University Press.

Berger, Peter L. 1979. *The Heretical Imperative: Contemporary Possibilities of Religious Affirmation*. New York: Anchor Press.

Berlinerblau, Jacques. 2001. "Toward a Sociology of Heresy, Orthodoxy, and Doxa." *History of Religions* 40 (4): 327–51.

Berlinerblau, Jacques. 2012. *How to Be Secular: A Call to Arms for Religious Freedom*. New York: Houghton Mifflin Harcourt.

Bhabha, Homi K. 1990. *Nation and Narration*. New York: Routledge.
Bialecki, Jon. 2009. "Disjuncture, Continental Philosophy's New 'Political Paul,' and the Question of Progressive Christianity in a Southern California Third Wave Church." *American Ethnologist* 36 (1): 110–23.
Bialecki, Jon. 2011. "No Caller ID for the Soul: Demonization, Charisms, and the Unstable Subject of Protestant Language Ideology." *Anthropological Quarterly* 84 (3): 679–703.
Bialecki, Jon. 2014. "Does God Exist in Methodological Atheism? On Tanya Luhrmann's *When God Talks Back* and Bruno Latour." *Anthropology of Consciousness* 25 (1): 32–52.
Bialecki, Jon. 2016. "The Genealogy of Ethical Life: Jon Bialecki on Webb Keane's *Ethical Life*." *Marginalia*, September 24. http://marginalia.lareviewofbooks.org.
Bialecki, Jon. 2017a. *A Diagram for Fire: Miracles and Variation in an American Charismatic Movement*. Berkeley: University of California Press.
Bialecki, Jon. 2017b. "Eschatology, Ethics, and Ethnos: Resentment and Christian Nationalism in the Anthropology of Christianity." *Religion and Society: Advances in Research* 8 (1): 42–61.
Bibby, Reginald W. 2017. *Resilient Gods: Being Pro-religious, Low Religious, or No Religious in Canada*. Vancouver: University of British Columbia Press.
Bielo, James S. 2008. "On the Failure of 'Meaning': Bible Reading in the Anthropology of Christianity." *Culture and Religion* 9 (1): 1–21.
Bielo, James S. 2009a. "The 'Emerging Church' in America: Notes on the interaction of Christianities." *Religion* 39 (3): 219–32.
Bielo, James S., ed. 2009b. *The Social Life of Scriptures: Cross-Cultural Perspectives on Biblicism*. New Brunswick, NJ: Rutgers University Press.
Bielo, James S. 2009c. *Words upon the Word: An Ethnography of Evangelical Group Bible Study*. New York: New York University Press.
Bielo, James S. 2011a. *Emerging Evangelicals: Faith, Modernity and the Desire for Authenticity*. New York: New York University Press.
Bielo, James S. 2011b. "'How Much of This Is Promise?': God as Sincere Speaker in Evangelical Bible Reading." *Anthropological Quarterly* 84 (3): 631–54.
Bielo, James S. 2016. "Creationist History-Making: Producing a Heterodox Past." In *Lost City, Found Pyramid: Understanding Alternative Archaeologies and Pseudoscientific Practices*, edited by Jeb J. Card and David S. Anderson, 81–101. Tuscaloosa: University of Alabama Press.
Bielo, James S. 2018. *Ark Encounter: The Making of a Creationist Theme Park*. New York: New York University Press.
Bielo, James S. 2020. "The Materiality of Myth: Authorizing Fundamentalism at Ark Encounter." In *Christian Tourist Attractions, Mythmaking, and Identity Formation*, edited by Erin Roberts and Jennifer Eyl, 43–57. London: Bloomsbury.
Bigelow, Anna. 2019. "Lived Secularism: Studies in India and Turkey." *Journal of the American Academy of Religion* 87 (3): 725–64.
Blanes, Ruy L. 2006. "The Atheist Anthropologist: Believers and Non-believers in Anthropological Fieldwork." *Social Anthropology* 14 (2): 223–34.

Bledstein, Burton J. 2001. Introduction to *The Middling Sorts: Explorations in the History of the American Middle Class*, edited by Burton J. Bledstein and Robert D. Johnston, 1–25. New York: Routledge.
Bloome, David, and Erine Theodorou. 1985. "Reading, Writing, and Learning in the Classroom." *Peabody Journal of Education* 62 (3): 20–43.
Bloome, David, and Judith Green. 2002. "Directions in the Sociolinguistic Study of Reading." In *Handbook of Reading Research*, edited by P. David Pearson, 395–421. Mahwah, NJ: Lawrence Erlbaum Associates.
Borg, Marcus J. 2001. *Reading the Bible Again for the First Time: Taking the Bible Seriously but Not Literally*. New York: Harper Collins.
Borg, Marcus J. 2003. *The Heart of Christianity: Rediscovering a Life of Faith*. New York: Harper Collins.
Bourdieu, Pierre. 1977. "The Economics of Linguistic Exchanges." *Social Science Information* 16 (6): 645–68.
Bourdieu, Pierre. 1990. *In Other Words: Essays toward a Reflexive Sociology*. Palo Alto, CA: Stanford University Press.
Bourdieu, Pierre. 1991. *Language and Symbolic Power*. Cambridge, MA: Harvard University Press.
Boyarin, Jonathan, ed. 1993a. *The Ethnography of Reading*. Berkley: University of California Press.
Boyarin, Jonathan. 1993b. "Voices Around the Text: *The Ethnography of Reading* at Mesivta Tifereth Jerusalem." In *The Ethnography of Reading*, edited by Jonathan Boyarin, 212–237. Berkley: University of California Press.
Boyer, Paul. 1992. *When Time Shall Be No More: Prophecy Belief in Modern American Culture*. Cambridge, MA: Harvard University Press.
Brooks, E. Marshall. 2018. *Disenchanted Lives: Apostasy and Ex-Mormonism among the Latter-day Saints*. New Brunswick, NJ: Rutgers University Press.
Brown, Callum G. 2009. *The Death of Christian Britain: Understanding Secularisation, 1800–2000*. New York: Routledge.
Brown, Callum G. 2012. *Religion and the Demographic Revolution: Women and Secularisation in Canada, Ireland, UK and USA Since the 1960s*. Woodbridge, UK: Boydell Press.
Brown, Candy Gunther. 2004. *The Word in the World: Evangelical Writing, Publishing, and Reading in America, 1789–1880*. Chapel Hill: University of North Carolina Press.
Brown, Delwin. 2008. *What Does a Progressive Christian Believe?: A Guide for the Searching, the Open, and the Curious*. New York: Church Publishing.
Brown, Karen McCarthy. 2002. "Writing about 'the Other,' Revisited." In *Personal Knowledge and Beyond: Reshaping the Ethnography of Religion*, edited by James V. Spikard, J. Shawn Landres, and Meredith B. McGuire, 127–33. New York: New York University Press.
Bruce, Steve. 2011. *Secularization: In Defense of an Unfashionable Theory*. New York: Oxford University Press.
Bullock, Josh. 2018. "The Sociology of the Sunday Assembly: 'Belonging without Believing' in a Post-Christian Context." PhD diss., Kingston University, London.

Burke, Tony, ed. 2017. *Fakes, Forgeries, and Fictions: Writing Ancient and Modern Christian Apocrypha: Proceedings from the 2015 York Christian Apocrypha Symposium.* Eugene, OR: Cascade.

Calhoun, Craig, Mark Juergensmeyer, and Jonathan VanAntwerpen, eds. 2011. *Rethinking Secularism.* Oxford: Oxford University Press.

Campbell, Heidi, and Ruth Tsuria, eds. 2021. *Digital Religion: Understanding Religious Practice in New Media Worlds.* New York: Routledge.

Cannell, Fenella. 2005. "The Christianity of Anthropology." *Journal of the Royal Anthropological Institute* 11 (2): 335–56.

Cannell, Fenella. 2006. "Reading as Gift and Writing as Theft." In *The Anthropology of Christianity*, edited by Fenella Cannell, 134–62. Durham, NC: Duke University Press.

Carrette, Jeremy, and Richard King. 2005. *Selling Spirituality: The Silent Takeover of Religion.* New York: Routledge.

Carwana, Brian. 2021. "Evangelicals, the Liberal State, and Canada's Family Values Debates: The Struggle to Shape Selves." PhD diss., University of Toronto.

Casanova, José. 1994. *Public Religions in the Modern World.* Chicago: University of Chicago Press.

Castanheira, Maria Lucia, Teresa Crawford, Carol N. Dixon, and Judith L. Green. 2000. "Interactional Ethnography: An Approach to Studying the Social Construction of Literate Practices." *Linguistics and Education* 11 (4): 353–400.

Cavalcanti, H. B. 2010. *The United Church of Christ in the Shenandoah Valley: Liberal Church, Traditional Congregation.* New York: Rowman and Littlefield.

Chappell, David L. 2004. *A Stone of Hope: Prophetic Religion and the Death of Jim Crow.* Chapel Hill: University of North Carolina Press.

Chaves, Mark. 2006. "All Creatures Great and Small: Megachurches in Context." *Review of Religious Research* 47 (4): 329–46.

Chidester, David. 1996. *Savage Systems: Colonialism and Comparative Religion in Southern Africa.* Charlottesville: University of Virginia Press.

Chidester, David. 2013. *Empire of Religion: Imperialism and Comparative Religion.* Chicago: University of Chicago Press.

Cimino, Richard, and Christopher Smith. 2015. *Atheist Awakening: Secular Activism and Community in America.* New York: Oxford University Press.

Clarke, Brian. 1996. "English-Speaking Canada from 1854." In *A Concise History of Christianity in Canada*, edited by Terrence Murphy and Roberto Perin, 261–360. New York: Oxford University Press.

Clarke, Brian, and Stuart Macdonald. 2017. *Leaving Christianity: Changing Allegiances in Canada since 1945.* Montreal-Kingston: McGill-Queen's University Press.

Clifford, James, and George E. Marcus, eds. 1986. *Writing Culture: The Poetics and Politics of Ethnography.* Berkeley: University of California Press.

Cobb, John B., Jr., ed. 2008. *Resistance: The New Role of Progressive Christians.* Louisville, KY: Westminster John Knox Press.

Coffman, Elesha J. 2013. *The Christian Century and the Rise of the Protestant Mainline.* New York: Oxford University Press.

Coleman, Simon. 2003. "Continuous Conversion: The Rhetoric, Practice, and Rhetorical Practice of Charismatic Protestant Conversion." In *The Anthropology of Religious Conversion*, edited by Andrew Buckser and Stephen D. Glazier, 15–28. New York: Rowman and Littlefield.

Coleman, Simon. 2006. "The Multi-Sited Ethnographer." In *Critical Journeys: The Making of Anthropologists*, edited by Geert De Neve and Maya Unnithan-Kumar, 31–46. Burlington, VT: Ashgate.

Cook, Ramsay. 1985. *The Regenerators: Social Criticism in Late Victorian English Canada*. Toronto: University of Toronto Press.

Cooperman, Alan, Gregory A. Smith, and Stefan S. Cornibert. 2015. "US Public Becoming Less Religious." Pew Research Center, November 3. www.pewforum.org.

Coser, Lewis A. 1964. *The Functions of Social Conflict*. New York: Free Press.

Cottee, Simon. 2015. *The Apostates: When Muslims Leave Islam*. London: C. Hurst.

Cotter, Christopher R. 2020. *The Critical Study of Non-Religion: Discourse, Identification and Locality*. London: Bloomsbury.

Crapanzano, Vincent. 2000. *Serving the Word: Literalism in America from the Pulpit to the Bench*. New York: New Press.

Crossan, John Dominic. 2007. *God and Empire: Jesus against Rome, Then and Now*. New York: HarperCollins.

Crossley, James. 2012. *Jesus in an Age of Neoliberalism: Quests, Scholarship and Ideology*. Durham, UK: Acumen.

Crossley, James. 2015. *Jesus and the Chaos of History: Redirecting the Life of the Historical Jesus*. Oxford: Oxford University Press.

Crossley, James. 2021. "The End of Apocalypticism: From Burton Mack's Jesus to North American Liberalism." *Journal for the Study of the Historical Jesus* 19 (2): 171–90.

Darnton, Robert. 2002. "What Is the History of Books?" In *The Book History Reader*, edited by David Finkelstein and Alistair McCleery, 9–26. New York: Routledge.

Daswani, Girish. 2013. "On Christianity and Ethics: Rupture as Ethical Practice in Ghanaian Pentecostalism." *American Ethnologist* 40 (3): 467–79.

Daswani, Girish. 2016. "A Prophet but Not for Profit: Ethical Value and Character in Ghanaian Pentecostalism." *Journal of the Royal Anthropological Institute* 22 (1): 108–26.

Daswani, Girish. 2019. "Ordinary Ethics and Its Temporalities: The Christian God and the 2016 Ghanaian Elections." *Anthropological Theory* 19 (3): 323–40.

Davidman, Lynn, and Arthur L. Greil. 2007. "Characters in Search of a Script: The Exit Narratives of Formerly Ultra-Orthodox Jews." *Journal for the Scientific Study of Religion* 46 (2): 201–16.

Davie, Grace. 1994. *Religion in Britain since 1945: Believing without Belonging*. Oxford: Blackwell.

Davie, Jody Shapiro. 1995. *Women in the Presence: Constructing Community and Seeking Spirituality in Mainline Protestantism*. Philadelphia: University of Pennsylvania Press.

Day, Abby. 2010. "Propositions and Performativity: Relocating Belief to the Social." *Culture and Religion* 11 (1): 9–30.

Day, Abby. 2011. *Believing in Belonging: Belief and Social Identity in the Modern World*. New York: Oxford University Press.
Delehanty, Jack, Penny Edgell, and Evan Stewart. 2019. "Christian America? Secularized Evangelical Discourse and the Boundaries of National Belonging." *Social Forces* 97 (3): 1283–1306.
Dempsey, Amy, and Jim Rankin. 2016. "'Sad Day' for United Church, Says Atheist Minister Gretta Vosper." *Toronto Star*, September 8. www.thestar.com.
Denham, Robert D., ed. 2003. *Northrop Frye's Notebooks and Lectures on the Bible and Other Religious Texts*. Vol. 13. Toronto: University of Toronto Press.
Devlin-Glass, Frances. 2001. "More Than a Reader and Less Than a Critic: Literary Authority and Women's Book-Discussion Groups." *Women's Studies International Forum* 24 (5): 571–85.
DiManno, Rosie. 2018. "By Swallowing Its Opposition to the Minister Who Doesn't Believe in God, the United Church Shows Just How Irrelevant It Is." *Toronto Star*, November 11. www.thestar.com .
Dochuk, Darren. 2011. *From Bible Belt to Sunbelt: Plain-Folk Religion, Grassroots Politics, and the Rise of Evangelical Conservatism*. New York: W. W. Norton.
Dorrien, Gary. 2001. "Berger: Theology and Sociology." In *Peter Berger and the Study of Religion*, edited by Linda Woodhead with Paul Heelas and David Martin. 26–40. New York: Routledge.
Dorrien, Gary. 1995. *Soul in Society: The Making and Renewal of Social Christianity*. Minneapolis: Fortress Press.
Dorrien, Gary. 2006. *The Making of American Liberal Theology: Crisis, Irony, and Postmodernity 1950–2005*. Louisville, KY: Westminster John Knox Press.
Dorrien, Gary. 2009. *Social Ethics in the Making: Interpreting an American Tradition*. Malden, MA: Wiley-Blackwell.
Douglas, Mary. 1982. "The Effects of Modernization on religious Change." *Daedalus* 111 (1): 1–19.
Drescher, Elizabeth. 2016. *Choosing Our Religion: The Spiritual Lives of America's Nones*. New York: Oxford University Press.
Droge, A. J. 2008. "Cynics or Luddites? Excavating Q Studies." *Studies in Religion/Sciences Religieuses* 37 (2): 249–69.
Dubuisson, Daniel. 2003. *The Western Construction of Religion: Myths, Knowledge, and Ideology*. Baltimore: John Hopkins University Press.
Dudley, Kathryn Marie. 1999. "(Dis)locating the Middle Class." *Anthropology Newsletter,* 40 (4): 1, 4.
Edles, Laura Desfor. 2013. "Contemporary Progressive Christianity and Its Symbolic Ramifications." *Cultural Sociology* 7 (1): 3–22.
Ehrenreich, Barbara. 1990. *Fear of Falling: The Inner Life of the Middle Class*. New York: Harper.
Elisha, Omri. 2008. "Faith beyond Belief: Evangelical Protestant Conceptions of Faith and the Resonance of Anti-humanism." *Social Analysis* 52 (1): 56–78.

Elisha, Omri. 2011. *Moral Ambition: Mobilization and Social Outreach in Evangelical Megachurches*. Berkeley: University of California Press.
Emberley, Peter. 2002. *Divine Hunger: Canadians on a Spiritual Walkabout*. Toronto: HarperCollins.
Engelke, Matthew. 2004. "Text and Performance in an African Church: The Book, 'Live and Direct.'" *American Ethnologist* 31 (1): 76–91.
Engelke, Matthew. 2007. *A Problem of Presence: Beyond Scripture in an African Church*. Berkley: University of California Press.
Engelke, Matthew. 2009. "Reading and Time: Two Approaches to the Materiality of Scripture." *Ethnos* 74 (2): 151–74.
Engelke, Matthew. 2013. *God's Agents: Biblical Publicity in Contemporary England*. Berkeley: University of California Press.
Engelke, Matthew. 2014. "Christianity and the Anthropology of Secular Humanism." *Current Anthropology* 55 (10): S292–301.
Evans, Christopher H. 2017. *The Social Gospel in America: A History*. New York: New York University Press.
Ewart, David. 2015. "An Open Letter to Gretta Vosper: In Response to Her Open Letter to the Rev. Gary Paterson, Moderator of the United Church of Canada" (blog). *David Ewart: Data. Analysis. Cheeky, Theological Reflections*, January 13. www.davidewart.ca.
Farr, Cecilia Konchar. 2005. *Reading Oprah: How Oprah's Book Club Changed the Way America Reads*. Albany: State University of New York Press.
Faubion, James D. 2011. *An Anthropology of Ethics*. Cambridge: Cambridge University Press.
Fitzgerald, Timothy. 2000. *The Ideology of Religious Studies*. New York: Oxford University Press.
Francis, Leslie, and Mandy Robbins. 2004. "Belonging without Believing: A Study in the Social Significance of Anglican Identity and Implicit Religion among 13–15-Year-Old Males." *Implicit Religion* 7 (1): 37–54.
Frei, Hans W. 1974. *The Eclipse of the Biblical Narrative: A Study in Eighteenth and Nineteenth Century Hermeneutics*. New Haven, CT: Yale University Press.
Fridell, Gavin. 2007. *Fair Trade Coffee: The Prospects and Pitfalls of Market-Driven Social Justice*. Toronto: University of Toronto Press.
Frye, Northrop. 1982. *The Great Code: The Bible and Literature*. Toronto: Academic Press.
Frye, Northrop. 1991. *The Double Vision: Language and Meaning in Religion*. Toronto: University of Toronto Press.
Frykholm, Amy Johnson. 2004. *Rapture Culture: Left Behind in Evangelical America*. New York: Oxford University Press.
Frykholm, Amy Johnson. 2016. *Christian Understandings of the Future: The Historical Trajectory*. Minneapolis: Fortress Press.
Funk, Robert W., Roy W. Hoover, and the Jesus Seminar. 1993. *The Five Gospels: The Search for the Authentic Words of Jesus*. New York: Macmillan.
Funk, Robert W. 1996. *Honest to Jesus: Jesus for a New Millennium*. New York: HarperSanFrancisco.

Funk, Robert W. 2000. "The Once and Future Jesus." In *The Once and Future Jesus*, edited by the Jesus Seminar, 5–25. Santa Rosa, CA: Polebridge Press.
Garriott, William, and Kevin Lewis O'Neill. 2008. "Who Is a Christian?: Toward a Dialogical Approach in the Anthropology of Christianity." *Anthropological Theory* 8 (4): 381–98.
Graybill, Rhiannon. 2021. *Texts after Terror: Rape, Sexual Violence, and the Hebrew Bible*. New York: Oxford University Press.
Griffith, R. Marie. 1997. *God's Daughters: Evangelical Women and the Power of Submission*. Berkeley: University of California Press.
Groys, Boris. 2003. "Back from the Future." *Third Text* 17 (4): 323–31.
Gunnemann, Louis H. 1977. *The Shaping of the United Church of Christ: An Essay in the History of American Christianity*. Cleveland: United Church Press.
Guyer, Jane I. 2007. "Prophecy and the Near Future: Thoughts on Macroeconomic, Evangelical, and Punctuated Time." *American Ethnologist* 34 (3): 409-50.
Hall, David D. ed. 1997. *Lived Religion in America: Toward a History of Practice*. Princeton, NJ: Princeton University Press.
Hande, D'Arcy, and Erich Schultz. 1990. "Struggling to Establish a National Identity: The Evangelical Church in Canada and Its Archive," *Archivaria* 30:64–70.
Hann, Chris. 2007. "The Anthropology of Christianity per se." *European Journal of Sociology / Archives Européennes de Sociologie*. 48 (3): 383–410.
Harding, Susan. 1987. "Convicted by the Holy Spirit: The Rhetoric of Fundamental Baptist Conversion." *American Ethnologist* 14 (1): 167–81.
Harding, Susan. 1991. "Representing Fundamentalism: The Problem of the Repugnant Cultural Other." *Social Research* 58 (2): 373–93.
Harding, Susan. 1994. "Imagining the Last Days: The Politics of Apocalyptic Language." In *Accounting for Fundamentalisms: The Dynamic Character of Movements*, edited by Martin E. Marty and R. Scott Appleby, 57–78. Chicago: University of Chicago Press.
Harding, Susan. 2000. *The Book of Jerry Falwell: Fundamentalist Language and Politics*. Princeton, NJ: Princeton University Press.
Harpur, Tom. 2004. *The Pagan Christ: Recovering the Lost Light*. Toronto: Thomas Allen.
Harris, Oliva. 2006. "The Eternal Return of Conversion: Christianity as Contested Domain in Highland Bolivia." In *The Anthropology of Christianity*, edited by Fenella Cannell, 51–76. Durham, NC: Duke University Press.
Harrold, Philip. 2006. "Deconversion in the Emerging Church." *International Journal for the Study of the Christian Church* 6 (1): 79–90.
Hatch, Nathan O. 1989. *The Democratization of American Christianity*. New Haven, CT: Yale University Press.
Hatch, Nathan O., and Mark A. Noll, eds. 1982. *The Bible in America: Essays in Cultural History*. New York: Oxford University Press.
Hedges, Chris. 2008. *I Don't Believe in Atheists*. New York: Free Press.
Hendershot, Heather. 2004. *Shaking the World for Jesus: Media and Conservative Evangelical Culture*. Chicago: University of Chicago Press.

Hillis, Bryan. 2008. "Outsiders Becoming Mainstream: The Theology, History and Ethnicity of Being Lutheran in Canada." In *Christianity and Ethnicity in Canada*, edited by Paul Bramadat and David Seljak, 247–86. Toronto: University of Toronto Press.

Hjelm, Titus. 2019. "Rethinking the Theoretical Base of Peter L. Berger's Sociology of Religion: Social Construction, Power, and Discourse." *Critical Research on Religion* 7 (3): 223–236.

Hobsbawm, Eric, and Terence Ranger, eds. 1983. *The Invention of Tradition*. Cambridge: Cambridge University Press.

Hoover, Roy W., Stephen J. Patterson, Lane C. McGaughy, Joe Bessler-Northcutt, Hal Taussig, Glenna S. Jackson, Charles W. Hedrick, and Francis MacNab. 2004. *The Historical Jesus Goes to Church*. Santa Rosa, CA: Polebridge Press.

Howard, Robert Glenn. 2010. "Enacting a Virtual 'Ekklesia': Online Christian Fundamentalism as Vernacular Religion." *New Media & Society* 12 (5): 729–44.

Howell, Brian. 2005. "The Anthropology of Christianity: Beyond Missions and Conversion—A Review Essay." *Christian Scholar's Review* 34 (3): 353–62.

Howell, Brian. 2007. "The Repugnant Cultural Other Speaks Back: Christian Identity as 'Ethnographic' Standpoint." *Anthropological Theory* 7 (4): 371–91.

Hughes, Aaron W. 2013. *Abrahamic Religions: On the Uses and Abuses of History*. New York: Oxford University Press.

James, William C. 2011. *God's Plenty: Religious Diversity in Kingston*. Montreal-Kingston: McGill-Queen's Press.

Janca, Aleksandar, and Clothilde Bullen. 2003. "The Aboriginal Concept of Time and Its Mental Health Implications." *Australasian Psychiatry* 11:S40–S44.

Jenks, Gregory C. 2000. Introduction to *The Once and Future Jesus*, edited by John Shelby Spong et al. (the Jesus Seminar), 1–4. Santa Rosa, CA: Polebridge Press.

Johnson, Luke Timothy. 1993. "Reshuffling the Gospels: Jesus According to Spong and Wilson." *Christian Century* (April 28): 457–58.

Jones, Robert P. 2008. *Progressive and Religious: How Christian, Jewish, Muslim and Buddhist Leaders Are Moving beyond Partisan Politics and Transforming American Public Life*. Lanham, MD: Rowman and Littlefield.

Jones, Robert P. 2016. *The End of White Christian America*. New York: Simon and Schuster.

Jones, Robert P., Daniel Cox, and Juhem Navarro-Rivera. 2014. "Believers, Sympathizers, and Skeptics: Why Americans Are Conflicted about Climate Change, Environmental Policy, and Science." *PRRI*. www.prri.org.

Jones, Robert P., Daniel Cox, Juhem Navarro-Rivera, E. J. Dionne, Jr., and William A. Galston. 2013. "Do Americans Believe Capitalism and Government Are Working?: Religious Left, Religious Right & the Future of the Economic Debate." *Findings from the 2013 Economic Values Survey*. Washington, DC: Public Religion Research Institute and Governance Studies at Brookings.

Jorgensen, Danny L. 1989. *Participant Observation: A Methodology for Human Studies*. Thousand Oaks, CA: Sage.

Juzwik, Mary M. 2014. "American Evangelical Biblicism as Literate Practice: A Critical Review." *Reading Research Quarterly* 49 (3): 335–49.

Kaell, Hillary. 2014. *Walking Where Jesus Walked: American Christians and Holy Land Pilgrimage*. New York: New York University Press.
Kaell, Hillary. 2017. "Place Making and People Gathering at Rural Wayside Crosses." In *Everyday Sacred: Religion in Contemporary Quebec*, edited by Hillary Kaell, 129–55. Montreal-Kingston: McGill-Queen's University Press.
Keane, Webb. 2002. "Sincerity, 'Modernity,' and the Protestants." *Cultural Anthropology* 17 (1): 65–92.
Keane, Webb. 2007. *Christian Moderns: Freedom and Fetish in the Mission Encounter*. Berkeley: University of California Press.
Keane, Webb. 2010. "Minds, Surfaces, and Reasons in the Anthropology of Ethics." In *Ordinary Ethics: Anthropology, Language, and Action*, edited by Michael Lambek, 64–83. New York: Fordham University Press.
Keller, Eva. 2005. *The Road to Clarity: Seventh-day Adventism in Madagascar*. New York: Palgrave Macmillan.
King, Rebekka. 2005. "Progressive Christians as Neo-Literalists: The Drive for 'Intellectual Integrity' in Contemporary Christianity." Master's thesis, Queen's University, Kingston, ON.
King, Rebekka. 2010. "Canada: Protestants and the United Church of Canada." In *Encyclopedia of Religion in America*, edited Charles H. Lippy and Peter W. Williams, 395–404. Washington: CQ Press.
Kingsolver, Barbara. 2002. *Small Wonder*. New York: Harper Collins.
Klassen, Pamela E. 2006. "Textual Healing: Mainstream Protestants and the Therapeutic Text, 1900–1925." *Church History* 75 (4): 809–48.
Klassen, Pamela E. 2011. *Spirits of Protestantism: Medicine, Healing, and Liberal Christianity*. Berkeley: University of California Press.
Knibbe, Kim, and Helena Kupari. 2020. "Theorizing Lived Religion: Introduction." *Journal of Contemporary Religion* 35 (2): 157–76.
Kort, Wesley A. 1996. *"Take, Read": Scripture, Textuality, and Cultural Practice*. University Park: Pennsylvania State University Press.
Krotz, Larry. 2016. "Atheist at the Pulpit: Can the United Church Survive without God?" *Walrus*, May 11. https://thewalrus.ca.
Kurtz, Lester R. 1983. "The Politics of Heresy." *American Journal of Sociology* 88 (6): 1085–1115.
Lambek, Michael. 1990. "Certain Knowledge, Contestable Authority: Power and Practice on the Islamic Periphery." *American Ethnologist* 17 (1): 23–40.
Lambek, Michael, ed. 2010. *Ordinary Ethics: Anthropology, Language, and Action*. New York: Fordham University Press.
Latour, Bruno. 1993. *We Have Never Been Modern*. Cambridge, MA: Harvard University Press.
Lebner, Ashley B. 2015. "The Anthropology of Secularity beyond Secularism." *Religion and Society: Advances in Research* 6: 62–74.
Lee, Lois. 2015. *Recognizing the Non-Religious: Reimagining the Secular*. Oxford: Oxford University Press.

Leggett, William H., and Ida Fadzilla Leggett, eds. 2021. *Field Stories: Experiences, Affect, and the Lessons of Anthropology in the Twenty-First Century*. Lanham, MD: Lexington Books.

Leonard, Henrietta L. 1989. "Childhood Rituals and Superstitions: Developmental and Cultural Perspectives." In *Obsessive-Compulsive Disorder in Children and Adolescents*, edited by Judith L. Rapoport, 289–310. Washington, DC: American Psychiatric Press.

Levitsky, Ihor. 1979. "The Tolstoy Gospel in the Light of the Jefferson Bible." *Canadian Slavonic Papers* 21 (3): 347–55.

Lindquist, Galina, and Simon Coleman. 2008. "Introduction: Against Belief?" *Social Analysis* 52 (1): 1–18.

Livingston, James C. 1974. *The Ethics of Belief: Essay on the Victorian Religious Conscience*. Tallahassee, FL: American Academy of Religion.

Lofton, Kathryn. 2011. *Oprah: The Gospel of an Icon*. Berkley: University of California Press.

Long, Elizabeth. 1993. "Textual Interpretation as Collective Action." In *The Ethnography of Reading*, edited by Jonathan Boyarin, 180–211. Berkeley: University of California Press.

Lopez, Donald S., Jr. 1998. "Belief." In *Critical Terms for Religious Studies*, edited by Mark C. Taylor, 21–35. Chicago: University of Chicago Press.

Low, William, and Eileen Davenport. 2005. "Postcards from the Edge: Maintaining the 'Alternative' Character of Fair Trade." *Sustainable Development* 13: 143–53.

Lutz, Catherine A. 1990. "Engendered Emotion: Gender, Power, and the Rhetoric of Emotional Control in American Discourse." In *Language and the Politics of Emotion*, edited by Catherine A. Lutz and Lila Abu-Lughod, 69–91. Cambridge: Cambridge University Press.

Mahmood, Saba. 2015. *Religious Difference in a Secular Age: A Minority Report*. Princeton, NJ: Princeton University Press.

Malley, Brian. 2004. *How the Bible Works: An Anthropological Study of Evangelical Biblicism*. Walnut Creek, CA: AltaMira Press.

Manning, Johanna. 2006. *The Magdalene Moment: A Vision for a New Christianity*. Vancouver, BC: Raincoast Books.

Manseau, Peter. 2020. *The Jefferson Bible: A Biography*. Princeton, NJ: Princeton University Press.

Marshall, David B. 1992. *Secularizing the Faith: Canadian Protestant Clergy and the Crisis of Belief, 1850–1940*. Toronto: University of Toronto Press.

Marti, Gerardo. 2020. *American Blindspot: Race, Class, Religion, and the Trump Presidency*. New York: Rowman and Littlefield.

Marti, Gerardo, and Gladys Ganiel. 2014. *The Deconstructed Church: Understanding Emerging Christianity*. New York: Oxford University Press.

Martin, Craig. 2009. "How to Read an Interpretation: Interpretive Strategies and the Maintenance of Authority." *The Bible and Critical Theory* 5 (1): 6.1–26.

Martin, Craig. 2010. *Masking Hegemony: A Genealogy of Liberalism, Religion and the Private Sphere*. New York: Routledge.

Martin, Craig. 2014. *Capitalizing Religion: Ideology and the Opiate of the Bourgeoisie.* New York: Bloomsbury.

Masuzawa, Tomoko. 2005. *The Invention of World Religions: Or, How European Universalism Was Preserved in the Language of Pluralism.* Chicago: University of Chicago Press.

Maul, Stefan M. 2008. "Walking Backwards into the Future: The Conception of Time in the Ancient Near East." In *Given World and Time: Temporalities in Context,* edited by Tyrus Miller, 15–24. New York: CEU Press.

McCloud, Sean. 2007. *Divine Hierarchies: Class in American Religion and Religious Studies.* Chapel Hill: University of North Carolina Press.

McCutcheon, Russell T. 1997. *Manufacturing Religion: The Discourse on Sui Generis Religion and the Politics of Nostalgia.* New York: Oxford University Press.

McCutcheon, Russell T. 2015. "The Category 'Religion' in Recent Publications: Twenty Years Later." *Numen* 62 (1): 119—41.

McDonald, Marci. 2010. *The Armageddon Factor: The Rise of Christian Nationalism in Canada.* Toronto: Vintage Canada.

McFague, Sallie. 1982. *Metaphorical Theology: Models of God in Religious Language.* Philadelphia: Fortress Press.

McGuire, Meredith B. 2008. *Lived Religion: Faith and Practice in Everyday Life.* Oxford: Oxford University Press.

McKinnon, Andrew M. 2002. "Sociological Definitions, Language Games, and the 'Essence' of Religion." *Method and Theory in the Study of Religion* 14 (1): 61–83.

Milne, Mike. 2015. "How to Deal with Clergy Who No Longer Believe in God." *Broadview,* May 1. https://broadview.org.

Milne, Mike. 2016a. "How Atheist Minister Gretta Vosper Tested the Limits of United Church Tolerance." *Broadview,* November 1. https://broadview.org.

Milne, Mike. 2016b. "United Church Committee Finds Atheist Minister 'Not Suitable.'" *Broadview,* September 9. https://broadview.org.

Milne, Mike. 2019. "Gretta Vosper Settlement Could Redefine the United Church." *Broadview,* March 1. https://broadview.org.

Mittermaier, Amira. 2011. *Dreams That Matter: Egyptian Landscapes of the Imagination.* Berkeley: University of California Press.

Mockabee, Stephen T., Kenneth D. Wald, and David C. Leege. 2012. "In Search of the Religious Left: Reexamining Religiosity." In *Improving Public Opinion Surveys: Interdisciplinary Innovation and American National Election Studies,* edited by John H. Aldrich and Kathleen M. McGraw, 278–98. Princeton, NJ: Princeton University Press.

Modern, John Lardas. 2011. *Secularism in Antebellum America.* Chicago: University of Chicago Press.

Moorhead, James H. 1999. *World without End: Mainstream American Protestant Visions of the Last Things, 1880—1925.* Indianapolis: Indiana University Press.

Morgan, David. 2010. Introduction to *Religion and Material Culture: The Matter of Belief,* edited by David Morgan, 1–17. New York: Routledge.

Mroczek, Eva. 2016. *The Literary Imagination in Jewish Antiquity.* New York: Oxford University Press.

Muse, Erika M. 2005. *The Evangelical Church in Boston's Chinatown: A Discourse of Language, Gender, and Identity.* New York: Routledge.
Myles, Robert J. 2016. "The Fetish for a Subversive Jesus." *Journal for the Study of the Historical Jesus* 14 (1): 52–70.
Newman, Katherine S. 1999. *Falling from Grace: The Experience of Downward Mobility in the Age of Affluence.* Berkeley: University of California Press.
Newton, Richard W., Jr. 2020. *Identifying Roots: Alex Haley and the Anthropology of Scriptures.* Sheffield, UK: Equinox.
Noll, Mark A. 2006. "What Happened to Christian Canada?" *Church History* 75 (2): 245–73.
Nongbri, Brent. 2013. *Before Religion: A History of a Modern Concept.* New Haven, CT: Yale University Press.
Nord, David Paul. 2004. *Faith in Reading: Religious Publishing and the Birth of Mass Media in America.* New York: Oxford University Press.
Oakes, Kaya. 2015. "Belonging without Believing." *CrossCurrents* 65 (2): 229–38.
Olson, Daniel V. A. 1994. "Making Disciples in a Liberal Protestant Church." In *"I Come Away Stronger": How Small Groups Are Shaping American Religion*, edited by Robert Wuthnow, 125–47. Grand Rapids, MI: William B. Eerdmans.
Olson, Laura R. 2007. "Whither the Religious Left? Religiopolitical Progressivism in Twenty-First-Century America." In *From Pews to Polling Places: Faith and Politics in the American Religious Mosaic*, edited by J. Matthew Wilson, 53–79. Washington, DC: Georgetown University Press.
Olson, Laura R. 2011. "The Religious Left in Contemporary American Politics." *Politics, Religion and Ideology* 12 (3): 271–94.
O'Neill, Kevin Lewis. 2010. *City of God: Christian Citizenship in Postwar Guatemala.* Berkeley: University of California Press.
O'Neill, Kevin Lewis. 2012. "Pastor Harold Caballeros Believes in Demons: Belief and Believing in the Study of Religion." *History of Religions* 51 (4): 299–316.
Orsi, Robert A. 2003. "Is the Study of Lived Religion Irrelevant to the World We Live In? Special Presidential Plenary Address, Salt Lake City, November 2, 2002." *Journal for the Scientific Study of Religion* 42 (2): 169–74.
Ortner, Sherry B. 1995. "Resistance and the Problem of Ethnographic Refusal." *Comparative Studies in Society and History* 37 (1): 173–93.
Packard, Josh. 2012. *The Emerging Church: Religion at the Margins.* Boulder, CO: First Forum Press.
Porter, Catherine. 2019. "A Canadian Preacher Who Doesn't Believe in God." *New York Times*, February 1.
Putnam, Robert D. 2000. *Bowling Alone: The Collapse and Revival of American Community.* New York: Simon and Schuster.
Radway, Janice A. 1997. *A Feeling for Books: The Book-of-the-Month Club, Literary Taste and Middle-Class Desire.* Chapel Hill: University of North Carolina Press.

Ramey, Steven. 2015. "When Acceptance Reflects Disrespect: The Methodological Contradictions of Accepting Participant Statements." *Method and Theory in the Study of Religion* 27 (1): 59–81.

Rauschenbusch, Walter. 1913 [1907]. *Christianity and the Social Crisis*. New York: Macmillan.

Redding, Jonathan D. 2021. *One Nation under Graham: Apocalyptic Rhetoric and American Exceptionalism*. Waco, TX: Baylor University Press.

Reed, Annette Yoshiko. 2008. "Pseudepigraphy, Authorship, and the Reception of 'the Bible' in Late Antiquity." In *The Reception and Interpretation of the Bible in Late Antiquity*, edited by Lorenzo DiTommaso and Lucian Turcescu, 467–90. Leiden, NL: Brill.

Reimer, Sam. 2003. *Evangelicals and the Continental Divide: The Conservative Protestant Subculture in Canada and the United States*. Kingston-Montreal: McGill-Queen's University Press.

Robbins, Joel. 2001. "Secrecy and the Sense of an Ending: Narrative, Time, and Everyday Millenarianism in Papua New Guinea and in Christian Fundamentalism." *Comparative Studies in Society and History* 43 (3): 525–51.

Robbins, Joel. 2003. "What Is a Christian? Notes toward an Anthropology of Christianity." *Religion* 33 (3): 191–99.

Robbins, Joel. 2007. "Continuity Thinking and the Problem of Christian Culture: Belief, Time and the Anthropology of Christianity." *Current Anthropology* 48 (1): 5–19.

Robbins, Joel. 2008. "On Not Knowing Other Minds: Confession, Intention, and Linguistic Exchange in a Papua New Guinea Community." *Anthropological Quarterly* 81 (2): 421–29.

Robbins, Joel. 2012. "On Becoming Ethical Subjects: Freedom, Constraint, and the Anthropology of Morality." *Anthropology of This Century,* no. 5 (October). http://aotcpress.com.

Robbins, Joel. 2016. "What Is the Matter with Transcendence?: On the Place of Religion in the New Anthropology of Ethics." *Journal of the Royal Anthropological Institute* 22 (4): 767–808.

Robbins, Joel. 2018. "Where in the World Are Values?: Exemplarity and Moral Motivation." In *Moral Engine: Exploring the Ethical Drives in Human Life*, edited by Cheryl Mattingly, Rasmus Dyring, Maria Louw, and Thomas Schwarz Wentzer, 155–73. Oxford: Berghahn.

Roseberry, William. 1996. "The Rise of Yuppie Coffees and the Reimagination of Class in the United States." *American Anthropologist* 98 (4): 762–75.

Ruel, Malcolm. 2002. "Christians as Believers." In *A Reader in the Anthropology of Religion*, edited by Michael Lambek, 99–133. Malden, MA: Blackwell.

Sapiro, Gisèle. 2004. "Forms of Politicization in the French Literary Field." In *After Bourdieu: Influence, Critique, Elaboration*, edited by David L. Swartz and Vera L. Zolberg, 145–64. Dordrecht, NL: Kluwer.

Schaberg, Jane. 1987. *The Illegitimacy of Jesus: A Feminist Theological Interpretation of the Infancy Narratives*. New York: Harper and Row.

Schaefer, Donovan O. 2015. *Religious Affects: Animality, Evolution, and Power*. Durham: Duke University Press.

Scheer, Monique, Birgitte Schepelern Johansen, and Nadia Fadil. 2019. "Secular Embodiments: Mapping an Emergent Field." In *Secular Bodies, Affects and Emotions: European Configurations*, edited by Monique Scheer, Birgitte Schepelern Johansen, and Nadia Fadil, 1–14. London: Bloomsbury.

Schmidt, Leigh Eric. 2005. *Restless Souls: The Making of American Spirituality from Emerson to Oprah*. San Francisco: HarperSanFrancisco.

Schreiner, Thomas R. 2006. "Penal Substitution View." In *The Nature of the Atonement: Four Views*, edited by James K. Beilby and Paul R. Eddy, 67–98. Downers Grove, IL: InterVarsity Press.

Segovia, Fernardo F., and Mary Ann Tolbert, eds. 1995. *Reading from this Place: Social Location and Biblical Interpretation in the United States*. Minneapolis: Fortress Press.

Selby, Jennifer. 2019. "Interrogating Categories with Ethnography: On the 'Five Pillars' of Islam." In *Constructing "Data" in Religious Studies: Examining the Architecture of the Academy*, edited by Leslie Dorrough Smith, 61–69. Sheffield, UK: Equinox.

Seljak, David. 2000. "Resisting the 'No Man's Land' of Private Religion: The Catholic Church and Public Politics in Quebec." In *Rethinking Church, State, and Modernity: Canada between Europe and the USA*, edited by David A. Lyon and Marguerite Van Die, 131–48. Toronto: University of Toronto Press.

Shoaps, Robin A. 2002. "'Pray Earnestly': The Textual Construction of Personal Involvement in Pentecostal Prayer and Song." *Journal of Linguistic Anthropology* 12 (1): 34–71.

Shoemaker, Terry. 2019. "Deconversion, Sport, and Rehabilitative Hope." *Religions* 10 (5): 341.

Slessarev-Jamir, Helene. 2011. *Prophetic Activism: Progressive Religious Justice Movements in Contemporary America*. New York: New York University Press.

Smith, Christian. 1998. *American Evangelicalism: Embattled and Thriving*. Chicago: University of Chicago Press.

Smith, Christian, ed. 2003. *The Secular Revolution: Power, Interests, and Conflict in the Secularization of American Public Life*. Berkeley: University of California Press.

Smith, Erin A. 2015. *What Would Jesus Read? Popular Religious Books and Everyday Life in Twentieth-Century America*. Chapel Hill: University of North Carolina Press.

Smith, Jonathan Z. 2004. "What a Difference a Difference Makes." In *Relating Religion: Essays in the Study of Religion*, 250–302. Chicago: University of Chicago Press.

Smith, Wilfred Cantwell. 1977. *Belief and History*. Charlottesville: University Press of Virginia.

Smith, Wilfred Cantwell. 1979. *Faith and Belief*. Princeton, NJ: Princeton University Press.

Spong, John Shelby. 1991. *Rescuing the Bible from Fundamentalism: A Bishop Rethinks the Meaning of Scripture*. New York: HarperCollins.

Spong, John Shelby. 1992. *Born of a Woman: A Bishop Rethinks the Virgin Birth and Treatment of Women by a Male-Dominated Church*. San Francisco: HarperSanFrancisco..

Spong, John Shelby. 1998. *Why Christianity Must Change or Die: A Bishop Speaks to Believers in Exile*. San Francisco: HarperSanFrancisco.

Spong, John Shelby. 2000. *Here I Stand: My Struggle for a Christianity of Integrity, Love, and Equality*. San Francisco: Harper San Francisco.
Spong, John Shelby. 2005. *The Sins of Scripture: Exposing the Bible's Texts of Hate to Reveal the God of Love*. New York: HarperOne.
Spong, John Shelby. 2007. *Jesus for the Non-Religious: Recovering the Divine at the Heart of the Human*. San Francisco: HarperSanFrancisco.
Spong, John Shelby. 2009. *Eternal Life: A New Vision—Beyond Religion, beyond Theism, beyond Heaven and Hell*. New York: HarperOne.
Spong, John Shelby. 2016. *Biblical Literalism: A Gentile Heresy: A Journey into a New Christianity through the Doorway of Matthew's Gospel*. New York: HarperOne.
Stevenson, Jill. 2013. *Sensational Devotion: Evangelical Performance in Twenty-First-Century America*. Ann Arbor: University of Michigan Press.
Storm, Jason Ananda Josephson. 2012. *The Invention of Religion in Japan*. Chicago: University of Chicago Press.
Streib, Heinz, Ralph W. Hood, Jr., Barbara Keller, Rosina-Martha Csöff, and Christopher F. Silver. 2009. *Deconversion: Qualitative and Quantitative Results from Cross-Cultural Research in Germany and the United States of America*. Göttingen, DE: Vandenhoeck and Ruprect.
Strhan, Anna. 2015. *Aliens and Strangers?: The Struggle for Coherence in the Everyday Lives of Evangelicals*. New York: Oxford University Press.
Stromberg, Peter G. 1993. *Language and Self-transformation: A Study of the Christian Conversion Narrative*. New York: Cambridge University Press.
Sutton, Matthew Avery. 2012. *Jerry Falwell and the Rise of the Religious Right: A Brief History with Documents*. New York: Bedford/St. Martin's.
Sutton, Matthew Avery. 2014. *American Apocalypse: A History of Modern Evangelism*. Cambridge, MA: Harvard University Press.
Taussig, Hal. 2006. *A New Spiritual Home: Progressive Christianity at the Grass Roots*. Santa Rosa, CA: Polebridge Press.
Taylor, Charles. 2007. *A Secular Age*. Cambridge, MA: Harvard University Press.
Thiessen, Joel. 2015. *The Meaning of Sunday: The Practice of Belief in a Secular Age*. Montreal-Kingston: McGill-Queen's University Press.
Thiessen, Joel, and Sarah Wilkins-LaFlamme. 2020. *None of the Above: Nonreligious Identity in the US and Canada*. New York: New York University Press.
Thiselton, Anthony C. 1995. *Interpreting God and the Postmodern Self: On Meaning, Manipulation and Promise*. Grand Rapids, MI: T&T Clark.
Threinen, Norman J. 2006. *A Religious-Cultural Mosaic: A History of Lutherans in Canada*. Vulcan, Alberta, CA: Today's Reformation Press.
Thuesen, Peter J. 1999. *In Discordance with the Scriptures: American Protestant Battles over Translating the Bible*. New York: Oxford University Press.
Thuesen, Peter J. 2002. "The Logic of Mainline Churchliness." In *The Quiet Hand of God*, edited by Robert Wuthnow and John H. Evans, 27–53. Berkeley: University of California Press.

Trollinger, Susan L., and William Vance Trollinger, Jr. 2016. *Righting America at the Creation Museum*. Baltimore: Johns Hopkins University Press.
Turner, James. 1985. *Without God, without Creed: The Origins of Unbelief in America*. Baltimore: John Hopkins University Press.
Tyrrell, George. 1913. *Christianity at the Cross-Roads*. London: Longmans, Green.
United Church of Canada. 2021. *The Manual*. Toronto: United Church Publishing House.
Urban, Greg. 1996. "Entextualization, Replication, and Power." In *Natural Histories of Discourse*, edited by Michael Silverstein and Greg Urban, 21–44. Chicago: University of Chicago Press.
Vásquez, Manuel A. 2011. *More than Belief: A Materialist Theory of Religion*. New York: Oxford University Press.
Veldman, Robin Globus. 2019. *The Gospel of Climate Skepticism: Why Evangelical Christians Oppose Action on Climate Change*. Berkeley: University of California Press.
Vliek, Maria. 2019. "'It's Not Just about Faith': Narratives of Transformation When Moving out of Islam in the Netherlands and Britain." *Islam and Christian-Muslim Relations* 30 (3): 323–44.
Vliek, Maria. 2021. *Former Muslims in Europe: Between Secularity and Belonging*. New York: Routledge.
Voas, David. 2003. "Is Britain a Christian Country?" In *Public Faith?: The State of Religious Belief and Practice in Britain*, edited by Paul Avis, 92–105. London: SPCK.
Vosper, Gretta. 2009. *With or Without God: Why the Way We Live Is More Important Than What We Believe*. New York: HarperCollins.
Vosper, Gretta. 2015. "A Letter to Gary Paterson Regarding Paris." *Gretta Vosper*, January 8. www.grettavosper.ca.
Walker, Randi Jones. 2005. *The Evolution of a UCC Style: Essays in the History, Ecclesiology, and Culture of the United Church of Christ*. Cleveland: United Church Press.
Ward, Graham. 1997. "Postmodern Theology." In *The Modern Theologians: An Introduction to Christian Theology in the Twentieth Century*, edited by David F. Ford, 585–601. Malden, MA: Blackwell.
Watkins, Steven Mark. 2014. "An Analysis of the Creation Museum: Hermeneutics, Language, and Information Theory." PhD diss., University of Louisville, Kentucky.
Weber, Max. 1959 [1919]. "Science as Vocation." In *From Max Weber: Essays in Sociology*, edited by H. H. Gerth and C. Wright Mills, 129–56. New York: Oxford University Press.
Webster, Joseph. 2013. *The Anthropology of Protestantism: Faith and Crisis among Scottish Fishermen*. New York: Palgrave Macmillan.
West Hill United Church. 2018. "We Are So Happy to Share." Facebook, November 7. www.facebook.com.
White, Ronald Cedric, Charles Howard Hopkins, and John Coleman Bennett. 1976. *The Social Gospel: Religion and Reform in Changing America*. Philadelphia: Temple University Press.
White, Stephen Ross. 1994. *Don Cupitt and the Future of Christian Doctrine*. London: SCM Press.

Whitehead, Andrew L., and Samuel L. Perry. 2020. *Taking American Back for God: Christian Nationalism in the United States*. New York: Oxford University Press.
Wilcox, Melissa M. 2003. *Coming Out in Christianity: Religion, Identity, and Community*. Bloomington: Indiana University Press.
Wilk, Richard. 1999. "Consuming America." *Anthropology Newsletter*, 40 (2): 1, 4–5.
Williams, Philippa. 2012. "India's Muslims, Lived Secularism and Realising Citizenship." *Citizenship Studies* 16 (8): 979–95.
Wimbush, Vincent L., ed. 2008. *Theorizing Scriptures: New Critical Orientations to a Cultural Phenomenon*. New Brunswick, NJ: Rutgers University Press.
Wolfe, Alan. 1998. *One Nation, After All: What Middle-class Americans Really Think About: God, Country, Family, Racism, Welfare, Immigration, Homosexuality, Work, the Right, the Left, and Each Other*. New York: Viking.
Wolfe, Alan. 2003. *The Transformation of American Religion: How We Actually Live Our Faith*. New York: Free Press.
Worthen, Molly. 2014. *Apostles of Reason: The Crisis of Authority in American Evangelicalism*. New York: Oxford University Press.
Wuthnow, Robert. 1986. "Religion as a Sacred Canopy." In *Making Sense of Modern Times: Peter L. Berger and the Vision of Interpretive Sociology*, edited by James D. Hunter and Stephen C. Ainlay, 121–142. New York: Routledge.
Wuthnow, Robert. 1994a. *Sharing the Journey: Support Groups and America's New Quest for Community*. New York: Free Press.
Wuthnow, Robert. 1994b. "The Small-Group Movement in the Context of American Religion." In *"I Come Away Stronger": How Small Groups Are Shaping American Religion,* edited by Robert Wuthnow, 344–66. Grand Rapids, MI: Eerdmans.
Young, Ralph. 2015. *Dissent: The History of an American Idea*. New York: New York University Press.
Zaleha, Bernard Daley, and Andrew Szasz. 2015. "Why Conservative Christians Don't Believe in Climate Change." *Bulletin of the Atomic Scientists* 71 (5): 19–30.
Zigon, Jarrett. 2007. "Moral Breakdown and the Ethical Demand: A Theoretical Framework for an Anthropology of Moralities." *Anthropological Theory* 7 (2): 131–50.
Zikmund, Barbara Brown, ed. 1987. *Hidden Histories in the United Church of Christ*. Cleveland: United Church Press.
Zubrzycki, Geneviève. 2016. *Beheading the Saint: Nationalism, Religion, and Secularism in Quebec*. Chicago: University of Chicago Press.
Zuckerman, Phil, Luke W. Galen, and Frank L. Pasquale. 2016. *The Nonreligious: Understanding Secular People and Societies*. New York: Oxford University Press.
Zwissler, Laurel. 2007. "Spiritual, But Religious." *Culture and Religion* 8 (1): 51–69.
Zwissler, Laurel. 2018. *Religious, Feminist, Activist: Cosmologies of Interconnection*. Lincoln: University of Nebraska Press.

INDEX

Page numbers in italics indicate Tables

accidental prayer, 22
action: belief as, 3; in ethics, 17
The Acts of Jesus, of Jesus Seminar, 97
Adams, Jim, 7, 21
affiliations, 9; Anglican Church of Canada diversity of, 214n6; belief linked to, 115–16; collective reading for religious beliefs and, 88
agnostics, 115, 134, 141, 200
already and not yet, of temporal language, 159–64
American Fascists (Hedges), 177–78, 182
Anglican Church of Canada, 213n2; affiliations diversity of, 214n6; *Book of Alternative Services* of, 62; diocesan financial structure, 67; study of, 27. See also St. Matthias Anglican Church; St. Peter's Anglican Church
Answers in Genesis: on creationism as scientific model, 190–91; evolution skepticism of, 191
anthropology of Christianity: on belief, 21; language and discourse role, 25–26; on language practices, 22–23; need for study of, 25–26; reflexive account, 29; research methods and reflexivity, 25–34; sincerity and, 21, 23
anthropology of ethics, 164–68, 222n14
anthropology of religion: ethical dimension of, 164–68; reading practices, 215n2; scripture and, 91–92

apocalypse: dispensationalists on, 149; Harding on knowing history on, 149; in theological temporality, 148
apostasy, Islamic, 35, 189; Cottee on, 191; ethics driving skepticism in, 191–92; religion rejection factors, 191; Vliek and, 192
Apostles' Creed, 85, 171–72
arbitration settlement, of West Hill United Church, 201–2
The Armageddon Factor (McDonald), 218n7
Asad, Talal, 19, 114
atheism, 35, 156–57; Christianity end and, 154; church attendance and, 1, 3; Engelke on, 204; eschatology and, 148; nontheism compared to, 43; progressive Christianity movement toward, 172–74; strong atheists and, 134, 218n4; Vosper religious beliefs of, 201
Austin, Diane J., 133
authenticity, Protestantism preoccupation with, 45
authority, of popular theology, 96–97, 103–4

baby-boomers: in field study churches, 47; at George Street United Church, 38; progressive Christianity well-educated, middle-class, 5, 38, 47
Barbour, John, 112–13
Baudrillard, Jean, 108

Bayart, Jean-François, 92
Beattie, Tina, 70
belief: as action or practice, 3; affiliation linked to, 115–16; anthropology of Christianity on, 21; Asad on activity in world, 114; from biblical criticism, 81–82; as Christian identity primary category, 164; collective reading for affiliation and, 88; conviction and, 21, 115; in creeds, 85; Day on social and performative functions of, 115, 116; deconversion and undoing, 114–19; discourse about, 153; in God immorality, 23, 156; in God rejection, 3, 5; identity and, 115; in Jesus rejection, 3; moral character and future, 165; rejection of supernatural, 6; rejection of traditional, 3, 163–64; skepticism or conviction generated from, 115; Smith, W., on, 221n13; still adverb and giving up of, 154; temporal language and, 147; as unethical, 21, 165; Vosper skepticism and practice of, 204. *See also* disbelief; ethics of belief
Belief and History (Smith, W.), 221n13
believer in exile, Spong on, 6, 36, 103
believing against, in progressive Christianity, 4
belonging: religious, 26, 71, 90, 203; without believing, 2
Berger, Peter, 175, 188–89
de Bernières, Louis, 184
Beyond Belief (Pagels), 216n5
Bialecki, Jon, 113–14, 159
Bibby, Reginald, 9
Bible, 11; Baudrillard on simulacrum, 108; Crapanzano on, 100–101; demytholizing of, 7; desire for popular and accessible version of, 95–96; extraction and excavation of, 105–10; historical analysis of, 3, 42, 71, 78; King James and Revised Standard Versions, 95; as living Word, 79; Masowe Apostolics rejection of, 80–81; progressive Christianity absence of, 79–80, 81, 137; purification and, 35, 108–10; as source of doubt and certainty, 121; Spong neoliteralism of, 100; Spong on interpretation of, 99–101; Spong on unscientific claims of, 101–2; West Hill United Church rejection of reading, 2. *See also* New Testament; Old Testament
Bible rewriting: feminism and, 104–5; on Jesus and Mary Magdalene, 104–5; of Ten Commandments, 12–17, 106
Bible study, 5, 72–74; Bielo on evangelical, 88–89
biblical criticism, 1, 34, 41, 121, 148; Christian origins and, 153; on Christian Right, 218n8; historical, 78, 95, 102, 206; liberal Christians, 95; religion evaluation through, 11, 168; religious beliefs from, 81–82; scientific method and, 107–8; Spong on, 42, 99; traditions evaluated through, 168
Biblical Literalism (Spong), 83
Biblical reception, 103–4, 191
Bielo, James, 29, 33; on collective reading, 88–89; on creationism poetics, 191; on evangelical Bible study, 88–89; on textual economy, 89, 91
Bigelow, Anna, 17, 18
Birds without Wings (Bernières), 184
Book of Alternative Services, of Anglican Church of Canada, 62
book study group, 87, 89, 173, 197–98; influence of, 126–29; Smith, E., on, 216n5; within St. Peter's Anglican Church, 27; on Ten Commandments rewriting, 12–17, 106; of Theological Studies Group, 42–43, 82–83; at West Hill United Church, 145–47, 177–89, 185
Borg, Marcus, 12, 49, 69–71, 75, 92, 93, 122

Born of a Woman (Spong), 104, 216n8
Bourdieu, Pierre: on authority of discourse, 135; on social competence, 96; on specialized discourses, 96
Brooks, E. Marshall, 112
Brown, Dan, 104, 216n5

CAA. *See* church alumni association
Canada: Anglican Church of, 27, 62, 67, 213n2, 214n6; Bibby on religious participation in, 9; evangelical Christianity in, 218n7; Evangelical Lutheran Church in, 213n2; Protestant proximate other in, 218n6; separation of church and state, 212n9
Canadian Centre for Progressive Christianity, 7, 9, 188, 212n6
The Center for Progressive Christianity (TCPC), 7, 21, 209, 210
charismatic Christian, 117, 218n5
Children's Prayer, at West Hill United Church, 169
choice: against, Christianity and, 175; in deconversion narrative, 113; fundamental to progressive Christianity, 176, 187; heresy and, 175; of heretics, 175–76; progressive Christianity and, 176, 187
Christian dogma, decentralization and deconstruction of, 15–16
Christian evolutionists, 35
Christian identity: belief as primary category of, 164; deconversion and retention of, 113; progressive Christianity God rejection and, 5; progressive Christianity retention of, 4, 202–3. *See also* religious identity
Christianity: atheism and end of, 154; Bialecki on plasticity in, 113–14; biblical criticism and, 153; choice against in, 175; future of, 138–44; heritage of, 1, 2, 203; progressive Christianity antagonism, 136–37; Robbins on ideal-typical notion of, 148–49; undesirable gifts in, 21; Vosper on metaphorical understanding of, 166
Christianity and the Social Crisis (Rauschenbusch), 150
Christian progressivism, of Social Gospel, 7–8
Christian Right, biblical criticism on, 218n8
church: atheism and attendance in, 1, 3; faith and community of, 142; social nature of studies in, 216n4
church alumni association (CAA), 43–44
citizenship, Williams on lived secularity and, 18
Claiborne, Shane, 160, 218n8
CNN debate between Nye and Ham, 190–91
Coffman, Elesha, 59
Coleman, Simon, 134, 165
collective liturgical revision, 168–73
collective reading, 215n9; Bielo on, 88–89; ethical significance of, 187; of progressive texts, 26, 28; for religious beliefs and affiliation, 88; in religious traditions, 87–88; solidarity engendered from, 89–90
Communion liturgy: at Holy Cross Lutheran Church, 54–55; of Vosper, 58–59; West Hill United Church, 142
community, 163; deconstruction influence from progressive Christianity, 167–68; faith and church, 142; liturgical revision and sense of, 172; membership and theme of, 57–58
congregational dynamics, 8, 45, 47, 189
conservative Christianity, 9, 117–18
contested spaces, in St. Matthias Anglican Church, 62–69
conversion: Coleman on continuous, 134; of Jamaican Pentecostals, 134; narrative, 112, 137

conviction, 3; belief and, 21, 115; in deconversion narrative, 113; ethics and discipline interlaced with, 16; faith weakening and, 21; skepticism relationship to, 4
Cottee, Simon, 191
Crapanzano, Vincent, 100–101
creation: fundamentalist Christianity on, 219n3; in temporality, 148
creationism, 189; Answers in Genesis on scientific model of, 190–91; Bielo on poetics of, 191; Creation Museum and, 190–91; Dawkins criticism of, 211n1
Creation Museum, 190–91
creeds: Apostles' Creed, 85, 171–72; corrupting effect of, 94; mainline Christianity recital of, 85; Nicene Creed, 85, 94; progressive Christianity examination of, 168, 171; sincerity and beliefs in, 85
Crossan, John Dominic, 12, 49, 75, 93, 98–99
Crossley, James, 98
cultural context, of lived religion, 17
cultural transformation, of middle-class, 51

The Da Vinci Code (Brown), 104, 216n5
Dawkins, Richard, 1, 20, 146, 191; creationism criticism, 211n1; New Atheist movement and, 211n1
Day, Abby, 115, 116, 135
decentralization, of Christian dogma, 15–16
deconstruction: of Christian dogma, 15–16; of deconversion, 133–38; progressive Christianity community influence on, 167–68
deconversion: Christian identity retention and, 113; in church setting, 218n8; deconstruction of, 133–38; Harrold on, 137; "Losing My Religion and Finding My Soul" presentation, 111–12; Shoemaker on, 217n1; skepticism as ethical imperative in, 113; transitional nature of, 112, 130, 133–34, 136; undoing belief in, 114–19; Vliek on, 192
deconversion narratives, 35, 119, 137; Barbour on, 112–13; Brooks on, 112; choice and conviction emphasis in, 113; cultural critique of former beliefs and practices, 112; emotional experience of Hedy, 123–30, 138–39; intellectual motivators of Thomas, 120–23, 139–41; shared ethical concerns of Sandra and Margie, 130–33, 141–44
deficiency of character of God, religious narrative on, 23
demythologizing, of Bible, 7
Desfor Edles, Laura, 7
detail, progressive Christianity attention to, 15, 108
dialogue method, of liturgical revision, 48
diocesan financial structure, of Anglican Church of Canada, 67
disbelief: as ethical act, 23; in God, 154, 156; in life after death, 220n9; Protestantism, 3–4; as religious expression, 4; religious identity and, 211n4; secular form of knowledge and, 25
discipline, ethics and conviction interlaced with, 16
discourse analysis: anthropology of Christianity on practices, 25–26; about belief, 153; Bourdieu on authority of, 135; Bourdieu on specialized, 96; future in progressive Christian, 194–95; Lutz on control in gendered, 70
dispensationalists, on apocalypse, 149
dissent: Protestantism, 3–4; Young on, 211n3
distant future, 152–53
divine figure, rejection of Jesus as, 108–9
doubt: Bible as source of, 121; in lived secularity, 22, 191

Drescher, Elizabeth, 193, 222n1
Dudley, Kathryn, 51

The Empire of Illusion (Hedges), 178
Engelke, Matthew, 213n14; on atheism, 204; Masowe Apostolics study by, 80–81; on secular humanism, 214n4
entextualization practice, 16, 212n11
eschatology, 147–51; atheism and, 148; fundamentalist Christianity on, 219n3; Social Gospel and, 149–50; temporality in, 148, 154–59
Eternal Life (Spong), 220n8
ethical act, disbelief as, 23
ethical commitment, in secularism, 20
ethical humanism, secular knowledge alignment with, 11
ethical imperative, of skepticism, 21, 113
ethics: action in, 17; anthropology of, 164–68, 222n14; conviction and discipline interlaced with, 16; Islamic apostasy and skepticism, 191–92; Lambek on practice of, 164; language attached to, 23
ethics of belief, 4, 24–25, 164–68; unethical beliefs, 21, 165
ethnography: of Canadian wing of progressive Christianity, 212n6; of field study churches, 46–47; Hann on lack of research on, 26; Lebner on secularity, 19–20; of progressive Christianity, 4–5
ethnography of interpretation, 92; interpreters interpretation, 93–105
ethnography of reading, 87–93
evangelical Christianity, 117–18, 122–23, 136, 140; Bielo on Bible study in, 88–89; in Canada, 218n7; mainline Christianity critiques by, 165; on Rapture, 220n5
Evangelical Lutheran Church in Canada, 213n2

everyday items, lived religion significance of, 17, 34
evolutionism, 35; Answers in Genesis skepticism of, 191; Creation Museum on, 190
exclusive humanism, Taylor on secularity and, 19
exorcism, of Pentecostals, 133

Fadil, Nadia, 20
A Fair Country (Saul), 178–79, 180
faith: Adams on, 21; church community and, 142; conviction and weakening of, 21; undesirable gifts classification with, 21; Worthen on, 212n10
Faith and Belief (Smith, W.), 221n13
Falwell, Jerry, 1, 119, 211n1
Felten, David, 93
feminism, Bible rewriting and, 104–5
fingers crossed, sincerity and, 82–87
The Five Gospels, of Jesus Seminar, 97
fundamentalist Christianity, 117–18, 138, 141, 143–44; on creation, 219n3; on eschatology, 219n3; in Gamrie, Scotland, 151–52; God agency insistence by, 219n3; progressive Christianity contrast with, 8
Funk, Robert W., 97
future: of Christianity, 138–44; discourses in progressive Christianity, 194–95; Guyer on, 152–53; Harrold on representations of, 137; moral character and belief, 165; proximate and distant, 152–53; symmetrical evacuation of, 153; uncertainty, 173–74

Gamrie, Scotland: church on Second coming of Jesus, 152; fundamentalist Christianity in, 151–52; Webster research on, 151–53
Gandhi, Mahatma, 109, 110
gendered discourse, Lutz on rhetoric of control in, 70

George Street United Church, 27, 31; Jesus view by, 37–38; nativity conflict at, 44–45, 86; service order in, 38; Spong visit to, 42–43, 82–84; theological diversity at, 37; Theological Studies Group at, 38–43, 47, 82–83, 105–6, 173, 188
Gibson, Mel, 100
glossolalia, of Pentecostals, 133
God: belief rejection of, 3, 5; disbelief in, 154, 156; fundamentalist Christianity insistence on agency of, 219n3; immorality of belief in, 23, 156; Masowe Apostolics on, 81; as moral symbol, 212n6; progressive Christianity rejection of intervention of, 24; religious narrative on character deficiency of, 23; Spong on divine authority of, 101; Spong on Jesus imbued with, 109; Spong on pro-Jewish, 23–24; traditional representation of, 146; unequal treatment of, 24
God and Empire (Crossan), 12
God Is Still Speaking motto, of United Church of Christ, 154–55
Gospels, inconsistency of, 93
Groys, Boris, 173, 222n17
Guyer, Jane, 152–53

Haley, Alex, 91–92
Half the Sky (Kristof and WuDunn), 184
Ham, Ken, 190–91
Hann, Chris, 26
Harding, Susan, 29; on knowing history of apocalypse, 149; temporal language and, 147
Harpur, Tom, 12, 133; Rethinking Christianity guest lecture of, 49
Harrold, Philip, 137
The Heart of Christianity (Borg), 12; St. Peter's Anglican Church study of, 69
Hedges, Christopher, 146, 177–78, 182–83, 185–86
Here I Stand (Spong), 135

heresy: choice and, 175; honesty compared to, 200; importance of, 94
heresy trial, against Vosper, 199–203, 220n9
The Heretical Imperative (Berger), 175
heretics, 36, 194–98; Berger definition of, 175; choice of, 175–76; progressive Christianity identity of, 3, 27
heritage, of Christianity, 1, 2, 203
historical analysis, of Bible, 3, 42, 71, 78
historical biblical criticism, 78, 95, 102, 206
history, shift from scripture to, 34
Hitchens, Christopher, 20, 191
Holy Cross Lutheran Church, 27, 31, 32, 188; Communion liturgy at, 54–55; leadership, location and like-mindedness at, 47–56; liturgical revision at, 170; Living the Questions curriculum of, 93; middle-class at, 50; as mission church, 48; Rethinking Christianity lecture series of, 49–50, 54; *Saving Jesus* video series at, 119
honesty, heresy compared to, 200
Hussein, Irtaza, 191–92

ideal-typical notion, of Christianity, 148–49
I Don't Believe in Atheists (Hedges), 185–86
inclusive language, 48
individualism, of middle-class, 51–52
intellectual integrity, 1, 6, 52, 212n6
intentionality: language attached to, 23; North American Christians religious speech acts, 23
interactive language, 167
interpretation: through Jesus Seminar, 97–98; popular authors authority from, 96–97, 103–4; progressive Christianity detail attention in, 15, 108; Spong on Bible, 99–101
intervention, temporal language of, 151–53
Islamic apostasy. *See* apostasy, Islamic

Jesus: belief rejection of, 3; Bible rewriting on Mary Magdalene and, 104–5; Crossan and Wright subversive versions of, 98–99; as divine figure rejection, 108–9; as ethical, religious teacher, 16; George Street United Church view of, 37–38; life and teachings reexamination, 71; as Son of God and Son of man, 73; Spong on fictitious story of, 42, 102; Spong on God imbued in, 109; St. Peter's Anglican Church reexamination of, 71; as transcendent, 63–64

Jesus Camp documentary, 218n5

Jesus for President (Claiborne), 218n8

Jesus for the Non-Religious (Spong), 39, 42, 82, 105

Jesus Prayer, 48

Jesus Seminar, 216n6; Crossley on, 98; Funk founding of, 97; historical context of, 98; Jesus revisions and, 98–99, 104; on New Testament historical accuracy, 97; scholars book discussion in, 97; Spong on, 97–98

Johansen, Birgitte Schepelern, 20

Joncas, Michael, 221n10

Journey of Transformation service, of West Hill United Church, 57–59

Keane, Webb: on moral vision and purification, 108; on religious language and moral character, 165; on sincerity, 23

King, Martin Luther, Jr., 109, 110

King James Bible Version, mainline liberal congregations on outdated, 95

Kingsolver, Barbara, 178, 182–83, 185

knowledge: disbelief and secular form of, 25; sincerity of inner self and, 22

Kristof, Nicholas, 184

Lambek, Michael, 164

language: anthropology of Christianity on practices of, 22–23, 25–26; Coleman, Stromberg and Keane on moral character and, 165; disagreements about traditional, 157; ethics and, 23; inclusive, 48; intentionality and ethic attached to, 23; as interactive, 167; liberal Christianity on metaphorical, 166–67; limited ritualized, 55–56; Protestantism on moral terms of, 165; sincerity and, 23; St. Matthias Anglican Church word emphasis, 63–64; temporal adverbs emphasis, 35. *See also* referential language

The Last Supper according to Mary and Martha (Beattie), 70

Latour, Bruno, 35; on purification, 107, 217n10

leadership, 37; against dominant orthodox, 175–76; at Holy Cross Lutheran Church, 47–56; Masowe Apostolics on God interpretation by, 81

Lebner, Ashley, 19; on secularity imprecision, 20

liberal Christianity, 186; on metaphorical religious language, 166–67; progressive Christianity attention to, 136; progressive Christianity compared to, 8; Social Gospel roots of, 149–50; Spong on, 10; Vosper on, 9–10

liberal humanism, 1, 168

Lippman, Thomas, 184

liturgical revision, 6, 129; collective, 168–73; through dialogue method, 48; examples of, 170; at Holy Cross Lutheran Church, 170; Jesus Seminar and, 98–99, 104; progressive Christianity examination for, 168; purification and, 108; sense of community and, 172; in St. Matthias Anglican Church songs, 63

lived religion: cultural context of, 17; everyday items significance in, 17, 34; McCutcheon on challenges to, 212n12; practice and identity in, 114; scholars on, 18, 20; text-based cosmology and, 216n3 lived secularity, 17–25, 35, 189–94; citizenship and, 18; as embodied experience, 20; on knowledge and sincerity of inner self, 22; progressive Christianity context of, 22; skepticism and doubt in, 22, 191; Williams and Bigelow on, 18

Living the Questions curriculum, 75, 215n7; on New Testament discrepancies, 93; Procter-Murphy and Felten creation of, 93; at St. Matthias Anglican Church, 63, 68

living Word, Bible as, 79

Lord's Prayer, mainline Christianity congregation unified through, 169

"Losing My Religion and Finding My Soul" presentations, 111–12

Luther, Martin, 50

Lutz, Catherine A., 70

mainline Christianity, 5, 9, 26; Coffman on, 59; creed recital in, 85; evangelical critiques of, 165; on King James and Revised Standard Bible Versions, 95; Lord's Prayer and congregation unification, 169; progressive Christianity classification in, 213n15; Thuesen on, 59

Mandela, Nelson, 109–10

Martin, Craig, 51–52

Mary Magdalene, 104–5

Masowe Apostolics: Bible rejection by, 80–81; Engelke study of, 80–81; leadership interpreters of God, 81

McCutcheon, Russell, 212n12

McDonald, Marci, 218n7

membership: community theme, 57–58; through online mediatory, 57–59; from Rethinking Christianity lecture series, 54; symbolic, 57; of United Church of Canada, 214n5; of West Hill United Church, 56–69; West Hill United Church departure of, 60–61, 129, 157

middle-class, 34, 213n15; cultural transformation of, 51; Dudley on, 51; at Holy Cross Lutheran Church, 50; individualism of, 51–52; in progressive Christianity, 5, 38, 47

millennial generation, nones and, 193

Milton, Giles, 184

ministers tests of faith, United Church of Canada on, 200

miracles, progressive Christian struggle with, 164–65

Mittermaier, Amira, 29

moral character: beliefs in future and, 165; Coleman, Stromberg, Keane on religious language and, 165

moral directive: Old Testament and, 106; of secular knowledge, 11–12

moral symbol, God as, 212n6

moral vision, Keane on purification and, 108

More Magazine, Vosper featured in, 60

Mortenson, Greg, 184

Mother Theresa, 109

narrative: conversion, 112, 137; religious, 23, 101, 104–5, 216n9; virgin birth, 104–5, 216n9. *See also* deconversion narratives

nativity scene: George Street United Church conflict on, 44–45, 86; historical context of New Testament on, 93–94; Spong rejection of, 105

neoliteralism, Spong on Bible, 100

New Atheist movement, 146, 211n1

New Testament: Jesus Seminar on historical accuracy of, 97; Living the Questions curriculum on discrepancies in, 93; nativity historical context, 93–94

Nicene Creed, 85, 94

nonbelief. *See* disbelief

nonempirical beliefs, rejection of, 6

nones, 35, 189; Drescher on, 193, 222n1; millennial generation and, 193; Religious Landscape Study by Pew Research Center and, 192–93; Thiessen and Wilkins-LaFlamme on, 193, 194

nonreligion, 211n4
nontheism, 134; atheism compared to, 43
North American religions: biblical interpretations of, 147; intentionality regarding religious speech acts, 23; movements within, 27; prayer in, 22; on progressive Christian, 7; secularization within, 211n5
not yet. *See* already and not yet
Nye, Bill, 190–91

Obama, Barack, 8, 92
Old Testament, moral directives and, 106
"On Eagles' Wings" (song), of Joncas, 221n10
online religiosity, 52–53; membership through, 57–59
oral history, 82, 212n11
origins of universe scientific explanations, 163
Osteen, Joel, 119

The Pagan Christ (Harpur), 12, 49
Pagels, Elaine, 75, 216n5
Paradise Lost, Smyrna (Milton), 184
parousiai (Second Coming of Jesus), 147; good and evil struggle resulting in, 152
The Passion of Christ (film), of Gibson, 100
Peck, Scott, 127
penal substitutionary view, 221n11
Pentateuch, legal system recorded in, 13–14
Pentecostals, in Jamaica: Austin study of, 133; conversion of, 134; glossolalia and exorcism of, 133; repetitious experiences of, 133–34; on spiritual practice universality and egalitarianism, 133
performative function of belief, Day on, 115, 116
personal belief, collective belief statements disconnect, 85
personal integrity, secular knowledge and, 11–12

political element, of progressive Christianity, 8–9
popular theology, authority of, 96–97, 103–4
practice: lived religion identity and, 114; temporal language and, 147
prayer: accidental, 22; Children's Prayer, 169; Jesus Prayer, 48; in North American religions, 22; progressive Christianity rewriting of ritual, 25, 169
Procter-Murphy, Jeff, 93
progressive Catholicism, 8
progressive Christianity: believing against in, 4; Bible absence in, 79–80, 81, 137; characteristics of, 163–64; choice fundamental to, 176, 187; Christian identity retention, 4, 202–3; Christianity antagonism by, 136–37; closeting in, 69–77; conviction and weakening of faith, 21; creeds and liturgical statements examination by, 168, 171; ethnography of, 4–5; fundamentalist Christianity contrast with, 8; future discourses in, 194–95; God rejection but Christian identity, 5; hegemonic movements in, 27; heretics identity in, 3, 27; intellectual integrity in, 1, 6, 52, 212n6; isolation feeling in, 90; liberal Christianity compared to, 8; liberal humanism in, 1, 168; lived secularity and context of, 22; miracles struggle by, 164–65; movement toward atheism by, 172–74; political element of, 8–9; Protestant proximate others comparison to, 117–18, 135–36; reason for leaving church, 212n7; referential language approach of, 166–67; rejection of intervention of God, 24; scientific empiricism, 1; supernatural and non-empirical beliefs rejection, 6; Taussig definition of, 30; theological questions in, 176; within United Church of Canada, 213n1; on unpopular scriptures, 222n15; Vosper on, 9; well-educated middle-class baby-boomers in, 5, 38, 47

Progressive Christians Uniting, 7
progressive evangelicals, Desfor Edles on, 7
pro-Jewish, Spong on God as, 23–24
Protestantism: disbelief, skepticism and dissent of, 3–4; on language in moral terms, 165; sincerity and authenticity preoccupation, 45
Protestant proximate other, 116, 144; in Canada, 218n6; progressive Christianity comparison to, 117–18, 135–36
proximate future, 152–53
proximate other: religious identity through comparison, 116–17; research on, 26; Smith, J., on, 116, 136, 217n2; theory of self and, 116, 117. *See also* Protestant proximate other
Public Religion Research Institute, on American religious progressives, 8–9
purification: Bible and, 35, 108–10; of historical and personal figures, 109; Keane on moral vision and, 108; Latour on, 107, 217n10; liturgical revision and, 108

Rapture, evangelical Christianity on, 220n5
Rauschenbusch, Walter, 150
referential language: Keane on, 215n1; progressive Christianity approach of, 166–67; West Hill United Church, 166
reflexivity: anthropology of Christianity, research methods and, 25–34; Bielo on, 33
reincarnation, 194–96
religion: biblical criticism evaluation of, 11, 168; Canada private and domestic realm of, 9; Islamic apostasy and rejection factors for, 191; secularism lack of dependence on, 18; secularization theory on decline of, 18; Vosper on freedom from, 200. *See also* lived religion
religious authority, diminished emphasis on, 17

religious belief. *See* belief
religious commitments, anthropology of Christianity on sincerity and, 21, 23
religious expression, disbelief as, 4
religious identity: Austin on, 133; belief and, 115; Coleman on, 134; lived religion practice and, 114; through proximate other comparison, 116–17; secularity, secularism and, 5
Religious Landscape Study, on nones, 192–93
religious narratives: on character of God deficiency, 23; Spong on, 101, 105; on virgin birth, 104–5, 216n9
religious pluralism, 2; Taylor on secularity and, 19
religious teacher, Jesus as ethical, 16
Relin, David Oliver, 184
Rescuing the Bible from Fundamentalism (Spong), 10, 83
research, 8–9; anthropology of Christianity on methods of, 25–34; Hann on lack of ethnography, 26; on nones, 192–93; on proximate other, 26; of Webster on Gamrie, Scotland, 151–53
Rethinking Christianity lecture series, of Holy Cross Lutheran Church, 49–50, 54
Revised Standard Bible Version, 95
rhetoric of control, in gendered discourse, 70
right-wing Christian, 117–18
ritualized language, limited, 55–56
ritual prayers, progressive Christianity rewriting of, 25, 169
The Road Less Traveled (Peck), 127
Robbins, Joel, 148–49
Robinson, Pat, 119
Roots (Haley), scripturalizing role of, 91–92

sacrifice, Spong on, 154
salvation, 221n11

Saul, John Ralston, 178–79, 180
Saving Jesus video series, at Holy Cross Lutheran Church, 118
Schaberg, Jane, 216n9
Scheer, Monique, 20
scholars: Jesus Seminar book discussion, 97; on lived religion, 18, 20
scientific empiricism, 1, 11, 168
scientific method: biblical criticism and, 107–8; Latour on social forces and, 107
scripture: anthropology of religion and, 91–92; shift to history in place of, 34; women experiences within, 216n8
Second Coming of Jesus. See *parousia*
secular humanism, Engelke on, 214n4
secularity and secularism: Bigelow political, state-structured, 17; disbelief and forms of knowledge, 25; as embodied experience, 20; ethical commitment in, 20; Lebner on, 19–20; religion lack of dependence in, 18; religious identity and, 5; religious thinking integration with, 5–6; Scheer, Johansen and Fadil on, 20; secularization supplanted by, 18; social context for, 19; Taylor on, 19, 213n13. See also lived secularity
secularization: in North American religion, 211n5; secularism supplanting of, 18; skepticism compared to, 4, 211n5; theory on religion decline, 18
secular knowledge, 11–12
service order, in George Street United Church, 38
Shoemaker, Terry, 217n1
simulacrum, 34, 108
sincerity: anthropology of Christianity on religious commitments and, 21, 23; beliefs in creeds and, 85; ethics of belief and discipline of, 24–25; fingers crossed and, 82–87; Keane on, 23; knowledge and inner self, 22; language and, 23; Protestantism preoccupation with, 45; skepticism relationship with, 24

The Sins of Scripture (Spong), 83, 99–100, 216n8
skepticism, 121, 134; belief generation of, 115; conviction relationship to, 4; in deconversion, 113; as ethical imperative, 21, 113; in lived secularity, 22, 191; Protestantism, 3–4; secularization compared to, 4, 211n5; sincerity relationship with, 24; of Vosper and belief practice, 204
Small Wonder (Kingsolver), 178, 182–83, 185
Smith, Erin A., 216n5
Smith, Jonathan Z., 36, 116, 136, 217n2
Smith, Wilfred Cantwell, 221n13
social competence, Bourdieu on, 96
social context, for secularity and secularism, 19
social forces, Latour on scientific method and, 107
social function of belief, Day on, 115, 116
Social Gospel, 7–8, 149–50
social justice, 6; Canadian Centre for Progressive Christianity and, 7; Vineyard Church and, 160
solidarity, from collective reading, 89–90
Son of God and Son of man, Jesus as, 73
Spong, John Shelby, 10, 49, 74–75, 90–91, 93, 121–22, 135, 220n8; authority from historical exegesis, 96; on believer in exile, 6, 36, 103; on Bible interpretation, 99–101; Bible neoliteralism, 100; on Bible unscientific claims, 101–2; on biblical criticism, 42, 99; George Street United Church visit by, 42–43, 82–84; on God as pro-Jewish, 23–24; on God divine authority, 101; on Jesus and Mary Magdalene, 104–5; on Jesus fictitious story, 42, 102; *Jesus for the Non-Religious* of, 39, 42, 82, 105; Jesus Seminar and, 97–98; on sacrifice, 154; *The Sins of Scripture* of, 83, 99–100, 216n8; on unequal treatment of God, 24; on virgin birth, 104–5

still adverb, in temporal language, 154–55
St. Matthias Anglican Church, 27, 188; congregational meeting and contested spaces at, 62–69; description of, 62; emphasis on words, 63–64; Living the Questions curriculum at, 63, 68
Stones into Schools (Mortenson and Relin), 184
St. Peter's Anglican Church, 188; description of, 69; directional change in, 69–77; *The Heart of Christianity* study, 69; on Jesus life and teachings reexamination, 71; study group within, 27
Stromberg, Peter, 165
strong atheists, 134, 218n4
stumbling block, 220n7
suburban religiosity, 34
supernatural beliefs, rejection of, 6
symbolic membership, 57
symmetrical evacuation of future, 153

Taussig, Hal, 30
Taylor, Charles, 19, 213n13
TCPC. *See* The Center for Progressive Christianity
temporality: creation and apocalypse in, 148; in eschatology, 148, 154–59; progressive Christianity representations of, 197; proximate and distant future, 152–53; Social Gospel on, 150
temporal language: adverbs emphasis, 35; of already and not yet, 159–64; beliefs and practices outgrowing and, 147; Harding on, 147; of intervention, 151–53; of still adverb, 154–55
Ten Commandments: book study group rewriting of, 12–17, 106; historical context of, 13–14
Texts of Terror (Trible), 216n8
textual economy, Bielo on, 89, 91
textual ideologies, 87; Bayart on operational acts of identification in, 92; Klassen on, 216n3

theism, 43, 204, 218n4, 220n8
theological diversity: at George Street United Church, 37; at Holy Cross Lutheran Church, 54
theological questions, in progressive Christianity, 176
Theological Studies Group, at George Street United Church, 38–41, 105–6, 173, 188; social setting and dynamics in, 47; Spong book study at, 42–43, 82–83
theology, continuous transformation of, 172, 174
theory of self, proximate other and, 116, 117
Theresa (Mother), 109
Thiessen, Joel, 193, 194, 211n4
Three Cups of Tea (Mortenson and Relin), 184
Thuesen, Peter J., 59
Toronto Conference, of United Church of Canada: on Vosper unsuitability as minister, 201; West Hill United Church and Vosper arbitration settlement, 201–2
traditional beliefs, rejection of, 3, 163–64
traditions: biblical criticism evaluation of, 168; collective reading on religious, 87–88; of God representation, 146; secular knowledge evaluation of, 11
transitional nature, of deconversion, 112, 130, 133–34, 136
Trudeau, Pierre Elliott, 212n9

Understanding Islam (Lippman), 184
undesirable gifts, in Christianity, 21
unethical beliefs, 21, 165
United Church of Canada, 27; membership of, 214n5; on ministers tests of faith, 200; progressive Christianity within, 213n1; on Vosper suitability as minister, 199–201
United Church of Christ, 220n6; God is Still Speaking motto of, 154–55

Vineyard Church, 159, 160
virgin birth narrative, 216n9; Spong on, 104–5
Vision Works document, of West Hill United Church, 211n2
Vliek, Maria, 192
Vosper, Gretta, 12, 60, 179–80, 188–89; atheism religious beliefs of, 201; Communion liturgy of, 58–59; on freedom from religion, 200; heresy trial against, 199–203, 220n9; on liberal Christianity, 9–10; on metaphorical understanding of Christianity, 166; on progressive and conservative Christianity, 9; skepticism of belief practice by, 204; United Church of Canada on minister suitability of, 199–201; as West Hill United Church minister, 2

War is a Force That Gives Us Meaning (Hedges), 177
Webster, Joseph, 151–53
West Hill United Church, 1, 27, 138–39, 172; arbitration settlement, 201–2; Bible reading rejection in, 2; book study group at, 145–47, 177–89, *185*; Children's Prayer at, 169; Communion service, 142; Journey of Transformation service, 57–59; membership departure, 60–61, 129, 157; membership of, 56–69; Vision Works document, 211n2; WE st'ill ad for, 155. *See also* Vosper, Gretta
WE st'ill advertisements, for West Hill United Church, 155
Why Christianity Must Change or Die (Spong), 6, 85, 122
Wilkins-LaFlamme, Sarah, 193, 194, 211n4
Williams, Philippa, 18
With or Without God (Vosper), 12, 115, 179–80
women, 104–5; experiences within scripture, 216n8; Schaberg on, 216n9
Worthen, Molly, 212n10
Wright, N. T., 98–99
WuDunn, Sheryl, 184

Young, Ralph, 211n3

ABOUT THE AUTHOR

REBEKKA KING is Associate Professor of Religious Studies at Middle Tennessee State University. She holds a PhD in the Study of Religion from the University of Toronto. She has published in *Critical Research on Religion*, *Religion and Society: Advances in Research*, and the Bloomsbury *Critiquing Religion* series. She is the current president of the North American Association for the Study of Religion.